Mott Street

ALSO BY AVA CHIN

Eating Wildly
Split

Mott Street

A CHINESE
AMERICAN FAMILY'S
STORY OF
EXCLUSION AND
HOMECOMING

Ava Chin

PENGUIN PRESS
NEW YORK
2023

PENGUIN PRESS
An imprint of Penguin Random House LLC
penguinrandomhouse.com

Photo Credits:
p. 4, courtesy of the Municipal Archives, City of New York; pp. 24, 230, courtesy
of Celeste Chin; pp. 34, 150, courtesy of the National Archives at Seattle; p. 156,
courtesy of the National Archives at New York City; pp. 73, 166, 168, courtesy of
the National Archives at San Bruno; p. 160, courtesy of Lois Wu; p. 191,
courtesy of Lung "Pop" Chin, Museum of Chinese in America (MOCA)
collection; p. 266, courtesy of Alison Ho; p. 288,
courtesy of the National Archives at Boston

LIBRARY OF CONGRESS CATALOGING-IN-PUBLICATION DATA

Names: Chin, Ava, author.
Title: Mott Street : a Chinese American family's story of
exclusion and homecoming / Ava Chin.
Description: New York : Penguin Press, 2023. |
Includes bibliographical references and index.
Identifiers: LCCN 2022040793 (print) | LCCN 2022040794 (ebook) |
ISBN 9780525557371 (hardcover) | ISBN 9780525557388 (ebook)
Subjects: LCSH: Chin, Ava—Family. | Chinatown (New York, N.Y.)—Biography. |
Chin family. | Doshim family. | 37 Mott Street (New York, N.Y.)—History. |
Chinese—New York (State)—New York—Biography. |
Immigrants—New York (State)—New York—Biography. |
Chinese-Americans—New York (State)—New York—Biography. |
Chinese American families—New York (State)—New York—Social conditions.
Classification: LCC F128.68.C47 C45 2023 (print) | LCC F128.68.C47 (ebook) |
DDC 974.7/100495100922—dc23/eng/20220927
LC record available at https://lccn.loc.gov/2022040793
LC ebook record available at https://lccn.loc.gov/2022040794

Printed in Canada
1   3   5   7   9   10   8   6   4   2

DESIGNED BY MEIGHAN CAVANAUGH

For Mei

Let the Chinaman come. . . . He will give
us the benefit of his skill.

FREDERICK DOUGLASS, "THE COMPOSITE
NATION," 1869

No greater calamity could now befall the
United States than to have the Pacific slope fill
up with a Mongolian population.

THEODORE ROOSEVELT, 1882

After many amazing adventures, he had become
a merchant in a city called Mott Street.

LEE CHEW WITH JOSEPH SINGLETON,
"BIOGRAPHY OF A CHINAMAN," 1903

And tell me what street compares
with Mott Street in July?

RODGERS AND HART,
"MANHATTAN," 1925

Contents

Author's Note

First, a note on names. No identities or names have been changed, apart from some minor spelling adjustments from Chinese into English. Whenever possible, I used the individual's preferred spelling, and in cases where names changed across lifetimes—American names, nicknames, baby names (milk names), and names acquired with marriage—I chose the one that was most commonly used.

The languages and dialects spoken by the majority of Chinese in America—including my family members—during these time periods were Cantonese (Gungdongwa) and Toisanese (Hoisanwa), often colloquially referred to as Samyup (3 Counties) and Sayyup (4 Counties). As there is no commonly agreed-upon standardization for these equivalent to Mandarin's pinyin, and given that this work is rooted in an oral tradition, I have used a combination of transliteration systems (Jyutping, Yale, etc.), modulated by how it sounds to my own ear. There are exceptions for commonly used proper nouns, like Peking and Huangdi.

Over the course of my research, I navigated various languages and dialects with the help of others, and when I couldn't understand something, I continued to observe, and to take in new information. I did this in our ancestral villages in China, where folks welcomed my friends and me into their homes, and over cups of tea shared with us their memories of my family; I did this as I joined the various family and veterans' associations in Chinatown that my relatives belonged to—some of which only a decade or two before had been closed to women. I interviewed folks who had known my family in these spaces, asking questions over the click of mahjong tiles shuffled across tabletops; other times, gathering in members-only family association rooms to bow before the altars of our common ancestors with offerings of incense, rice wine, and intention—performing three deep bows under a pressed tin ceiling just like my great-grandfather had done in that very room when he arrived in New York City in the late nineteenth century.

As much as I could, I allowed the family stories to lead the way down a cavernous tunnel—the voice of the original speaker echoing before me. But ultimately, I had to make a choice. Whose story was this anyway? The people who lived it—or my own, and that of my daughter's and the future generations?

Since I was not present, or even born, when most of the folks I have written about were alive, I built dialogue based on what surviving family members remembered in retrospect, told from their points of view, and what I could surmise from my own vantage point. Sometimes, I had to imagine their conversations, their multitude of voices, clamoring to be heard, with all of their local color and multilingualism. I have placed such exchanges *in italics*. Whenever possible, I cross-referenced these stories against the written record, but often the written record itself had to be approached skeptically, especially when nineteenth-century anti-Chinese bias was outright blinding—a real lesson in reading against the grain.

The deeper that I delved into this rich, loamy terroir, the more I realized that I was writing a narrative that was part ghost book. As I entered my ancestors' world on Mott Street, their spirits began speaking to me, leaving a trail of breadcrumbs to the story, materializing as letters, notes, even a seal chop bearing my Chin grandfather's name. My family is a noisy, bothersome bunch—bursting through the walls and hallways as I tried to doze; talking to me through the memories of old friends, eyes brimming with recollection like a teacup about to overflow; egging me on to continue, *Write faster—what are you waiting for?*; even daring to show up on the sofa, like one great-grandmother—demanding to be heard.

Mott Street Family Tree
(WONG, NG, CHIN FAMILIES)

WONG FAMILY
黃

Wong Yuan Son
(born c. 1849) m. wife

Wun Man "George"
(b. 1893) = 2

Sow Lei
(born c. 1895–d. 1954)
m. Mei Lam = 6

Gene Kai Fei Wong
(b. 1922–d. 1998)
m. Rose Mai Doshim

NG FAMILY
伍

Ng Hong Dong
m. Madam Lum

Dek Foon
(b. 1860–d. 1938)

m.1 Madam Gee   m.2 Elva Lisk
(d. 1890) = 1   *(b. 1870–*
                        d. 1945)

Wu Chow
(b. 1883–d. 1941)

m.1   m.2
"Dai Mah"   "Sai Mah"
= 1   = 1

Normon   Edith
(b. 1911–   *(b. 1915–*
Oilily *d. 1916)* Johnny *d. 2004)*
(b. 1909–   *(b. 1913–* = 2
d. 1981)   *d. 1977)*
= 4   = 3

Kenith   Wesley   Laura
(b. 1941)   *(b. 1943)*   *(b. 1945)*
                            m. Stanley Chin

Ava Chin *(b. 1970)*
m. Owen Brunette
(b. 1967)

Mei Rose Brunette
(b. 2012)

CHIN FAMILY

陳

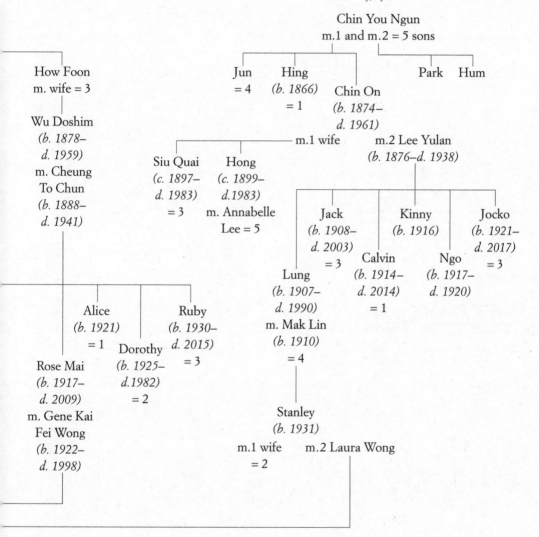

Chin You Ngun
m.1 and m.2 = 5 sons

How Foon
m. wife = 3

Wu Doshim
(b. 1878–
d. 1959)
m. Cheung
To Chun
(b. 1888–
d. 1941)

Jun
= 4

Hing
(b. 1866)
= 1

Chin On
(b. 1874–
d. 1961)

Park   Hum

m.1 wife

m.2 Lee Yulan
(b. 1876–d. 1938)

Siu Quai
(c. 1897–
d. 1983)
= 3

Hong
(c. 1899–
d.1983)
m. Annabelle
Lee = 5

Jack
(b. 1908–
d. 2003)
= 3

Kinny
(b. 1916)

Jocko
(b. 1921–
d. 2017)
= 3

Calvin
(b. 1914–
d. 2014)
= 1

Ngo
(b. 1917–
d. 1920)

Lung
(b. 1907–
d. 1990)
m. Mak Lin
(b. 1910)
= 4

Alice
(b. 1921)
= 1

Ruby
(b. 1930–
d. 2015)
= 3

Dorothy
(b. 1925–
d.1982)
= 2

Rose Mai
(b. 1917–
d. 2009)
m. Gene Kai
Fei Wong
(b. 1922–
d. 1998)

Stanley
(b. 1931)

m.1 wife
= 2

m.2 Laura Wong

PART ONE

1970s–Present

1

The Elbow of Mott Street

Chinatown, New York City

As I walk past the restaurants, vegetable stands, and open-air shop fronts that line Mott Street—the main artery that pulses through the heart of Chinatown—the sights and smells here are as familiar to me as my grandparents' kitchen. Roast duck and slabs of salted pork. Vast bins of varying grades of dried shiitakes, baby shrimp, flower teas wrapped in cellophane packages. Plump dried oysters—plucked from their shells and naked, but for some black bearding and a spray of salt—so provocatively laid out that it almost hurts to look at them.

When I was a kid growing up in Flushing, Queens, before it became the "new" Chinatown, we used to come here nearly every week. Sometimes it was to see my grandmother Rose's family, or to go shopping for roast pork or Chinese beef jerky, items difficult to make at home. It always involved good food. Giant, elaborate meals of long, pan-fried egg noodles with sliced beef, chicken, pork, and verdant gai lan vegetables as long as my chopsticks. Lobster Cantonese with minced pork and lacy egg whites. A whole flounder steamed from head to tail—topped with a medley of ginger, scallions, and soy sauce—right before we devoured it down to the delicate skeleton, when it was time to flip it over and start again. Chinatown was where my maternal grandfather, Gene Wong, went on his days off to visit friends, place horse-racing bets at the local off-track betting office, and purchase in-season crabs or lobster. The smaller, younger female crustaceans were our favorite: tender, succulent, and if we were lucky, packed with rich, unctuous eggs.

I didn't know, on any of the innumerable weekend excursions we took here, that a whole other side of my family, one that I had never met, was just around the corner from our favorite Cantonese restaurant. They were there, even as we marveled at the tiny turtles or Mexican jumping beans, or sucked on sweet hawthorn berry candies or preserved plums from the Hong Kong sweets shop with the Japanese name, or tossed

37 Mott Street
c. 1939–1941

white gunpowder-filled pellets to make snapping noises against the pavement. If I had looked up, perhaps I would have seen them, residing right there in the elbow of Mott Street—37 Mott Street—an apartment building that had been the epicenter of the Chinese community for almost seventy-five years.

Built in 1915 after a fire destroyed a funeral parlor and a stable, the red brick building that locals called Sun Lau, or New Building, was considered the height of luxury when it rose from the ashes. The most prominent families of Chinatown flocked to live there, including members of both my maternal and paternal sides. There, they occupied the choicest apartments with views of the cross section of Mott and Pell Streets.

It's a bustling three-pronged, panoramic view here at the intersection of Mott Street and Pell, and this is where our family's story in New York begins.

So many generations of my family have lived in this building—great-grandparents, grandparents and their siblings, parents, uncles, aunts, cousins, and now, me. When I last counted, I tallied forty-nine Chins and Ng-Doshims in total, many of whom took their first breaths as wailing newborns here.

Each wing of the family can trace its lineage back to an ancestor born and raised in the same fertile Pearl River Delta, an ocean and a continent away. Although each of them had lived out west collectively through the eras of Lincoln, Grant, Harrison, and Cleveland, it would take decades for their descendants to settle some three thousand miles away, in the apartment building that stood at the heart of the community they called Tong Yun Gai. It was here on Tang People's Street that their descendants became neighbors, lovers, classmates, sworn enemies, and eventually, as fate would have it—through my own birth—family kin.

IN THE GLASSY BUILDING ENTRANCE, I catch a glimpse of myself as I pull out a hefty key and open the door to 37 Mott Street.

It's a little like Alice through the looking glass as I enter the lobby—to anyone else it resembles an ordinary entrance with stairs leading to a narrow corridor, but for me it's a portal to my family and to our history in this country. I feel that rush every time I'm here. Soon, I am climbing the front staircase, the banister worn smooth by the hands of so many generations who lived here from childhood to old age. The stairway walls look like they are covered in a century's worth of dirt and grime. I often find garbage along the steps or cigarette butts on the windowsills, and if I run my finger along the soot in the screens it's as if I am temporarily disturbing the building's sedimentary layers before they settle back down again.

I arrive on the fourth floor of what was once our family domain. Chins have lived in the building in successive generations for over a hundred years, and aside from a few sporadic paint jobs and some strategically placed security cameras, the place is pretty much as it was when my great-grandparents lived here. The hallway walls are now painted-over bricks that make the place feel a bit like a bunker, and each door along the corridor is a different color and material style—classic painted-over tenement, white suburban prefab, complete with peephole and knocker, some even with patched-up screen doors. The effect is a janky individuality that I find strangely comforting.

It is a relief, after so many years of visiting this vibrant neighborhood—exoticized by outsiders, journalists, and even, I'll admit it, by me—to finally have a space to write here. Neighbors still keep their doors open in the summer, so that the smells of home cooking and the ringing tones of our language bounce through the hallways. Cantonese and Toisanese, which my grandfather spoke—a country dialect my grandmother considered backwards, but which I find charming—prevail here. While these southern dialects, with more than double the tones of standard Mandarin, are so familiar to me, I still have difficulty deciphering their meaning. (Once, when a neighbor asked me a question and I answered her in English, she looked at me startled. "You're not Chinese?" To her, my inability to speak Cantonese or Hoisanwa meant that I must be another ethnicity.)

I turn my key and enter a small T-shaped apartment.

The first time I walked into my writing studio, my footsteps audible against the wooden floors, I felt disoriented. I kept feeling like someone was going to shock me awake from my sudden good fortune of being here, and poof, I'd be out on the street again, looking up at the building from the outside.

When my generation moved in—the fourth to live here—we found old Chinese medicine bottles and "Sloan's Liniment" in the original kitchen cabinets, with doors that refuse to shut due to a thick century's worth of paint. The old Acme food storage safe, built into the wall— every unit has one—where my family used to burn lucky paper to honor our ancestors, is now flung open and transformed into a meditation area with a yoga cushion, incense, and a singing bowl.

I am standing in the kitchen, which doubles as a living space, where my great-uncle and great-aunt raised their family, just down the hall from my grandfather's apartment, and diagonally across from my great-grandparents' old unit.

This was the place where I was going to be writing the story I had been trying to uncover ever since I was a child, estranged from my father and his whole side of my family. Back then, I grappled with so many questions that spilled over to even the folks who raised me. Who were these pioneering family members who came before us? Who were they in relation to each other? Who was I in relation to them?

Then, as now, the dark shadow of the Chinese Exclusion Act hovers over us all. Chinese Exclusion laws (1882–1943)—the country's first major federal immigration restrictions that closed its borders to a specific nationality—not only halted the majority of our legal immigration but also blocked Chinese from citizenship for sixty-one years. Coupled with earlier legislation that prevented women from freely immigrating, and had excluded Asians from naturalizing, these laws left a devastating impact on our communities across America for generations. These discriminatory laws shaped the histories of Chinatowns up and down the West Coast and reached all the way east, laying down the foundation for the very neighborhood in which I'm standing, a community that, with the COVID-19 pandemic and the ensuing anti-Asian violence, has been embattled and shaken to its very core. Still, despite these many years of racism, Chinatown is the only place for me that truly feels like a refuge.

As a writer, I believe it is important to uncover the truths from our collective past—no matter how painful or unsettling the discoveries. And so much of Chinese Exclusion has felt personal. As I tried to piece the puzzle together, I was forced time and time again to contend with my own feelings of exclusion, even from within my own family. No matter how old I was—a twenty-something writer seeking my father out for the first time, or a professor/mom to a sixth-generation New Yorker—no matter how many times I tried to understand and interview my father, I always found myself here alone, engaging in a solitary dance with the shadowy specter of having been excluded from my Chin side for so very long.

It wasn't the only erasure I felt. Growing up, my maternal grandfather, Gene, regaled me with stories of our ancestors on his side, stories about working on the railroad out west that held me in thrall throughout my childhood, well into my school years. In the sixth grade, when my teacher began the lesson on the nation's first transcontinental railroad, I thought that I already knew everything about it. But when I opened my big textbook on American history, I stared in disbelief at the official photograph. What was this nonsense? Why weren't we in the picture?

To understand what really happened, I needed to collect as many of our stories as possible. As a college student, I started interviewing my family members, and made my way out to the Church of Jesus Christ of Latter-day Saints' genealogy library in Salt Lake City to look for traces of my railroad worker ancestor. Decades later, I continued the journey as a professor—zigzagging my way across the country to consult archives and experts, and to visit my families' many places of detention, the border towns where they crossed over, and their sites of greatest achievement. I even moved my family across the globe as a Fulbright scholar to visit the villages in China that we had left behind. Eventually, I uncovered the Chinese Exclusion Act files on each of my major family members—manila folders filled with intrigue, half-truths, and in some cases, outright lies.

It is a general rule of thumb, among researchers and historians alike, that it is the written record that is the gold standard, and the family stories that are long on twisted falsehoods, embellishment, and tall tales. But when you're Chinese in America, with roots that stretch back to the Exclusion era, it is the historical record that is a fabulist fabrication, and the oral stories, passed down from generation to generation, like rare, evolving heirlooms, that ultimately hold the keys to the truth.

At noon, the bells from Transfiguration Church ring throughout the building and the neighborhood, just as they did when my maternal grandmother, Rose, and paternal grandfather, Lung, were children, just as they did for my father and his siblings, and for my cousins a generation later, our family spilling out and taking over this floor. I pause at my writing desk—by the window, overlooking rooftops, fire escapes, and a tenacious understory tree in the courtyard, sitting in the midst of my family's long history—and note every chime.

2

The Crown Prince
of Chinatown

Chin Family

I first saw my father as a pair of feet in Italian leather shoes, bounding down the carpeted staircase of his office building, on one of the oldest streets in Chinatown.

It was a cold, rainy late afternoon in mid-February. When I arrived, only ten minutes before, I had stood at the threshold hesitating, every button on my black peacoat fastened, my breath fogging up the windows flanking the double doors. No one else in my family knew that I was here, or that I was meeting my father for the first time. If they did, they might have stopped me—and I couldn't risk losing my nerve.

I tried to stay calm and take deep, even breaths.

I had never hidden anything this big from the family who raised me, but I had been waiting my entire life for this moment.

Finally, I pushed the buzzer.

His building, the Edward Mooney House—the only townhouse dating back to the American Revolution in all of Manhattan—was a short two-block jaunt from Mott Street that I had walked numerous times before, as a child on family outings, and later, as a young activist in the community. I had no idea back then that if I looked up to the third floor of this red brick edifice, I could see his office, and perhaps even catch a glimpse of this elusive, mysterious man.

At the barbershop next door, hairdressers were busy fashioning buzz cuts, flattops, and layer upon layer of Jennifer Aniston *Friends*-style haircuts. A few doors down, a crowd of tourists was entering the soup dumpling restaurant, the city's first xiao long bao joint, for dumplings so juicy one had to eat them with both a spoon and chopsticks. Pell Street was a scant two blocks long, but it had everything—ATMs, a curio shop, even a Baptist church—though it was so narrow that sometimes trucks had to traverse it with one front and back wheel hiked up on the sidewalk. I noticed that my father's name had been outside, on the street-level buzzer that I had just pressed, at eye level, the entire time. As a writer, I liked to think of myself as an observant person, but what other important things had I simply walked past dozens of times, lost in my own head?

Then, finally, I heard the sound of feet running down stairs, and saw those black leather shoes.

Suddenly, the doors were flung open, and a small face with a thin protective smile was carefully peering down at me.

I had the sensation that I was meeting someone very familiar yet very odd—it was rather like being studied from across time and down the long end of a very old, unfolding telescope.

This was my father.

In that moment, as he stared at me, I knew that I had to be perfect, even if it meant that I had to contort myself into someone completely unrecognizable. Someone who spoke softly and reasonably, who wasn't loud and impossible—an A+ Asian daughter with perfect emotional pitch who wouldn't scare him with her anger, or give him cause to push her away.

The thought of him rejecting me all over again made the surface of my skin buzz like glass just before the cracks appear.

When I was a child, I had recurring visions of meeting him. I imagined my father showing up at my honors ceremony, or any number of graduation convocations—grade school, middle school, high school—waiting there with a bouquet of flowers in the audience, clapping enthusiastically when they announced my name.

In Flushing, I pined after him—searching for clues in the few objects he had left behind. A diamond engagement ring my mother kept for years in a box in her dresser drawer, until she finally hocked it to pay the rent. A stuffed toy koala bear he'd given her in the early days of their courtship, the black paws of which I gnawed at and cut my baby teeth on as a toddler. A gold cross given to me when I was still a newborn by my Chin grandmother, a woman whose name I did not know growing up because the rift between the families was so great that I had never met her.

In other daydreams, inspired by Cecil B. DeMille Technicolor Hollywood films, my father would call for me from his deathbed, like Pharaoh did for Moses. I would rush to him, somehow just managing to make it in time for this, our first and final reunion. In this overblown, gauzy fantasy, despite the fact that my father has other daughters, it is my name that he repeats on his last dying breath.

Sometimes, while taking a bus home from high school, I'd think I'd seen him from the window, a tall thin man walking out of the local pizza parlor, or putting money in the meter for his car—as if I could inherently pick him out of a crowd of strangers, because he was my father and because I supposedly looked just like him.

Was it true? Did I really look like him? Did I really sound like him too, "when I was being obnoxious," like my mother claimed? ("How is it possible she sounds so much like him when we were the ones who raised her?" my grandmother asked.) I just shrugged and chalked it up to my family's touchy, but very justifiable anger toward him for walking out.

The only image I had ever seen of my father was a square photograph that my mother produced one day, on a whim when I was in the third grade. I had been told throughout my childhood that I looked just like him, like a Chin, but I did not really know what that meant until that moment. In the photograph, he was sitting cross-legged, ankle over knee, in my grandparents' mid-century yellow armchair, smiling for the camera. He had the debonair air of a player—a man with cojones, as the boys in my neighborhood liked to say. His expression and posture emanated such effortlessness, as if such willful virility could barely be contained by the simple boundaries of the photographic record, or apparently, even the responsibilities of fatherhood itself.

I caught a glimpse of the resemblance—the high forehead and cheekbones, the long neck, a propensity for dark circles under the eyes—right before my mother burned the picture with a kitchen match. I lunged at the image, seeking to save it.

The picture vanished in a brief orange blaze and a lingering curl of smoke.

Only my grandmother Rose would talk to me about my father and the Chins.

"You come from a big, big family," Grandma would sometimes say, usually on a late Friday night, as we sat together in front of the television. We were alone, my grandfather not yet back from his restaurant shift, and nestled together in that same armchair my father had been pictured in before he walked out of the frame. "Too bad they don't look you up.

"Your father was much older than your mother—closer to our age than to hers," she revealed, as the glare of the television credits scrolled up and down her glasses. "He used your mother, then threw her away."

Then, sighing, before standing up to get ready for bed. "Oh well. What can you do?"

I always teared up a little whenever Grandma said things like that, not knowing what to do or how to react. Was I to blame? How could I save my mother and myself from the gaping hole he had left?

My father never did show up to any of those graduations and honors ceremonies, no matter how much magical thinking I engaged in, so once I hit my twenties, I did the next best thing—I set about stealthily researching my Chin family from afar. If I couldn't meet Stanley, at least I could start to puzzle together who the rest of my family was. After I graduated from college and became a freelancer at *The Village Voice*, at the height of the grunge era, I had access to a database. In those last innocent years before the internet, it seemed rather like an oracle.

I plugged in the only search terms I knew—"Chin," "obituary," and the year that my Chin grandfather passed away, "1990" (my grandma Rose had seen it in one of the many newspapers she read)—before hitting enter.

Lung Chin, 84, Is Dead; Leader in Chinatown
Section B; Page 10, Column 3; Metropolitan Desk

Lung Chin, a merchant and community leader in Chinatown for more than 60 years, died of cancer on Tuesday at St. Vincent's Hospital. He was 84 years old and had lived at 37 Mott Street since 1915, several months after emigrating from China. Mr. Chin, a raconteur, was co-manager of two stores, Ying Chong and Sun Yuen Hing. In 1931, he converted Sun Yuen Hing into the Sugar Bowl, the first coffee shop in the neighborhood. . . .

Mr. Chin attended Stuyvesant High School and was an alumnus of the Mount Hermon School in Northfield, Mass. He was a longtime leader of Boy Scout Troop 50, a basketball coach for neighborhood youths, a spokesman for the Chinatown Democratic Club and an oral-history contributor to the Chinatown History Project.

Surviving are his wife, Mak Lin; three sons, Stanley, of Manhattan, Stephen, of Tappan, N.Y., and Stewart, of Atlantic City; a daughter, Janice Wong of Southington, Conn. . . . 15 grandchildren, and three great-grandchildren. . . .

My eye stopped at my father's name, Stanley. I didn't know that he was the first son in his family—a position of filial privilege. I had so many questions for so many years, and now here was a wealth of information in 205 words that seemed to beg even more questions: Lung Chin? Cancer? Raconteur? (As a slam poet and an activist, I considered myself a bit of a raconteur.) I had fifteen first cousins on my father's side? Stuyvesant and Mount Hermon prep school? Who knew there were Chinese boys in prep school in the 1920s? And then my eye doubled back to his "oral-history" contribution to the "Chinatown History Project," and the address in Chinatown, 37 Mott Street.

LATER THAT SAME WEEK, I climbed the magnificent silver wrought-iron staircase of the old Public School 23, where my grandmother and her siblings had attended, which housed the Chinatown History Museum. I had been to the building for rehearsals with a local Asian American dance company, but I hadn't known that an important family archive was housed steps away. When I arrived at the front desk, an apologetic staffer raised his head. "I'm sorry, but the museum is closed for renovations."

I just stared at him. The panicky feeling of being shut out—so close to the Chins but so very far away—started to rise up in my chest.

I thrust the obituary printout at him and, in the mad rush of a near-crazy person, said, "I'm looking for my grandfather Lung Chin's oral history."

It was the first time that I had ever said his name aloud, and it felt vaguely as though I were lying.

To my relief, the museum staffer's expression brightened.

"You're Lung Chin's granddaughter?" he said, smiling. He jumped up from his seat. "Please, come with me."

And just like that I followed him into a dark, empty gallery space. Someone would get back to me about the oral history, he informed me, but in the meantime, "There's something you should see."

He flipped on the light, and on the far wall was a large, blown-up, photographic portrait of a white-haired man in profile.

Everything seemed to fall away as I walked closer, my footsteps audible against the creaky wooden floors. It slowly dawned on me that I was looking at my grandfather Lung Chin for the very first time.

Lung was lean and elegant, gazing out placidly at something beyond the picture's frame, chin resting on bony fingers. Under his thinning hair, he had bags under his eyes, just like I had when I didn't get enough sleep. And there was that very high forehead.

I struggled to hold back the tears welling up in my eyes.

Next to his portrait was another photograph, a rather ragtag picture of Lung and his brothers—tall, formerly athletic, gray-haired men in midconversation, sitting on white folding chairs in a backyard in Bradley Beach, New Jersey. I searched for clues of myself in their features, but they were too old and their faces too fuzzy, the photograph blown up larger than its resolution could withstand. The images dated from the mid-1980s, when I was still a teenager, and in the background, a band of blurry school-aged kids, my cousins presumably, and perhaps even my half siblings, were chasing one another.

Looking at the picture of so many generations of Chins at their New Jersey Shore summer home (Chinese on the Jersey Shore?), I felt happiness, pain, anger, relief, and gratitude. Growing up, our family orbit had felt so small—just me, my mother, and my maternal grandparents, and the endless ruminations about my estranged family.

Before I went home, I left my contact information with the staffer, who promised to help me obtain the oral history.

I never received a phone call.

ONE DAY, A FEW YEARS LATER, as I was juggling a magazine career with my creative writing, my mother accidentally ran into my half sister, Stanley's oldest daughter, at a work conference in Queens.

"Does she ever want to meet him?" my sister asked.

My mother, a former beauty queen, whose anger toward my father only flared out more brightly in the intervening years after he had left, flat-out lied. "No," she said.

"Of course I want to meet him," I said, after she had told me about the encounter. "How could you *say* that?"

Now, some months later, here was Stanley, standing in the ornate, run-down doorframe—tall, good-looking, and distinguished. When he shook my hand, his long, elegant fingers were cold, bony. There was no awkward hug, just an awkward pause.

"Come in, come in," he said, beckoning me up the stairs.

Then, I was following him, the carpeted steps bouncy under our feet. Even though he was in his early sixties, my father seemed both younger—as a former basketball player, he still had what ballet dancers call "ballon," that springy lightness on the feet—as well as strangely frail. He had a kind of impish quality that favored sons sometimes have. From the moment he opened the door, I got the sense that if I was not careful he might dissolve into a puff of smoke. (I always had the lingering feeling that I could run my hand right through him like a ghost.)

Stanley had a small side office on an upper floor, which was large enough to accommodate his desk, cabinets, and a chair for clients, along with a side-facing window through which you could see a sliver of Pell Street. Numerous pictures hung on the walls—I couldn't help but stare at them, one by one, marveling at this life I never had. Family on a row-

Stanley in his high school yearbook, 1940s

★ ★ ★ ★ ★ ★ ★ ★ ★ ★ ★
★ **DEMOCRATIC PRIMARY** ★

STANLEY CHIN
ASSEMBLYMAN
62nd ASSEMBLY DISTRICT
VOTE TUESDAY JUNE 20th

Stanley's campaign poster, 1972

Stanley playing guitar

boat on the Jersey Shore. His oldest daughter from his first marriage, my half sister, wide-eyed and beaming, sitting in our father's Triumph convertible sports car, the top off. My father with different girlfriends and ex-wives—the singer, the stewardess/dance partner whom he had married and divorced, twice. Black-and-white photos of him in a cowboy hat, midstride across a platform, one hand extended toward Robert F. Kennedy. A photo of Donald Manes, the disgraced former Queens borough president. I was trying to take it all in—my father as a tangible reality. I had so many questions: Why was he shaking hands with Bobby Kennedy? Why was Donald Manes, who had killed himself several years before, on his wall? A Triumph sports car?

One of the images that captured my attention was a framed campaign card from when my father ran for state assembly, two years after he walked out on us. It was an outdoor shot, with natural light. He was not looking at the camera, instead focused on something just outside of the frame. His hair was rakishly wavy—lush 1970s hair, parted on one side—and his face framed by a row of stars ("Stanley Chin Assemblyman 62nd Assembly District—Vote Tuesday June 20th"). It was in that moment that I realized my family was right—we *did* look alike.

What else had I inherited from him?

My father sat back in his swivel chair, the current, older version of himself, and regarded me. He was such the picture of ease that I knew right away it was fake—a false projection, a pretense.

In truth, we were aliens to each other.

He had grown up a firstborn son in a large Chinatown family where my father, as a boy, was the little prince.

He had no clue what it was like to grow up like I had, cut off from an entire side of my family, in a culture that traditionally revered the family as sacred.

I was his daughter, but I was as alien to him as if I had just dropped down from the movable sky.

"So how can I help you?" he asked, one leg crossed over the other, as if I were a client, here for an initial consultation.

I searched his face for traces of myself. It was all there: the high forehead, the deep brown eyes that appeared almost reddish brown in sunlight, eyes that had a propensity for bags and dark circles. Even the shape of our face was the same.

"Are you upset?" he asked. "Is that why you came?"

I opened my mouth, but I was walking on a wire. I couldn't let him know how scared I'd been to meet him, or any of my mixed emotions about being here. The need for precision was key—*Give him no reason to reject you.*

"I've always wanted to know you," I said, putting a toe out. "Can you tell me about yourself, about your life?"

I pointed to the photograph on the back wall. "Why are you shaking hands with Bobby Kennedy?"

"I used to be involved in politics," he said, smiling a little.

"What was your platform?" I asked, the reporter kicking in, taking notes in the journal always tucked into my bag.

My father leaned in across his desk, and for the first time looked me straight in the eye. "I firmly believe in abortion, and a woman's right to choose."

He said it so smoothly that for a moment he became Stanley Chin for State Assembly again, back on the campaign trail ("Paid for by Citizens Committee to Elect Stanley Chin").

Back when they were engaged, my father got my much younger mother pregnant—and suddenly, he was pressuring her to get an abortion. My mother, a twenty-three-year-old schoolteacher, refused. It wasn't just that the procedure was a dangerous, illegal operation done under questionable conditions—she wanted to get married, start a family.

What did he mean he didn't want to have any more children?

Shouldn't he have told her this before he got down on one knee and proposed?

Before he slipped it to her, without a condom?

A woman's right to choose. Was he kidding? I suppressed the urge to laugh—it was so shocking and full circle: tell the adult daughter to her face on the very day that you first meet her that you believe in abortion. Hers.

Anyone else might have punched him. Called him a jerk. Hurled a thousand and one curses upon his head until he wished that *he* had never been born. I envisioned rising up and summoning the strength to overturn his heavy wooden desk onto his lap, the piles of paper, legal documents, and framed photos sliding onto the floor. Then turning on my heels, and leaving his office in an array of broken furniture, strewn papers, and personal mementos.

Instead, I blinked it off. Stanley was not going to throw me off the trail when I was so close to fulfilling my childhood dream of knowing him, and where I came from.

I smiled. "So what happened with the race?"

My father stared at me, paused, then amazingly began recounting the story of his adult life and career. Since it was getting dark, he suggested continuing the conversation over dinner.

We walked out onto the street, where it had stopped raining, but the pavement was slick with moisture. It was that kind of inky mid-February early evening that's pitch-black outside, but where the streets are as crowded as midday. Grandmas were shopping in pairs, talking a mile a minute, their arms weighed down by bags of groceries. The soup dumpling restaurant, with its front window festooned with Zagat reviews, was even more crowded than before.

He pointed out the store with the best jung, sticky rice in bamboo leaves stuffed with savory lap cheong, pork belly, and a salty, powdery duck egg yolk. "Our family opened Chinatown's first coffee shop here— the Sugar Bowl," he said.

I already knew this from his father's obituary, but it was still startling to see the site up front, and right here.

Up ahead, past the lampposts, the flags, and the vertical signs, Pell

Street seemed to dead-end into a six-story red brick building on Mott Street—my Chin grandfather's last address listed in his obituary. Its facade was festooned with Chinese characters—the only ones that I would later be able to make out were "Toi San," the Pearl River Delta county in Guangdong Province from which we all originally hailed—and Old Glory paired with the Nationalist flag of the Republic of China, its white sun framed by a blue sky, postage-stamped on a field of red. The building appeared to encompass the neighborhood like a giant open book—there was even a bend in the middle like a spine, where Mott Street suddenly hooked southeastward. If I cracked it, what stories might fall out?

"I was born there," my father said.

I followed his finger, up the green fire escapes along its brick facade, startled that I must have seen this building dozens of times without ever realizing my Chin family lived there. He was pointing out a floor and window on the left, but it was difficult for me to make out one apartment from the other.

Stanley as a baby with his father, Lung, 1931

"Back then," he continued, "people were born at home, not hospitals.

"My grandparents, your great-grandparents, lived there," he added, indicating another apartment to the right.

I paused.

My father was born here, where my grandparents lived. And now I knew that my great-grandparents resided here as well.

I stood there marveling at this great brick building that seemed to open before me. I could practically see the great-grandmothers and their children rushing about their individual apartments, the theater of the domestic, and the grandmother that I had never met bearing down with all her might, before giving birth to the crying infant who would become my father.

Something about this hooked its way into my heart, sprouting a tentacle, even as I raced to catch up to my father, who was already walking ahead up the block.

For a time, I lived off the high of knowing him.

I learned that he was born in 1931, and just like me, his father—Grandfather Lung, the same gray-haired elder I saw in the museum photograph only a few years before—had also grown up separated from his dad. Lung had left written documents that I scooped up from various family members, who were eager for someone else to read the unedited materials he'd been working on before he died, plus that oral history, which was still tied up in red tape at the museum. A charismatic character, who ran numbers and lived most of his life in Chinatown, Grandfather Lung was always spinning tales, and roping in some young woman to write them all down.

Then, one day, I was on the phone with my maternal grandmother, Rose, when she told me the address where she was born.

I paused, above my pen and paper, where I was scribbling it down, unsure of what I was hearing.

Chin On family, 1929

"Can you repeat that?" I asked. "What number Mott Street?"

When she confirmed it, I was so flustered that I quickly got off the phone.

Thirty-seven Mott Street.

She was born in the same apartment building as my father, the tenement on Mott Street with the bend in the middle.

It was then that I realized that long before my parents met, their families must have known one another.

It would take another few years before I discovered, on a trip out to see the Chinese enclave of Bradley Beach for myself, that both families had not only kept summer homes in the same community on the Jersey Shore, but they had also once been upstairs and downstairs neighbors from each other in Chinatown.

My families, whom I had never before seen in the same room together—whose only connection I had formerly understood to be me— had been *upstairs-downstairs neighbors*.

It got stranger.

As I got to know my father, little by little, the information started to flow, but it was often completely contradictory from what I learned from the people who raised me.

"Your grandmother is very stiff and proper," he said one day.

Grandma Rose, like most parents, could not suffer having her daughter stood up at the altar.

"I had to meet him to insist he marry her," she later told me. "She was already pregnant with you, and here he was calling off the wedding!"

"My father, Lung, was a court interpreter," he said, on another occasion, when I asked about our Chin side.

When I told my grandmother, she scoffed. "He swept the floors!"

"My father, Wu Doshim, was a VP of the Bank of Canton," she said, proudly.

"Doshim was a loan shark!" my father proclaimed.

What was the truth?

It was hard to know.

Although both sides had been part of the same community in lower Manhattan, right now, because of what had happened between my parents, these people hated one another.

To understand the truth for myself, I had to go back generations, to the villages they had left behind in China, and all the places where they originally landed in America—Angel Island, Seattle, Malone, New York. But no matter how far I traveled, and how many time zones I jumped, all paths eventually led me back to the Chinese Exclusion Act—the country's most restrictive and longest-running immigration law—and our six-floor building on Mott Street at the very center of old Chinatown.

3

Such Treasures

—

Wong-Ng-Doshim Family

黄伍

As a child, I spent countless weekends at my grandparents' Queens home, where in the kitchen, Grandpa Gene was the towering gourmand at the center of it all. Through the hefty power of his cleaver, chopping block, and pantry stockpiled with ingredients carefully chosen by way of color and smell—dongu mushrooms, dried, with cracked caps that smelled like the forest floor, and chewy abalone that resembled imperial boat-shaped gold ingots (he required only the best, no matter the cost)—Grandpa created meals that were nothing short of magical.

Even if it was just the three of us, my grandparents and I, while my mother was off on a date, Grandpa would produce a parade of food: stir-fried pepper steak; soy sauce chicken wings dripping in a brown sugar glaze that had me sucking on the bones and lapping up the last grains of sauce-soaked rice; winter melon and pork soup in a clear consommé with

*Gene and Rose at their
wedding, 1941*

bobs of floating medicinal dongquai root that Grandpa said was *good for
when I became a woman*. It was here in the kitchen and upon my plate
that he and Grandma Rose placed the choicest morsels from each dish—
the biggest crab legs bursting with lumps of meat, ready to be dunked in
Chinese vinegar, or the largest pieces of lobster still clinging to shiny red
shells. At the end of every epic meal, Grandpa would suck his teeth, slap
his ever-expanding belly, and order me to bring him a toothpick.

Years later, when I was an adolescent and he'd gambled away whatever savings he had—Grandpa had a fondness for the horses that was
second only to his appetite—he informed me that *his wealth was located
right there in his stomach*, where not even the bank could take away such
treasure.

THOUGH GRANDMA WAS BORN here like me, my grandparents had a
split work schedule like many immigrant families. While she held a day

job as a bookkeeper, Grandpa worked afternoon and night shifts as a bartender and general manager of a restaurant. They rarely saw each other, except for the weekends, when Grandpa would cook, carefully timing the prep so that he could lower everything to a slow simmer, and conveniently slip away to the racetrack.

Some of my earliest memories are of rolling out of bed on Sunday mornings, and listening to Grandpa recount stories about our family in his deep, resonant voice. These were fragments of a larger narrative that not only pointed to something valuable about our Wong ancestors and Grandpa's boyhood in China, but also about our family's larger contributions to American history.

By far the best stories were about his grandfather Yuan Son, who, as a teenager, crossed the Pacific Ocean and landed in the American West to work on the nation's first transcontinental railroad. Although I never saw a picture of my great-great-grandfather, I envisioned him looking like a cross between handsome Grandpa and the Marlboro Man.

When Yuan Son arrived in the 1860s, he and the others still referred to California, and by extension the entire country, by its Gold Rush name—Gum San—the Gold Mountain. Although that era had long since passed, the feeling among the new arrivals was that through their luck and determination, like maan mah ban tang—ten thousand stampeding horses galloping full steam ahead—they were going to strike it rich.

Together, Yuan Son and his countrymen labored in California's high Sierra Nevada—dangling off rugged cliffs in baskets loaded with explosives, blasting tunnels through miles of granite, laying grade even in the deepest winter, sometimes in over forty feet of snow.

They hauled rocks and chipped away at boulders, built massive trellises across yawning canyons, and laid down track armed only with hand tools—shovels, picks, sledgehammers, spikes—engaging in a grueling kind of *bone work* that reverberated up Yuan Son's arms and shoulders, making his teeth chatter.

In winters, they braved snowstorms and freezing temperatures, camping out in snow tunnels dug, once again, by their own hands. Many froze to death or were swept away by avalanche while working or sometimes sleeping, whole camps felled by the weight and gravity of tons of crushing snow. Some would be found the following summer, as the ice melted away drip by drip from the needles of wet conifers, still clutching their hand tools or blankets—the same area that decades earlier had halted the Donner party in its tracks.

But somehow, Yuan Son survived.

When they breached the other side of the mountain range, they discovered that the earth cracked red beneath their feet, and a vast desert sprawled out before them. The nights were cold, and the days long, but still they persisted, in rotating shifts, the work an unrelenting rhythm like a muscle, until it seemed to move with the very pace of Yuan Son's beating heart. They raced forward laying down that track, even while the land transformed from desert to windswept, arid plains, and they were joined by others—Mormons, and freed Black men.

Then, one of the Big Bosses boasted that they could lay down ten miles of track in one day—wagering $10,000 to back it up.

The other railroad company to the east was incredulous. Many white men laughed and claimed it was impossible.

No workforce in the world had ever laid down that many miles of track that quickly.

On the day they hit a flat, uncurving part of the land, a spot where the very horizon appeared to shimmer and lighten with the clear rays of morning, Yuan Son and his countrymen sensed a glimmer of opportunity.

At the first trill of the whistle, they were off.

He and the others forged ahead, singing songs about love and longing, the sound of their spikes pounding into rails ringing out across the desert like the traditional wooden knockers folk musicians back home used while talking story. They worked until their hammers became extensions of their arms, movements resembling golden arcs as they bore down with all their weight, then rose up again, as fast as their earthly bodies would allow. The men and their work inched forward ever eastward, toward the rising sun, at a pace never seen before, all to prove to their bosses, the nation, and perhaps even themselves, exactly what they could accomplish.

Hoi-lah! Hoi-lah! Hoi-lah!
Figh-di! Figh-di! Figh-di!

They called out like parents urging small children to "hurry it up," but they were now men, on their own, building something important in this foreign land.

By noon, they had progressed an unprecedented six miles. While the others chowed down in their Whites Only dining cars, Yuan Son and his countrymen ate lunch right there on the line.

When break time was over, and the white men returned, Yuan Son and his countrymen were already waiting on the grade, tools at the ready.

By the time the sun had lowered, and the sweet sound of the final whistle blew, Yuan Son and the other workers reluctantly put down their hammers and shovels and picks, and found themselves bathed in reddish light, the setting sun at their backs, their silhouettes reaching out across the empty stretch of desert.

Suddenly, a plume of smoke appeared, accompanied by a noise so loud it could only have been steam powered, and then the appearance of a giant locomotive heading their way, a test run across their track.

The locomotive chugged forward, slowing down at the end with a satisfying screech of the brakes, all without a hitch.

When they made the announcement—the bosses shouting so loudly their voices rang across the desert like a bell—he could actually hear the white devil *kai ai*s shouting in their flat, monotone language, but he didn't fully comprehend it until a great murmur went up among his countrymen and someone yelled:

Sup miles! Mm sup lok!
十 miles! 五十六!

Ten miles, fifty-six feet of track. All in a single day.

The newspapers back in Dai Fo, the "Big City"—San Francisco—were ecstatic. California's *Daily Alta* claimed, "No such feat has ever before been accomplished in the history of railroading." Another newspaper declared it "the greatest work in track laying ever accomplished or conceived by railroad men."

That night, at their campsite, sitting around the natural rock formation in the middle of the Utah desert, Yuan Son and the others layered up against the blistering cold.

Gazing at the stars, so close to the completion of the railroad, he could almost feel the metallic edge of driving that last spike into the ground. He felt happy that they were nearly finished, but couldn't help thinking of the many who'd died along the way. Ever since he had started working for the Central Pacific Railroad, train-car loads of the dead had been sent back to California for burial. And because it took so long for the bodies to return to their villages in China, only the skeletal remains made it back home—transported in boxes the length of femur bones.

Sitting under the shadow of the stony arch, Yuan Son wondered why he had been one of the lucky ones.

When they finally did finish a week and a half later, the transcontinental railroad was hailed by the bosses, newspapers, and politicians alike as the nation's greatest engineering marvel of the nineteenth century. Four years after the Civil War, Lincoln's dream had been fulfilled. At long last, Americans could easily travel from coast to coast.

The country was finally unified.

When the photographer's bulb flashed on the great celebration day as the ceremonial golden spike was driven into the ground by officials surrounded by politicians and men from both railroads, there were no Chinese faces staring back at the photographer. Even so, after the festivities, and when most of the officials and photographers had left, a crew of Chinese workers remained to pound in the working spikes for the very last rail.

Because he had no wife back home, Yuan Son took his earnings and pressed on: first working on the Southern Pacific Railroad, and then eventually moving out to silver mining country in southern Idaho, where the state population was nearly 30 percent Chinese by 1870. It was near Boise, in the basin of a valley that overlooked mountain ranges that reminded him so much of home that Yuan Son, no longer a teenager, set up shop, opening a dry goods store and a gambling parlor.

WHAT MY GRANDPA NEGLECTED to mention in his retelling of this story was that not long after Yuan Son and his countrymen completed the railroad in 1869, a great depression roiled Europe and America.

First, the Vienna stock market crashed in May 1873.

Then, one of the biggest banks in New York, which financed and speculated on a bloated railroad industry, suddenly failed—sparking a panic and a run on banks across the country. When the New York Stock Exchange was forced to close for the first time in history, it ushered in the worst depression the young country had ever seen.

They called it the Great Depression, and later, the Long Depression and the Panic of 1873.

Ignited by years of suffering throughout the depression and fueled by racism, violence tore through the western United States like a wildfire. Congress, swayed by senators and congressmen riding a wave of populism, enacted the Chinese Exclusion Act in 1882—blocking the immigration of Chinese laborers and their rights to citizenship. Later, in Boise, Idaho, after almost three decades of living in America, Yuan Son heard an angry knock at his front door. When he opened it, he confronted a mob of his white neighbors yelling, "The Chinese must go!" Some didn't even bother to mask themselves, as they drove him out of the home he had been living in for decades.

Because this part of the story was so difficult to stomach, and I was so young when I first heard it—a preschooler who begged for pony rides at the local amusement park, who still believed in the magic of her grandfather's storytelling—Grandpa chose to focus on other aspects: the great engineering marvel of the railroad, and the names of the individual railroad companies—Central Pacific, Union Pacific, Southern Pacific. That they were the first words he learned in English only highlighted their importance.

Grandpa stressed these accomplishments and never mentioned the Exclusion laws. I would have to read about those later, when I grew older, in Asian American literature. It was only then, as I perused the works of Maxine Hong Kingston, *Woman Warrior* and *China Men*, in a college English class, that I realized they were there all along, even though no one in my immediate family actually explained them to me.

One day, when I was still in grade school, a piece of mail arrived addressed to "Sun Ming Wong" at my grandparents' house. My mother and I had moved twice by that point, but wherever Grandma and Grandpa lived would always be home.

"Who is that for?" I asked my grandmother.

"Grandpa," she said.

I frowned. My grandfather's Chinese name was Kai Fei, his American name, Eugene. The barflies that he served every day at the restaurant he managed since I was in pre-K called him Gene.

"It's his paper name," Grandma continued, before dismissing me to open yet another bill that had piled up in the hallway.

I don't remember when I began to realize that this was unusual. None of my friends' family members' mail came addressed to a different name.

Did that mean Grandpa was illegal—living here under an alias?

But why was he illegal when his grandfather came to this country so long ago, and helped build the railroad?

I forgot about this, until one day, decades later, as a college professor and a mom of a chatty four-year-old daughter, I attempted to follow the paper trail and uncover what existed of the family history. I flew out to Seattle, Washington, where Grandpa had first landed in America, and

Exhibit in case of
WONG SUN MING
Seattle file # 7030/11729.
TO BE RETURNED TO SEATTLE OFFICE

State of Washington, :
                      : ss
County of King, ---- :

29489/13-5

Wong Ging Teng, being duly sworn, depoese and says: That he was born in Canton, China, some forty-five years ago and came to the United States in 1913, being landed at the port of Vancouver as the son of Wong Hong Ho, a native born American citizen, and therefore as an American citizen in his own right under Section 1993 of the Revised Statutes of the United States; that as evidence of his American citizenship he holds certificate of identity No. 10076, issued to him by the immigration Service May 13, 1913; that he now resides at 44 west 34th Street, New york City;

That since admission affiant has visited in China some three times, the first time through Boston in Rep. 10; the second time thru Seattle in Rep. 20, and again in Rep. 25; that while in China in Rep. 10 he took a wife, one Lew Shee; that by this wife affiant has four children, as follows:

Wong Sun Ming, born Rep. 11-4-21, or May 17, 1922,
Wong Sun Ock, born Rep. 12-8-15,
Wong Kim Yuen, born Rep 21-1-11,
Wong Kim On, born Rep. 26-2-XX 15,

That the children named now live with their mother in the village of Tung On, China;

That it is the desire of affiant to have his son Wong Sun Ming jpin him in the United States to claim his American citizenship and to learn American ways, and this affidavit is made for his identification and use in obtaining transportation; that the photograph in the upper left corner thereof is that of affiant, and the photograph in the upper right corner is that of the said sonm Wong Sun Ming who shortly will seek admission at the Port of Seattle as the son of affiant, a citizen, and therefore as an American citizen in his own right under Section 1993 of the Revised Statutes of the United States.

Wong Ging Teng

Subscribed and sworn to before me this 1st day of June , 1938,

Henry A. Maurd
                        Notary Public.

Sun Ming Wong affidavit, 1938

where I was given clearance to review his Chinese Exclusion Act file at the National Archives offices.

The deposition contained a photograph of Grandpa at sixteen years old, and another man who claimed to be his father, whom no one in my family could identify.

I had never seen my grandfather at that age. When I was growing up he was still movie-star handsome, but back then, as a new immigrant, he was so pretty that if not for the short-cropped haircut, the starched white collar, and the jacket and tie, he could have been mistaken for a girl.

He was heart-meltingly young and fleeing the Japanese invasion of China, and here he was stuck in a facility that was essentially a jail.

The name listed in the file was Sun Ming Wong.

Suddenly, all the old unanswered questions came rushing back.

Who was Sun Ming Wong? Why had my grandfather taken this identity? Who was this man who claimed to be his father? How could the authorities believe this man, listed as Wong Ging Teng, was related to Grandpa, when they didn't even look alike? Why did Grandpa have to endure this charade when Yuan Son had lived out west for almost thirty years?

I looked down at the official file before me, an inch thick.

It would take me another few years and a move to China before I learned that this elaborate scheme—a part of the larger Exclusion apparatus—had turned his real uncle into a "paper father," rendering Grandpa a "paper son."

The Chinese Exclusion Act file was a complete and utter fiction.

SHORT AND PLUCKY GRANDMA ROSE had her own stories too. While Grandpa was busy creating elaborately timed feasts in the kitchen, she and I were busy bonding over her family sagas like mother and daughter.

Grandma had a kind of all-seeing eye that belied her actual near blindness and thick, round glasses. Although rarely physically demonstrative, when no one was looking, she would occasionally give me a wink from across the kitchen table.

She was the smartest person in our family, and the first woman to attend college. New Chinese arrivals were impressed with her language abilities—she spoke flawless Cantonese, and English with a lower Manhattan accent, and understood our village dialect and even Mandarin. On the weekends, she pored over the *Daily News*, the *New York Post*, and the Chinese newspapers with each serving of her morning coffee.

Other Americans were forever surprised that she had never been to China or set foot outside of the country. "Why would I need to leave when there are so many great places to visit here?" she always retorted.

Since I was a latchkey kid, coming home to an empty apartment after school each day, it was Grandma who taught me things that my overworked mother had no time for:

She taught me how to type on a giant IBM Selectric typewriter that hummed and rattled under my fingers.

She gave me skeins of golden yarn and a book on macramé, and soon I was making hanging baskets for her spider plants and their dangling springtime babies.

On Friday nights, we spent time together, huddled in my grandparents' mid-century banana-colored armchair in front of the television, where she allowed me to rub Jergens lotion on the back of her neck, and set her hair in rollers, so it would be ready for the weekend.

We slept in her big bed, chatting all night in matching pajamas, until the room grew dark and she made me go to sleep. My grandfather stayed in his own room because, she always said, *Grandpa snores*. But when I later learned that I snored too, she never complained.

Even in my teenage years, when other kids were busy rejecting their families, I saw my grandparents almost every weekend, when they spoiled me with attention and the giant feasts that I began to think of as my birthright.

I loved to sit at our kitchen table and leaf through Grandmother

Rose's giant photo albums, thick as bibles, and pester her about her family. Unlike Grandpa Gene, who fled war-torn China with few worldly possessions, my grandmother had plenty of photographs to sift through. Most of the time Grandma ignored me, or brushed off my questions ("Why do you want to talk about that old stuff for?"), but sometimes, if I was lucky, she'd start talking.

One day, when I was a college senior, I discovered a large, sepia-toned family studio portrait in one of her oldest albums. It was taken in 1926 and showed everyone sitting stiffly on hard-backed chairs in front of one of those pastoral painted backdrops so popular during the Victorian era.

"Grandma, who's this?" I asked, pointing to a distinguished, white-haired man in the center of the photograph.

"That's Dek Foon," she said, peering down at the portrait through thick eyeglasses. "He was my great-uncle."

"Who's that woman sitting next to him?"

Doshim family portrait, 1926

"His wife, Nana." Nana was a roundish white woman with light-colored eyes. She resembled the kind of pioneering women I'd read about as a grade-schooler obsessed with *Little House on the Prairie*, women who with seemingly just a few stirs could churn milk into butter.

"What was her *name*?"

My grandmother shrugged. "She just used to say, call me Nana. They lived in a big house in Brooklyn."

There they were, Dek Foon and Nana, the unlikely patriarch and matriarch of Grandma's family, sitting in the center of the portrait, flanked by my grandmother's banker father, her sweet beauty of a mother, and all six of their children. I'd never seen a portrait of a Chinese and white couple from that era. But here it was, an interracial marriage from earlier in the century within my own family. And here was my beloved grandmother, on the cusp of turning nine, sitting cross-legged in a white frock at Dek Foon's knees, a clear favorite—a future salutatorian and college student—her hair cut into a classic bob, sporting a string of her mother's pearls, her hair so shiny it gleamed even in sepia, looking at the camera lens with big luminous eyes. "What did your great-uncle do?"

"He was a translator and a banker—like my father. He was the one who sponsored my father over from China," she said matter-of-factly, offering nothing more that day.

A DECADE LATER, I stumbled across a profile of Dek Foon in Louis Beck's *New York's Chinatown*, describing him in 1898 as a "self-made man" and "one of the most highly respected men in Chinatown." I showed the book to my grandmother on my next visit.

"It says Dek Foon came to the U.S. eighteen years before the book was published," I said, slowly subtracting the years in my head. "He arrived in the 1880s."

"I've never seen such a young picture of him," my grandmother said, hovering low over the photograph. Her macular degeneration had gotten

Dek Foon in Louis Beck's New York's Chinatown, *c. 1898*

worse through the years, and she could see the image only from out of the corners of her eyes. Unlike me, she did not seem at all surprised to see her uncle there.

Uncle Dek was somewhere in his midthirties and wearing Western clothing—a suit buttoned to the top with a starched white collar that made me think of missionaries. As a Christian progressive (another rarity), he was certainly considered a missionary by his Chinese contemporaries. He was dark, with a proud nose and prominent cheekbones, and a generous mouth that I instantly recognized as a family trait we had all inherited. Noticeably, he wasn't wearing a queue—the long braid that Chinese men wore for hundreds of years under the Ching dynasty. Instead, his hair was thick and combed into a side part—a Western-style short cut that would put him at risk of beheading under Imperial law if he returned home with it.

Something about these two pictures, the Uncle Dek from this short profile, and the family portrait, took hold of my interest and refused to let go. From that moment on, I started piling on the questions.

Maybe the never-ending inquiries that popped out of my mouth grew out of my being estranged from my father and his family. And because no one, not even Grandma Rose, could bear to even talk about my Chin side without turning red with anger, or they'd mention them only in whispers, *bigwigs in Chinatown*—what did that even *mean*?—these mysteries remained like itches under the surface of my skin that I was constantly seeking to scratch.

And then there were the other unanswerable questions:

Why was it that despite our long history in the U.S., I grew up as an anomaly—the only Asian girl in my neighborhood, and one of a handful of Chinese Americans in my elementary and middle schools? And why, when I did run into another Chinese girl around my age in our two-fare zone, out-of-the-way neighborhood in Queens, did we invariably end up discovering that *we were indeed* related to each other, like someone's idea of a big fat joke? This feeling of unrest grew even as I gazed at that official Chinese-less transcontinental railroad photograph, and watched white actors like David Carradine portraying Chinese in the American West on television. Even though there was a hundred-year gap between the railroad's completion and the airing of *Kung Fu* on network TV, the two felt emotionally similar. Although I wasn't able to articulate it at the time, the word that arises now is *erasure*.

So I set about trying to uncover the history of the family who raised me, and stumbled upon the long-buried bones of a much larger story.

PART TWO

1880–1906

4

Dek Foon

Ng-Doshim Family

伍

Dek Foon, whose full name was Ng Dek Foon, and who lived in a village entirely populated by members of the Ng family, was a native son of southern China's Pearl River Delta region—where three major rivers, a maze of canals and streams, and a semi-tropical climate provided a year-long growing season. Farmers grew winter melon, leafy vegetables like gai lan and bok choy, an assortment of fruit, and green beans that grew as long as women's hair. Local brick builders dug gray-blue clay from the earth with their hands, fashioning bricks and building houses. It was also plagued by cycles of massive flooding, followed by years of severe drought.

Dek and his wife lived in a slate-colored brick house provided by his uncle, who had adopted the young man when he and his brother were boys, after Dek's parents could no longer provide for them. Although his parents' story is lost to history, for many young boys of Sun Ning (now called Toisan), this was not uncommon. The Opium Wars with the West, a fourteen-year civil war, and interethnic conflicts between locals and northern newcomers had split families apart when Dek was a child in the 1860s.

Shortly after Dek and his wife welcomed the birth of their son, the region suffered from a severe drought and food shortage. Wells ran to a trickle, and crops shriveled on their stems all the way down to their withering roots. In order to survive, they, along with the other villagers, were forced to eat bark, leaves, and mud. But when even the mud began to dry out, transforming into flaky, powdery dirt in his bowl, Dek Foon knew that he had to do more to provide for his family.

So he decided to seek his fortune in America, borrowed what money he could from his uncle, and boarded a ship bound for San Francisco.

When he was a boy, Dek Foon had learned English from a Christian missionary, who was so impressed with his intelligence and character that he was convinced that Dek Foon should become a man of the cloth. While his English was far better than most of his fellow compatriots', Dek Foon still had work to do if he was going to make something of himself in America. The only two books my uncle brought with him on the long journey over, besides a writing tablet, were two versions of the Bible: one in Chinese, the other English. Every day, in the darkness of steerage, while the others gambled, told stories, or slept the long hours away chewing on tiny bits of cloth formerly soaked in opium, Dek prepared for what he would say in English to the immigration officials until it became a kind of catechism. He whiled away the endless stretch of days and nights below deck by studying his bibles side by side, even after dinner and before preparing for bed.

On the day of their arrival, some three and a half weeks later, the excitement in their living quarters became muted when they weren't allowed to disembark with the other passengers. No one knows how long their wait was, but it would have seemed interminable. Officials were so backlogged trying to process recent immigrants under the Chinese Exclusion laws that had gone into effect in 1882 that San Franciscans complained of the massive "floating Chinese alien population on the Bay."

It's more likely than not that when the doors officially opened, and Dek Foon and his countrymen were ushered through, instead of being able to land, they were simply shuttled into the hold of a different ship—penned in with those recent Chinese arrivals—until the whole dismal cycle started all over again.

Although the first official documents are lost, I know from Dek Foon's Chinese Exclusion Act files housed in New York's National Archives that when he was finally interviewed by a *green government man*—all the immigration officers wore dark green uniforms—Dek Foon told the official in English that:

He was born in Shun On, in Sun Ning county—a district in Canton, where a majority of Chinese in America at that time originated.

His sponsor was his doctor cousin, and his occupation was "translator" for his cousin's medical practice.

Every answer that Dek Foon gave was carefully listed out as a record for future interviews going forward, so that inspectors could flag any errors or inconsistencies.

His face was heavily scrutinized for scars, pockmarks, moles.

The shape of his ears was noted, whether they were large or small (medium), whether they stuck out or were close to the head (close), whether they were long or short (longish).

His hands were checked to see if they were smooth or callused (smooth).

Finally, because these were the early days of Exclusion, and Dek's case was a fresh open file with no prior testimony with which to compare notes, the inspector admitted him.

The freedom must have felt exhilarating as he left the dock and headed with the other Chinese straight toward Chinatown. For the next several days, he stayed at the association clubhouse for Ng family members, a landing place for new arrivals, while acclimating to life in a new country. It would have been here, over his first hot meal in Gum San, that he heard the stories of the anti-Chinese riots igniting across the state.

JUST WEEKS BEFORE DEK FOON ARRIVED, a mob of white townspeople in the coastal town of Eureka, California, had attacked 310 Chinese men and women, forcing them out of their homes. Vigilantes tried to lynch one young man—slipping a noose around his neck—until someone from his church intervened and saved his life. At the docks where the entirety of the town's Chinese population were being held at gunpoint, the local Methodist minister tried to negotiate with the mob, but all Chinese, including the new Christian converts, were driven out.

This paai waa sparked similar sweeps in other parts of northern California's Humboldt County. Arcata. Salmon Creek. Ferndale. Hydesville. Garberville. Springville. . . . In San Francisco, while my uncle was just getting his footing, many of the Eureka victims were assembling a lawsuit against the town for the value of their stolen property.

The Chinese Exclusion Act had made its presence known by holding Dek Foon captive on the floating ships in the docks, but he would not feel the pressure of the Page Act until actually arriving in San Francisco's Chinese Quarter. Passed in 1875, just seven years before Chinese Exclusion, Page ostensibly barred Asian forced laborers and prostitutes from entering the country. But the act cast a veil of suspicion over all Asian women—forcing them to undergo a series of lengthy, humiliating examinations in order to prove that they *weren't* prostitutes. The practice served the government's goals—it dissuaded the majority of women, married or single, from immigrating, and also prevented the next generation of Asian American citizens from being born. Whenever Dek Foon walked the streets of Chinatown, catching glimpses through windows or open doors, the absence of women and children was startling.

. . .

AFTER THE COMPLETION OF the transcontinental railroad and the onset of the Long Depression, Dek found, as Yuan Son had, that the environment out west was drastically different from the stories he had heard. White immigrants searching for jobs arrived in droves from the East, transported by the very railroad that Chinese had been so instrumental in building. Many of the recent arrivals, themselves new to America, grew resentful when they discovered that the large contract jobs were dominated by Chinese workers—and not just in silver and quartz mining, but also in manufacturing, fishing, farming, and lumbering.

These men flocked to Denis Kearney's Workingmen's Party, the Order of Caucasians, the Caucasian League, the Knights of Labor—various organizations whose platforms rallied around "White Labor" while stoking the fires for Chinese expulsion. At the time, the Cigar Makers' Union label showed the white hand of Labor knifing a Chinese dragon. Many local judges, politicians, and business owners joined this anti-Chinese movement.

By 1880, as the Long Depression entered its second decade, anti-Chinese sentiment was so high that the California State Senate passed measures to explicitly prohibit all Chinese from living within city limits. These restrictions included places where Chinatowns had been flourishing for decades.

Although these ordinances were later struck down as unconstitutional, it provided a template for the federal Chinese Exclusion law, and inspired white extremists in many cities and towns, who used them as tacit approval to attack their Chinese Quarters—executing massacres and lynchings, looting and torching homes and businesses. Afterward, if any arrests were made, these men and women were let go—judges and juries often agreed with the anti-Chinese sentiment, so there were few, if any, ramifications. Chinese, like Blacks and Native Americans, were not allowed to testify in courts of law against whites.

By the time Dek Foon left San Francisco in the late spring of 1885, and headed northeast on a steamboat snaking up the Sacramento River to the foot of gold mining territory, organizations waving the banner of *white-only labor* were organizing to drive Chinese out of towns up and down the state of California.

According to his Chinese Exclusion Act file, Uncle Dek stayed in Nevada City for close to a year, acclimating to mountain life and opening his own hand laundry.

My uncle quickly set up shop. The humble work of a hand-laundry operation was one of the few businesses that Chinese could do that did not raise the ire of white townspeople. Even men who hated them, who boycotted a Chinese presence in the mines or factories, still needed clean clothing. Because Dek Foon knew little about doing laundry, he hired men with experience, Sayyup men—displaying skills they had learned from white matriarchs, who had hired them as domestics to help in the household. The laundry arrived at the shop in a rush: shirts, trousers, petticoats, undergarments, suspenders, socks, corsets, dickeys, clerical robes, dungarees, aprons. At a Chinese hand laundry, a poor man's overalls were washed in a tub along with a judge's robes or a rich man's three-piece suit. The same powder dissolved the accumulation of soil, grime, sweat, manure, and salts that caked the townspeople's clothing, before finally being rinsed away in a steady stream of soapy water.

My uncle saw firsthand the deficiencies in laundry equipment—the giant water wringers, the troubles of trying to fish hot irons out from a fire, the terrible burns his men suffered up and down their forearms—and began taking meticulous notations on how to improve them.

But Uncle Dek's contribution went unnoticed. During that time, other nearby frontier towns began organizing against people like us.

That November, as President Grover Cleveland was proclaiming the date for the National Day of Thanksgiving, the *Truckee Republican* published a brisk editorial for queue cutting—hacking off the long braid Chinese men wore (a "sure cure for the Chinese pestilence"). It suggested a reward system, and a kind of display, or trophying, "as is the case with pelts of wolves, coyotes, and like vermin when they become a pest."

Every time I read this article from the safety of my studio, it makes my breath catch. *They thought of us as animals.*

Insurance companies, anticipating arson—a common way of expelling Chinese residents—canceled the policies of Chinese businesses in Truckee and Nevada City.

As the local newspaper continued churning out anti-Chinese, pro-boycott editorials, Dek Foon's neighbors began hammering and screwing in extra locks and safety fasteners to their front doors and windows. Some even ordered guns and rifles from San Francisco.

Reading these articles over 130 years later makes me grow cold.

So many of these news accounts have the barest of information—it's just white people attacking nameless Chinese while they're working, or even while they're sleeping.

In nearly every one, the passive voice is dominant, as if the violence simply occurred like a force of nature, an act of God.

Fifty-four Chinese were driven out of Carbonado, in the Washington Territories, by a large crowd of white miners. (Who were these fifty-four Chinese men from our villages? What were their hopes and dreams for this life in America?)

> *More Chinese Driven Off. Portland, Or., March 1.—Between midnight and 2 o'clock this morning 180 Chinese working as woodchoppers and grubbers . . . were driven away from their camps, marched to the ferry landing and ferried across to this city. A crowd of eighty whites, most of them masked, divided into squads of twenty each, visited the camps and ordered the Chinese to leave, which order they obeyed without resistance.*

Dek Foon is much too close to these dangers for my liking—I feel like I have the weight of an anvil pressing down upon my chest. I have to get up from the file of newspaper articles and walk away.

A DAY AFTER DEK FOON's local newspaper ran its story about canceling the insurance policies of local Chinese business holders, 270 miles up the Pacific coast at the port of Seattle, church bells rang a coordinated signal at eleven o'clock throughout the entire town. It was the weekend. White residents stopped whatever they were doing and, from wherever they were, unlocked their doors and headed out to the streets. Some rode wagons, while others came on foot, boots kicking up dirt, clambering across the wooden sidewalks outside storefronts. (I'd love to call them vigilantes, but the group included the leading local suffragist, the acting chief of police, and nearly the entire police force.) When they arrived at the Chinese Quarter—a crowd of upwards of 1,500—they fanned out, knocking loudly on every door. *All Chinese out by one p.m.!*

Madame Lenoi Louie, the thirty-something wife of a merchant, was at home, in the boardinghouse she and her husband ran for Chinese workers. Even if she had heard the bells, she would not have known what they meant. It was Sunday, their busy day. Her husband, Chin Gee Hee, one of the most prominent Chinese merchants in town—a man famous in Guangdong Province for his later work on the Sun Ning railroad—was a major labor contractor for companies across the Pacific Northwest. He was connected to local sheriffs, judges, attorneys, and customs officials, as well as the Chinese consulates in San Francisco and Washington, DC, and he had business contacts as far out as New York, Hong Kong, and England.

Although a successful merchant's wife, Madame Louie wasn't afraid of hard work—when she first came to America, she had cooked hundreds of meals for the Chinese lumber mill workers who worked with her husband. In addition to feeding dozens of men who lived at their boardinghouse, hungering for the food of their hometowns, she also took care of their growing American family—giving birth to their son Chin Lem, a pudgy happy boy, doted on by all who resided with them, who in 1876 was one of the first Chinese Americans born in Washington Territory. His birth was followed by a daughter, and now there was yet another child on the way.

Although she had lived in the U.S. for a decade, Lenoi's interactions outside the community were limited. Surrounded as she was by her countrymen, she found little chance to learn or practice English. She would have been reminded by her husband how unsafe it was for her outside their home, as one of the few Chinese women in Seattle. If she ever went outside the store, perhaps running after one of her children out onto the street, everyone would have stopped and stared at her—the gwai lo cowboys with their rude eyes and gaping mouths, and their sons who threw rocks. She learned to stay indoors, watching the street only from the upstairs windows, instructing their son to look after his little sister when she sometimes strayed outside.

Lenoi was upstairs that morning, and I like to think of her enjoying the latter months of her pregnancy, that golden trimester when you could almost forget you were pregnant. Did she hear the mob yelling from outside, busting down doors and breaking windows, or was she completely unaware, busy in the back room, caught up in sorting things for the newborn? She must have heard them entering the front door, a wall of sound rising to the second floor as the clamor of footsteps approached. She stood up from her chair, belly rising first, the great yawning of pregnancy.

They were a motley crew—*these damned white ghosts* (even in America, she would have called them *foreign devils, barbarians*) who broke into her home. What was she thinking in that moment—of her children playing in the backyard, or of her husband, who had left the house earlier that morning, who had promised he would be back shortly, before any trouble erupted?

While Lenoi Louie's husband was fluent in English, she was most certainly not. And even if she could summon up the proper words of protest, in English, when has "Stop!" ever stymied a seething mob intent on forcing out people like you?

They yelled at her, *Get out!* but Lenoi just stood there, unsure of what to do. *What are you, stupid?* one of them said, before grabbing her. She hit him, but the more she protested, the more forceful they became, pushing her out into the hallway. When she tried to run, a gwai lo grabbed a fistful of her hair and began pulling her down the corridor. She had never been so close to *barbarians* before. She smelled something familiar off this man, mixed with the sweat and dirt on his hands, so close to her face, off their bodies crowding so close around her—a scent so subtle she couldn't quite place it.

She tried to slap him as he dragged her down the stairs, but it was like punching someone in a dream. Soon she was sliding down the steps in only her house slippers. When she grabbed the hand railing, barbarian hands peeled her fingers back, until she cried out in pain. *Why were they doing this? Where were her husband and children?* Chin Gee Hee had successfully resisted intimidations by townspeople before, and even brokered deals with the most ardently racist leaders to allow them to live here in peace—but it had never come to gwai lo breaking in.

The crew pushed her outside, where the air was cold and sharp, and Lenoi Louie found herself shivering on the wooden deck in only her lightweight house clothes. There were jeering gwai lo all around her, yelling, grabbing her hair and ears, and soon she was covering her face and head trying to protect herself. Suddenly, someone pushed her, and she was flung out onto the street and into the bright sunlight, where the wagons were waiting, where the horses shat. She fell onto her hands and knees, the dirt rising in clouds around her.

There were other Chinese amassed there too, shouting when they saw the pregnant merchant's wife. She was piled onto a wagon with the old people, the few Chinese women and crying children, while the others were ordered to march. Did the woman next to her curse the barbarians as *uncivilized dogs*, or did she sit, like the others, in terrified silence, even as the wagon moved forward and they were pelted with rocks?

When they arrived at the crowded docks, the home guard militia—composed of clergy, citizens, and nervous students—was in a tense standoff with anti-Chinese rioters. In the harbor, the *Queen of the Pacific* passenger ship and its crew lay in wait. Through the shouting and the threats, they were told that *Chinamen who wanted to leave* could board the ship, while *Chinamen who wanted to stay* would be brought back home with the militia. (Although the guard seemed to offer a reprieve, a few members extorted money—"jokingly" cutting off the braided hair of one terrified man, before brandishing it in the air like a trophy.) Was Lenoi Louie there when the guns went off, bullets ringing out into the air like firecrackers, and everything was thrown into chaos—blood, the acrid smell of gun smoke, a tangle of pushing bodies, shouts and cries? Later, they learned that five were wounded, including a man who died soon after, but Lenoi Louie would not remember any of this.

For only moments after she was pushed onto the street in front of her home, Lenoi had felt a searing ache in her womb that was like falling down an echoing well. Before she knew it, she was curled up into a ball and the world blackened, as if the sun above had turned its back on her.

Over the course of the next three days, Governor Squire of the Washington Territory, initially hesitant to ask for help, declared martial law—salons were shuttered and business ground to a halt. Lenoi Louie was removed to her bed, where the bruises and shock of being pushed out of her own home had prompted excruciating contractions. Finally, forty-eight agonizing hours later, she gave birth to the baby.

It was a preemie.

She held the infant so tiny and faint like a distant star in her arms.

Her breasts swelled with milk until they threatened to burst, desperate as a stream with no outlet, but no matter what Lenoi Louie did, the baby would not latch. Lenoi was despondent. It was only then that she realized what the scent was. Familiar, not familiar. The men who grabbed her smelled like nu nai, like cow's milk, like dairy.

A few weeks later, while 2,500 protestors, defying the federal government and the governor's orders, marched through the streets of Seattle, holding signs that read "Discharge Your Chinaman," "Down with the Mongolian Slave," and "Get off the Fence, Either For or Against," Lenoi Louie's baby died.

WHEN DEK FOON LANDED in New York with his bibles in his bag and an address to find in Chinatown, it was unlike any city he had ever seen. Unlike the Sierra Nevada mountain town he had fled—selling his laundry "at a profit," according to Louis Beck—New York had an ad hoc mix of Beaux Arts architecture and brownstones, and its own chaotic transportation: noisy but wonderful elevated train lines; horse-drawn cars and hansom cabs, breakneck cable cars, and streetcars that criss-crossed up and down Manhattan; and numerous ferries shuttling passengers between Manhattan and Brooklyn beneath the Gothic arches of the Brooklyn Bridge, the first steel-wire suspension bridge in the world.

It was sometime in the late spring of 1886.

For Dek Foon and other Chinese landing in the city, the Chinese Quarter was the epicenter of their world. Just three small, interconnected blocks, it was rich with gambling parlors, opium dens, Chinese joss houses (smoky places of worship filled with burning incense and joss paper to honor both deities and the dead), and a growing population of cooks, cigar rollers, candy makers, and sailors living in $1.50-to-$3.00-a-week boardinghouses.

In May 1880, only six years before his arrival, the United Christian Brethren of the Moravian Church—one of the biggest landlords along lower Mott and Pell Streets—had evicted their Chinese tenants and strictly forbade the subletting of apartments to Chinese or Blacks. Although these sentiments were just another iteration of "The Chinese must go!" I was particularly pained to learn that it had happened here in my hometown.

Chinese, who were charged higher rents, moved farther up the block or around the corner to nearby Park Street (today's Mosco). Some steadfastly refused to go, as in the case of one Mott Street shop owner, quoted in *The Evening Post*, insisting, "I stay here," while his clerk tallied up accounts on an abacus.

Despite the hostility, the neighborhood progressively became more Chinese as hundreds upon hundreds of refugees like Dek Foon arrived in the city. Local newspapers reported an exodus from the western states in the late 1870s and early 1880s: "Chinamen Coming East," "The Chinese Quarter Expanding: Many of the Victims of San Francisco 'Hoodlums' Coming to New York," and "Is It a Chinese Exodus? Rapid Growth of the Almond-Eyed Element in New York." Despite the best efforts of the local churches, by the time my uncle stepped off the streetcar, this was the largest Chinatown east of the Sierra Nevada.

On Mott Street, he soon discovered a rich and vibrant community of other Toisan transplants. Huie Kin, a thickly mustached Christian missionary with a deep center part, who would later become a trusted friend, described Chinatown's main artery as "a little Monte Carlo, but without its glamour," in his memoir *Reminiscences*.

The Reverend Huie, who arrived in New York the year before, was the elder statesman of a group of Chinese Christian intellectuals who were young and full of life. They were eager to root out the gambling parlors in Chinatown, which they considered the major vice of their brethren—meeting at a rented parlor on University Place and at Huie's Presbyterian Sunday school for Chinese, one of only four in the city.

They were Guy Maine (Yee Kai Man), a man of tireless energy who headed up the Chinese Guild of St. Bartholomew's Church and who came to the defense of Chinese across the city and Brooklyn whenever they suffered from harassment and attacks on their laundries; the charismatic and wiry interpreter Joseph Singleton (Jeep Man Sing), himself a noted Congregationalist minister; and Dr. Joseph Thoms (Tom Ah Joe), who worked his way up from being a young domestic to becoming the first Chinese in the country to graduate from a medical university.

To signal that they were progressive Americans, they cut off their queues, donned Western suits, and anglicized their names. Most of them had married or would go on to marry white women. Together, these exceptional men were like blood brothers.

A year before Uncle Dek befriended them, Huie Kin and the band of brothers had begun tackling the gambling dens directly.

It was dangerous work. On Leong tong, an organization composed of the earliest established businessmen and merchants in Chinatown, was getting a cut of all gambling profits. On Leong took a dim view of anyone attempting to interfere.

The gambling dens were loud, boisterous affairs at the back of storefronts, filled with men standing around and playing fan tan, a kind of Chinese roulette without the wheel, all while smoking and socializing. Huie, Maine, Singleton, and Thoms, dressed in workmen's clothing, mingled around the tables and got to know the proprietors, lookout men, and operators. But when they later reported these establishments to the authorities, the police were reluctant to get involved. Most officers turned a blind eye to what was going on in Chinatown, mainly because it was easier, and, more often than not, they were getting kickbacks from On Leong.

Soon, Huie and the others began pressuring top city officials to do something.

When police protested they could not differentiate between Chinese individuals, Huie and company offered to take part in the raids themselves. Once the arrests started rolling in, the band garnered a reputation as notorious do-gooders (twun nin a bow, or gow shee goon) and soon were targeted and threatened, even at their own churches. When threats proved ineffectual, gambling den proprietors switched tactics—offering the men a share in the profits. Huie and friends refused. From this work, they forced the police to shut down all the gambling parlors up and down Mott Gai. But less than a year later, by the time Dek Foon was getting his footing, it had all started back up again.

While I enjoy thinking of these men battling the evil forces that drain Chinese of their money (read, *Chinese draining money from other Chinese*), I don't exclusively see these as fun tales of my uncle's circle of heroic friends. I am a gambler's granddaughter, after all, and while I don't do it myself, nor condone it, I can see how the pressures of being apart from one's family, and living under discriminatory laws that created these family separations, would foster conditions where men would gamble, and gamble *often*, in their free time. And when coming to this country in and of itself was a huge gamble, they must have thought, *What could be so wrong with engaging in a few more games of chance at places where you might see many of your friends who were in exactly the same boat?*

In the Chinese Quarter my uncle found work with one of its oldest laundry suppliers, Wong I Gong. Uncle Dek clerked, kept the books, and even ran deliveries for his new employer on the windy bend of Doyers Street. Years before 37 Mott Street would become our family homestead, the building site around the corner from Dek Foon's workplace, and newfound home, was a funeral parlor and horse stable owned by James Naughton, an Irish undertaker. Naughton, who had purchased a set of connected buildings, 31–37 Mott, from an absentee Irish landlord, was an industrious nineteenth-century businessman who understood the neighborhood. He hired workers to paint "James Naughton" and "Undertaker" in giant letters between the floors of the three-story brick and frame building and ran advertisements in the *Cristoforo Colombo*, describing himself as "the biggest entrepreneur of Italian funerals in the city . . . many cars, carriages, and everything necessary for weddings, baptisms, and parades"—in Italian, naturally.

His popular stable at 37 Mott Street, with its ever-present piles of manure leading up to its wide entrance at the mouth of Mott and Pell Streets, provided horses for the police department and exemplary funerary services. It was likely here that Dek Foon got the horse to transport his boss's supplies.

Dek Foon was busy learning about the twin cities of New York and Brooklyn through his long horse and cart rides through various cobble-stoned neighborhoods, delivering supplies to laundrymen. He sent money back home to his wife through a channel his employer had set up, but even as the company clerk, Dek had to pay a small fee like everyone else (*a good business*). He had dreams of bringing his family over, although he soon learned that there were no provisions allowing them in under the Chinese Exclusion laws—it was entirely up to the whim of the immigration officer in charge. No other nationality had to contend with this—Dek Foon's Italian, German, Dutch, and Irish neighbors on the Lower East Side could simply bring their wives over for the price of passage.

His wife hired the local letter writer to send news from the village, messages that are now entirely lost to history.

Then, one day in 1890, Uncle Dek received a letter that she had died.

It's not hard to imagine that feeling of disconnect Dek Foon felt as he read the news, that moment when a letter becomes a vehicle to the past. News traveled slowly from China to New York, and the message had taken well over a month and a half to reach him. It was like looking at the night stars, and suddenly becoming aware that the light he was seeing had been emitted years ago.

He contemplated what he had been doing that day. When she was dying in their village, was he readying the horse for the journey into Brooklyn, making sure all the merchandise—the boxes of soap and liquid bluing ("Whiten White Clothes Safely!")—was securely tied down? Or was he already traversing the bridge, the sun coming up over Brooklyn, the wind at his face, horse, man, and cart reaching that midpoint juncture between the two cities, suspended over the rippling water flowing north toward the Harlem River and Long Island Sound, neither in Manhattan nor in Brooklyn?

It was his favorite part of the journey, apart from the pleasure of seeing laundrymen and merchants, who greeted him now like an old friend, as he brought supplies and goods from the Chinese Quarter—vegetables, dried noodles, herbs. Greeting their friendly faces in his native dialect as he descended made up for the parts of the journey where he was forced to duck as white boys pelleted rocks at him from the street (or worse, when they lobbed them from high windows).

Now, any enjoyment Dek felt that day would have been seen through a new veneer of guilt.

Dek Foon's first impulse was to return to China and fetch Wu Chow, now seven years old. He had not laid eyes on his son since he was just beginning to walk. But there were several obstacles: there was the problem of his having cut off his queue—a crime in China; also, there were no guarantees that Dek himself or his child would be able to get back into the U.S. Dek Foon no longer owned his own business, and he suspected that working as a clerk and part-time deliveryman for Wong I Gong was not going to pass muster with immigration officials at the border.

And even in the unlikely chance that Dek could manage to get both of them into the country, what would happen to the boy here? Who would take care of his son while Dek worked? If Dek Foon had to shield himself from rock-throwing children cursing him to hell across the city, how much of this would his son endure?

Dek's prospect of remarriage to a Chinese woman on the East Coast was slim to impossible, and the idea of marrying outside the race was not only frowned upon in most social circles, it was also illegal in many states, although, luckily, not in New York. No, Dek's brother would take care of the boy until arrangements could be made for him to attend a nearby boarding school. This was the same school that Dek's nephew Shim, an earnest bespectacled twelve-year-old who broke out into a sweat every time he had to recite classical poetry, attended. Shim would look out for Chow once there.

Better to have Wu Chow get a good education and enjoy the comfortable life back in the village, son of a "Gold Mountain man."

5

Dek Foon

Ng-Doshim Family

Over the course of the next few years, back when the sounds of carriage wheels and horse hooves resounded against the cobblestoned streets, Dek Foon's network widened across New York City.

He attended Guy Maine's Chinese Guild Episcopal church, and later went into a kind of "everything" business with Joseph Singleton. They offered local advertising, and personal banking for those who didn't belong to a tong, or who wanted to borrow more funds than their family or village association allowed, or who simply needed to wire money to their wives and families back in Toisan or any of the other towns throughout Guangdong Province and beyond. In the evenings, after dinner, he drafted plans for an ironing press that he had been considering ever since he closed up shop in Nevada City.

Both Maine and Singleton were interpreters at the Immigration Service and, impressed with Dek's fluency, they introduced him to their bosses, who needed part-time translators for dealing with the many Chinese coming through their doors because of the Exclusion Act. He may have been told that for someone with his language abilities it would be easy. The Office of the Chinese Inspector was just a short walk from Chinatown on the southern tip of Manhattan, and the procedures for screening his countrymen were familiar to him, having gone through it so recently himself.

Still, I can imagine how my uncle's heart raced when he was called into the interrogation room that very first time on the job. He was wearing his best Western suit, and his hands were perspiring when he removed his hat before sitting down at the big wooden table with the inspector and the stenographer. The new arrival was sitting across the table, and in that moment, Dek Foon regarded a pair of eyes whose nervousness was even deeper than his own.

This was the first time he faced this dilemma—whether to help his fellow Sayyup Chinese or remain as neutral as possible in this impossible situation under which they all found themselves—but it would not be the last. It would take years before he figured out the nuances of how to give aid without raising suspicions. In that time, he would have made mistakes, and he would have had to learn how to not get too attached to a case when officials deported someone whose answers didn't align with what they thought they should hear.

THE CONNECTION HE FORMED with writer Wong Chin Foo, an orator, charismatic trailblazer, and champion of our civil rights in America, whom he had met in the Chinese Quarter—a place so small that everyone knew each other—would be Uncle Dek's political awakening. Championed by a media eager to sell papers, Wong refuted popular stereotypes of Chinese in American culture.

"I never knew rats and puppies were good to eat until I was told by American people," he wrote in an essay.

When Chinese were blamed for lowering the living standards of white workers by the likes of sandlot orator Denis Kearney, an immigrant himself, Wong Chin Foo was out in the public square, ardently defending our countrymen with lectures and incisive essays in *Puck*, *The Cosmopolitan*, and *The North American Review*. He challenged Kearney to a public duel of "his choice of chopsticks, potatoes, or Krupp guns." When the two engaged in a lively debate at the editorial offices of *The World* in 1887, Wong, the superior debater, was declared the winner ("Denis Kearney Defeated" and "Downed by a Hated Chinaman").

By 1892, the Chinese Exclusion Act was coming to the end of its ten-year term. Although a subcommittee of Congress recommended a rubber-stamped renewal, this wasn't enough for a newbie congressman from California. Thomas J. Geary proposed his draconian Geary Act, requiring that all Chinese be interviewed and registered with the government; obtain identification papers with their photographic likeness; provide white witnesses to verify their identities; and keep these papers on them at all times, or risk arrest and deportation. Some have likened this to an internal passport system, but if folks were caught by the police or immigration without the paperwork, they were automatically presumed guilty—no "innocent until proven guilty" if you were Chinese—and denied bail during habeas corpus proceedings.

After hours of argument and testimonies that stretched over a month, the Geary Act passed the Senate by voice vote, and the House by an overwhelming majority of 186 to 27.

Under the new law, all Chinese would need to be photographed and registered by the following year.

The New York Times lambasted the new measures: "The act of Congress was one of political cowardice. . . . It is one of the most humiliating acts of which any civilized nation has been guilty in modern times."

Even New York's Chamber of Commerce declared Chinese Exclusion and the Geary Act as "unjust, unwise, and inexpedient."

The Six Companies, a consortium of Chinese American mutual aid organizations in San Francisco, called for mass civil disobedience—forbidding anyone from registering—and prepared to challenge the law in court as unconstitutional.

The Chinese government demanded its repeal on the grounds that it violated both the U.S. Constitution and bilateral treaty terms.

In New York, Wong Chin Foo sprang into action, reaching out to all Americanized and naturalized Chinese to fight the new law. Dek Foon and his friends joined him.

THAT VERY YEAR, they formed the Chinese Civil Rights League, and quickly renamed it the Chinese Equal Rights League (CERL). Uncle Dek met other English-speaking Chinese, all of whom sported Western haircuts and suits, and many of whom were naturalized before the Exclusion laws were enacted. In addition to Uncle Dek and Dr. Thoms, Wong Chin Foo served as secretary. The group worked tirelessly to build a coalition across the city—drumming up opposition to the law.

On the evening of September 22, a crowd began amassing at the Great Hall at Cooper Union in lower Manhattan.

The choice of venue was strategic. Not only was it conveniently located a block from the League's office, it was also the historic building where Lincoln had given his famous "right makes might" speech against the expansion of slavery, and where the U.S. women's suffrage movement was jump-started by Susan B. Anthony and Elizabeth Cady Stanton.

Although he did not speak, Dek Foon was in the audience, sitting prominently in the front.

By eight o'clock, hundreds of people were streaming in, and the sounds of their collective gathering filled the assembly.

While Wong Chin Foo and Joseph Thoms assembled onstage, other members of the League sat with Uncle Dek, including Singleton and his wife. I'm tempted to think that Dek, ever the optimist, shook hands like an American, smiling and engaging in the kind of jokey rhyming convention that folks from our villages often made up on the fly. ("It's a *great* evening—in the *Great* Hall.")

Newspapers reported there were as many women in the crowd as men—including white Sunday school teachers and their Chinese pupils. Several ministers in their clerical garb, mostly white, but some African Americans, made the rounds of the assembly. Outside the hall, an interloper circulated anti-Chinese pamphlets, but most ignored him.

By the time the first speaker stood up, a *Times* reporter noted, the Great Hall was two-thirds full. Dek and his friends were elated. For them, this event was personal and nothing short of momentous. In California, Washington, and Oregon, where the tides were so against them that they could not hope to petition whites or other naturalized citizens to join their side—here in New York, where the anti-Chinese sentiment was less prevalent, all hecklers aside, here they stood a chance.

As he watched Wong Chin Foo, and local Black and Irish ministers vehemently denouncing the Geary Act, I imagine that he felt something akin to pride.

According to League estimates, over a thousand prominent Americans as well as nearly two hundred Chinese, mostly merchants, attended that night, adopting a resolution declaring the Geary Act "monstrous, inhuman, and unconstitutional," and pledging support to protest the bill.

Uncle Dek left the meeting buoyed and so energized that when Wong Chin Foo asked him to be on the board of the Chinese Equal Rights League, as assistant secretary, he gladly accepted.

CERTAINLY THEY WERE BUSY that winter. The League garnered signatures from across several states and held another public meeting in Boston, aided by civil rights activist William Lloyd Garrison, Jr., son of the famous abolitionist. That night, Garrison acknowledged that the League's aim to stop only the Geary Act additions was modest, and argued that if he were Chinese, he "would demand nothing short of the rights and privileges due a citizen of the world," prompting a call throughout the assembly to end Chinese Exclusion in its entirety.

Garrison persuaded Massachusetts congressman John Forrester Andrew, who served on the Committee on Foreign Affairs, to draft legislation replacing the Geary Act. Andrew landed them a hearing before Congress, for which it was decided that Wong Chin Foo should testify as head of the League.

In early January 1893, Congressman Andrew presented a giant sheaf of signatures from across many different legislative districts, demanding the repeal of the Geary Act (the repeal of the entire Exclusion Act was not included, perhaps being seen as too drastic). *The New York Times* deemed it "a monster petition," when it appeared before the House of Representatives.

WHEN WONG CHIN FOO presented himself before the House Committee on Foreign Affairs in Washington, DC, on a fair winter's day, January 26, 1893, not four months after that energizing meeting at Cooper Union, he was making history. It's widely believed that this was one of the first times that a Chinese person had ever appeared before Congress. No one could remember any Chinese testifying at a congressional hearing before this point.

The newspaper reports from California, where Wong's address made front-page headlines, list only one person from the League accompanying Wong, and that was Tom Yuen, a board member who had seniority over Dek.

"Gentlemen of the Committee on Foreign Affairs," Wong Chin Foo began. "We represent and speak for the 150,000 Chinamen of this country, who are no longer emigrants, but bona fide residents of the United States."

Although he was inflating the numbers, in making his point about Chinese, who "have their families and their business interest in this country, who understand and abide by its laws" and "have been educated in your schools, and converted to your religion," Wong was refuting the commonly held belief that Chinese were unwilling to assimilate to American culture. And he was defining his cadre as those Chinese Americans who had been living here for years, if not decades.

"We do not ask for favors—we appeal for simple justice."

The San Francisco Call's report, where I'm reading an edited transcript of the proceedings, is an exercise in reading against the grain—like most West Coast publications, it had a decidedly anti-Chinese stance, and was prone to downplaying the strength of Wong's arguments, as well as taking cheap shots at his accented English.

Still, it's likely that this committee, which included the bespectacled junior California congressman Geary himself, regarded Wong with a mixture of curiosity, hostility, and bemusement. Although Congress had debated "the Chinese Question" for decades, this was probably the first time most had witnessed a Chinese addressing them like a peer—an Americanized Chinese, in a three-piece suit, who wasn't their domestic or laundryman, or even a soft-handed diplomat who had made his way up through the ranks of the imperial system in China.

"Is it then a crime, punishable by law, to be a Chinaman?" Wong posited. "Shall I be dragged from my bed at midnight because I shall refuse to be photographed? No, I will not be photographed against my will like a criminal. I would be hanged first."

Wong then held up a sheaf of national newspaper articles. "Ninety-five percent of these are against the Geary Act," he said, waving them above his head. "They are from newspapers all over the country, except California and Oregon, where we do not expect them to treat us with justice."

(This dig at the West Coast publications, although true, did not go over well with the California reporter, who defensively characterized Wong as "almost pathetic.")

When Geary himself asked Wong what Chinese from the League were advocating for, Wong said, "We want a law that won't photograph us. We do not wish to be treated as criminals."

"Now, Wong," Geary interjected, his tone overly familiar, as if placating a child, "there is no use in your talking like that. This is a most humane law. Under old conditions the Chinese were harassed by arrest and imprisonment. You have only to provide yourself with a certificate to render you free from molestations."

In my imagination, Geary transforms into a snake when he says this. A snake in a collar, pearl tie pin, and jacket.

"Certificates are impossible for many Chinamen," retorted Wong. He would not have liked Geary's tone of voice, from a man seven years his junior. "And besides, there is the disgrace. We don't wish to be photographed like felons. We are law-abiding."

"Yet you admit that there are 150,000 Chinese in America," said Geary, consulting his notes. "A few years ago, there were only 90,000. How do you account for the increase of 60,000? Surely it does not come from natural causes.

"They were smuggled in," Geary continued, without waiting for an answer, "everybody knows that!"

He regarded Wong through spectacles so small they appeared almost microscopic. "How many Chinamen wear short hair and clothes like yours? That is why you must be photographed. Your people are not law-abiding. That is why they must be regarded as they are in the United States."

And there it was. Surely Geary's characterizations of his countrymen smarted like vinegar onto a wound, but instead of arguing that the laws were unfairly stacked against us, and how the entire apparatus needed to be reformed or, better yet, *thrown out*, Wong Chin Foo stood before the congressional committee, unable to respond.

Wong Chin Foo was caught. He couldn't back down from the grandstanding of his opening statement and admit that he had inflated the numbers from the get-go, just to bolster the importance of the League and the size of the community it purported to represent.

"If this law is barbarous, you should insist on its enforcement and its own barbarity will soon bring about its repeal," Geary said smugly.

Chairman James Blount, a Redeemer Democrat from Georgia, intent upon maintaining white supremacy in the south, interjected. "Are you willing we should restore the old law allowing the entry of visitors, merchants, teachers, travelers and students, and prohibiting the entry of the working classes?"

"Yes, that is what we want," Wong said.

"But how could we make such a law more effective than in the past?" Blount queried.

If Wong gives an honest answer, he's doomed. (What does Wong know about enforcement? He's not a police officer.) The sensible approach would be to deflect away from the question—and toward equality for all Chinese to freely immigrate like *all other nationalities.*

But Wong thinks he knows all the answers. "By holding the steamships responsible, as well as the Chinese government," he said.

"But how could we hold the Chinese government responsible?"

"By fining her for each infraction of the law."

At this, several of the congressmen looked at each other and laughed.

"Would we have to send our army over there to collect the fine?" Blount asked incredulously.

"That would be unnecessary, I think," said Wong, "for China would pay up."

The California newspapers noted that this caused an outburst of laughter from the committee members.

It was in many ways a losing battle for Wong Chin Foo, surrounded by so many politicians who were dead set against him, in addition to the ones who didn't see any reason to stop the Geary Act or Chinese Exclusion because they didn't believe in equality or they needed to curry favor with colleagues from the western states or because Chinese were so disenfranchised without voting power that *in the eyes of these politicians, we did not matter.* In some cases, it was a combination of all of these.

I couldn't get over the fact that Wong hadn't argued against Exclusion in its entirety. Why not speak out on behalf of your fellow countrymen? Why be so shortsighted to the reality that in another generation their numbers would be so depleted, given miscegenation laws and the Page Act, that Chinese like us would eventually cease to exist—even in places where we were a significant part of the population? Without those numbers, they, or rather, *we* would have trouble establishing a large and vocal voting bloc in this country.

But maybe that was just it. Just as I had grown up unaware of this legacy, and was concerned with that which seemed to be most directly related to me, this was *their* reality. Dek Foon, Wong Chin Foo, Huie Kin, Guy Maine, Singleton, and all the others encountered this racism and the way it was embedded in nineteenth-century American law firsthand, and just like polypore mushrooms I find growing in the wild, they had to navigate this formidable obstacle by growing slowly and tenaciously around it.

Just as I was used to constant questioning from strangers—immigrants and other Americans alike—along the lines of "Where are you from?"—the implication being *you aren't from here*—so did they become used to this environment. They simply didn't know anything otherwise.

That day, the Committee on Foreign Affairs adjourned soon after Wong's testimony, without taking any further action.

The same Congress that had signed off on the Geary Act simply shrugged, and allowed it to stand with the new restrictions.

The Chinese Exclusion Act would continue for another ten years.

Soon, thousands of Chinese across America were scrambling to register.

In New York, Guy Maine noted that his Chinese Sunday school students were demoralized by the news. "The scholars seem to have no desire to further advance their knowledge of English and religion. I know men who hardly missed a Sunday in the Sunday School for years, who are idling away their time on Sunday in public parks and on the streets. When pressed for reasons, their simple reply is: I have no mind to study."

The League continued, but when Wong Chin Foo left New York City, it was greatly diminished. Then, on a trip to visit family in China in 1898, Wong Chin Foo died of heart failure at fifty-one years old.

Geary lost his congressional seat in the election the very next year, but the damage was done. The Geary Act would affect the lives of countless Chinese in America for generations to come.

ACCORDING TO HIS EXCLUSION FILE, Uncle Dek applied for his Geary Act certificate of residence while living out in Cincinnati, Ohio. The official record is muddled here—Dek's Chinese Exclusion Act file puts him in Cincinnati with a doctor cousin, which was his reason for entering the country, while another family member's file has him returning to China in 1889. Louis Beck's profile places him solidly in New York City from 1886 onward. I believe he traveled a bit (including to Boston, which had its own thriving Chinatown), and may have spent time in Ohio, but mainly called New York home. Wherever it was taken, in the photograph attached to his certificate, Dek, in three-quarter profile, looks steadfastly and decidedly away from the camera, resigned, but complying, and not liking it one bit.

By 1895, Dek Foon was back in Chinatown, residing at 55 Bayard Street, just around the corner from Naughton's stables and funeral parlor on Mott Street.

The next year, Dek's studious nephew, Shim, sent him a letter politely requesting his sponsorship to the United States. In China, there was a growing sense of resentment toward the tightened Exclusion restrictions, which only added to the ire toward Western countries for enacting the Opium Wars, and the eventual handing over of Hong Kong and concessions in Canton and Shanghai to foreign powers. The seeds for the Boxer Rebellion had taken root and spread, and now Christian missionaries were being attacked and murdered across the country.

Despite this, and perhaps even fueled by a sense of urgency, Shim, a Christian undeterred, was ever more anxious to become a missionary in order to spread the gospel to his countrymen. *Wouldn't it be better to do that by getting a good Christian education in the United States?*

Dek Foon contemplated the request. He and his brother, How Foon, Shim's father, were children when they were adopted by their uncle, who had no sons of his own, and here in New York, Dek was certainly doing well enough to support his nephew.

Although it had always been difficult for Christians like them in China, these days tensions had only grown worse—it wasn't just lofan missionaries being attacked, but more often their Chinese converts. Dek's son, Wu Chow, now a teenager, was content to stay at their local boarding school, but if things went well for Shim, who was now like an older brother, it would pave the way for Chow to see the benefits of coming to America too.

Dek wrote back with an invitation for his nephew to come join him in New York.

6

Chin On

—

Chin Family

When my paternal great-grandfather Chin On stepped into the small boat and huddled with the others, also attempting a midnight crossing of the St. Lawrence River from Canada into the Beautiful Country—head down, chin tucked into his collar, so his breath could warm him—he must have known that the odds were stacked against him.

Family reports vary over the date, but it was likely sometime in the mid-1890s, when Exclusion was in its second decade.

Great-Grandfather wondered, Whose crazy saap ngong idea was it to cross the Canadian-U.S. border in the last months of winter, when the frost still clung to tree branches and their breath hung in the air like clouds?

How like Hing, his second-oldest brother, to not inform him how cold the journey across Canada would be, and instead put his own needs before others. . . .

Chin On, 1913

Back in Sun Ning, Chin On was known as the quiet, learned son of his family. He had just completed the imperial exams, from which he had earned the quite respectable rank of teacher, and was waiting for a permanent position to become available anywhere in the Four Counties, when he received his older brothers' invitation to join them in Gum San.

Business was booming on Mott Street, and the Chin brothers needed someone literate like Chin On to keep the books and write to their suppliers and retail customers who were buying up as much of their merchandise as they could get their hands on.

The only wrinkle was that government officials would allow the store only two merchants' visas, which were now being used by the two eldest brothers.

Great-Grandfather Chin On may have been a learned scholar well versed in the doctrines of Confucius, Lao Tze, and Mencius, but he was also the son of the local kung fu master, and, like the men of his filial generation, he had trained at the family martial arts school since he was a boy. He knew how to defend himself in a fight, and he wasn't beyond taking risks.

After careful consideration, he decided that crossing into Gum San illegally across the Canadian border was a gamble he was willing to take.

Only now, with the gwai lo captain warily eyeing all Chinese passengers as if he were prepared to toss them into the river to save his own neck, Chin On was having second thoughts.

Why hadn't he just stayed home? Why was he coming to a land where the ways of the people were so strange?

Chin On had the misfortune of living in a period when the only real chance for entering the country for folks like him was to pay exorbitant amounts to white smugglers to skirt the system.

Suddenly, a flash of bright light appeared from a watchtower along the shoreline, beaming down to the river along which they drifted.

Did the man next to Chin On stiffen and call out in alarm? Did the captain hiss-bark an order for everyone to shut up?

Chin On was certain that the captain was going to toss them into the river, and that would be it—his adventure on Gold Mountain would be over before it even started. He was a strong swimmer, and the river was not too wide, nor even very deep near the shorelines, but the frigid temperatures would have greatly lowered his chances of survival. And even if he did make it over safely to the other side, what then? He still needed the *horse that carries people ten thousand miles* smuggler to bring him to shelter and safe passage.

They watched the searchlight crisscrossing the water, looking for crafts like theirs. The only thing Chin On could hear was the water lapping against the boat over his own breathing, which, for some reason, sounded louder to him than if he had swum out there himself.

Just then, a wind picked up, whistling through his ears and riffling his hair, and then he felt something cold against his face—big, giant snowflakes—before a blustery gale kicked up and they were engulfed in a howling white tunnel. The searchlight, confronted by the sudden snowstorm, swung from side to side, like a lone dog sitting forlornly at a window.

It was said afterward, within our family, that the small boat with the human cargo was hurtled toward shore on the other side, as if Providence itself had pushed it.

So even with the odds against him, Chin On considered himself extremely lucky. Later, safely in New York, he recounted this origin story to Grandfather Lung, who wrote the bones of it down—the pages of which fell into my hands after meeting my father, more than a decade later.

As soon as I read it, I knew Chin On wasn't the only lucky one.

BACK IN CHINA, the Chin brothers had been gamblers and kung fu fighters, working at their father's martial arts school. Although the family had been glorified generals and military nobility throughout the Ming dynasty, in the waning years of Manchurian rule, they and the men who worked for them were mere hired bodyguards, providing protection to ordinary citizens against bandits and merciless warlords. When the organizers of a nascent anti-foreigner movement began recruiting fighters, the Chin family was among the first approached in their village.

Ever since Marco Polo wrote about his travels to China (Cathay), foreigners had been seeking to establish a foothold, pushing trade for native items—tea, silk, porcelain *chinaware*. Only, China was uninterested in anything except silver. When the emperor cracked down on the British East India Company's flooding of the country with opium, the British army attacked—launching the Opium Wars in the 1830s, and then again in the 1860s. During this Century of Humiliations, China was forced to pay high reparations—granting foreigners diplomatic-like immunity in Shanghai and Canton, and handing Hong Kong, Kowloon, and the New Territories over to England. Soon, envoys of proselytizing missionaries arrived to convert the *heathens*.

It is time to get rid of the foreign devils, the movement leaders said, *including the missionary families and the traitors they converted.*

But the Chin brothers refused to fight on the side of the Manchurian government. Despite their dislike of foreigners, they hated the Manchus even more—northerners, who for centuries had forced them to shave their hairlines and braid their hair into long queues.

Instead older brother Hing, a risk-taker by nature, signed a contract with an American labor company. After a month at sea, he landed at one of the many fish canneries that had cropped up along the Columbia River near Seattle, Washington. Once he found his footing, he promised, he would send for the others, including younger brother Chin On.

Until then, Hing logged in long days, slogging on a work line with a machete doing dangerous manual labor hauling, gutting, and cleaning fish—Chinook, sockeye, and coho salmon. In his downtime, he drank and gambled (*ho yum, ho dou*), and in between seasons, he made trips down to Dai Fo, where he enjoyed the action that only a big city like San Francisco could provide. In Chinatown, he engaged in all of the Four Vices—gambling, drinking, visiting prostitutes, smoking opium. One night, after having a dream of a far-flung eastern capital, he bought a ticket for the White Pigeon Lottery. Two characters seemed to pop out at him, blocking all the rest.

Hing, who was guided by visions—visions of fortune, of opportunity—and gifted with the brute strength and determination to manifest his own luck, took all the money he had, his earnings from an entire season of laboring in the Pacific Northwest cannery and the whole of his gambling wins, and did what he did best—wagered it all on a single bet.

According to my grandfather's papers, Uncle Hing was lucky that day—to his delight, the characters "Go" and "Eastern Palace" won him $1,000.

If he had been home, this could have been interpreted as Japan or Hawaii, or even Gold Mountain itself, but in California, these characters could mean only one city—New York.

New York's a good place to go if you have money, they told him.

Melting pot.

New immigrants.

Fortunes to be made.

He carried his winnings tucked into a leather pouch that he wore strapped under his shirt like a belt.

ON THE TRAIN RIDE OVER, he met a Cantonese missionary based in New York—the young reverend Lee To, a friend of Dek Foon's. The good reverend offered Hing lodging, English lessons, and the gospel at the Morning Star mission on windy Doyers Street. It was here in the Chinese Quarter where Hing settled and soon met a German called "Big Louis" who sold odds and ends of pork—ham hocks, pork bellies, bacon sides—from the back of a horse-drawn wagon on Pell Street.

Hing saw a golden opportunity and hatched a plan. Buying from locals like Big Louis and Sayyup vegetable farmers from the outer boroughs, he used his gambling money and set up one of the first grocery stores on Mott Street—Ying Chong, or Grand Eagle. Situated among the curio shops, gambling parlors, and opium dens, Ying Chong was directly across the street from Naughton's funeral parlor and stable—Naughton, who also owned Ying Chong's building, was his landlord.

Business flourished. Gamblers flush with winnings bought groceries for a little taste of home—succulent pork belly, pristine lo bok, and hairy taro root. Even the poorest workers could afford the cheaper cuts of meat—pig ears and pork trotters—to feed themselves and their roommates. The cooks at gambling parlors, which provided food for patrons in order to keep everyone full, happy, and betting at the tables, began buying their ingredients directly from him. Because sales were so good, Hing sent for his kin.

The eldest brother, Jun, their father's favorite, and who, as firstborn son, inspired the most jealousy among the siblings, arrived next. He was quiet, with a stoic face covered in pockmarks.

And then, because business was booming with everyone from the cigar rollers and candy makers to Chinese merchants like Singleton and Dek Foon hankering for ingredients that tasted like home, and they needed someone literate to keep their books, they requested that the third brother, Chin On, my paternal great-grandfather, come join them.

After Chin On completed his harrowing border crossing, catching a train from Malone, a tiny border town in upstate New York, to the center of Manhattan, he lived in the back of the store with his older brothers. Ying Chong's success had cemented the Chin brothers' reputation on Mott Street, and a few years before Chin On's arrival they had been invited to join the society of other business owners, the On Leong tong.

On Leong, a.k.a. the Peaceful Chamber of Commerce, or the Merchants' Association, may have been composed of elite businessmen, but it was not a civic organization like Dek Foon's Chinese Equal Rights League. It was also different from the regional or family associations that other Chinese relied upon. Tong, which roughly translates to "chamber," would take on a whole different meaning by the next century, inspiring fear in the hearts of ordinary Chinese residents. (Decades later, when I was growing up, tongs would be linked to notorious street gangs and referred to in the press as "the Chinese Mafia.")

Tammany Hall, the dominant political machine in New York City, courted the city's immigrant communities for their votes, but because the Chinese Exclusion Act and the earlier Naturalization Act rendered Chinese in America ineligible to vote, Chinatown was at an extreme disadvantage. Despite this hurdle, the community still found a way of influencing city government by lining the pockets of its various politicians, "bosses," and local police officers. Tammany Hall favored its payoffs coming from a single, easily accessible neighborhood source, and that position was happily filled by Tom Lee.

Although my Chin family claims that the first president of On Leong was Hing, and its first secretary Chin On, the beginnings of On Leong's charter started years before, as the Lun Gee tong, before settling on its current name, with the bilingual Tom Lee as its public face. In the years before the Chin brothers made their way to New York City, Lee made it his business to personally knock on the door of every gambling parlor in Chinatown, flashing a sheriff's badge and accompanied by a police officer, to collect the "rent."

Wiry Tom Lee was a mercurial figure—the bane of Huie Kin's Christian brotherhood, he had been a good friend and supporter of Wong Chin Foo's Chinese civil rights campaign, even sitting beside Wong at Cooper Union, heckling orator Denis Kearney on his anti-Chinese road show in the mid-1880s. He had married a German woman and was raising a family on Mott Street, just doors down from both On Leong headquarters and the Chinese Consolidated Benevolent Association—the newest iteration of the Six Companies, and Chinatown's de facto city hall. In the summer of 1888, Lee, who enjoyed sporting a diamond stickpin in the lapel of his three-piece suit and smoking cigars, rented a ferry on behalf of On Leong and threw a giant two-hundred-person picnic in mixed company with both a Chinese and a German band.

The Chin brothers, on the other hand, were still struggling with the nuances of operating in another language and culture. When they joined On Leong, they did so in the order in which they immigrated, Hing gaining a foothold first, and then bringing in younger brother Chin On. While they lacked Tom Lee's and Dek Foon's ability to navigate white society, with the exception of Chin On, who was a favorite with certain illustrious women of Mott Street, the brothers made up for it with a certain kind of arrogance and flair that would later become known as a distinctively Chin quality.

7

Elva Lisk

Ng-Doshim Family

伍

Back when Dek Foon's ship was arriving in the San Francisco Bay in 1885, three thousand miles away in Brooklyn, Elva May Lisk, the fifteen-year-old, blue-eyed, fair-haired, precocious daughter of a Civil War veteran of Vicksburg and his wife, still had not yet experienced her menstrual period.

Her father, Benjamin, had returned home after the war in 1865, and for reasons that no one remembers anymore the couple, with their son, Charles, settled in a rural part of Pennsylvania not too far from Scranton. There, mother Sarah gave birth to twins—William and Lillie. Then, not two years later, Sarah, in her mid- to late thirties, with her hands full raising three children, made the surprising discovery that she was pregnant again.

Elva May was born in the fall of 1870 and was what my grandmother liked to refer to as the "P.S." baby. Sarah was at home when her contractions came on fast and strong, and she sent her oldest son out the door to fetch the midwife. But Sarah's womb, so efficient after having supported the twins two years prior, was way ahead of any child messenger or fleet-footed midwife. Before Sarah knew it, she was hunched over, ready to give birth in the darkness of the couple's bedroom.

By the time the midwife arrived, Sarah was in bed, and the baby already cleaned by her expert hand, wrapped in cotton swaddling, thoroughly attached and suckling. It was, by all accounts, a rather unremarkable birth. Nothing survives on paper saying otherwise.

By the time Elva was five years old, in 1875, the Lisk family was listed in the New York state census as residing in Brooklyn, living on the top floor of a house in a rough-and-tumble section of Red Hook, better known for its port culture of seamen and dockworkers, warehouses, and saloons than residential family life. Benjamin found employment as a police officer, likely off his credentials as a former Union soldier. It was the era of the Long Depression, when law enforcement was pitted against striking railroad workers, Civil War vets among both sides.

Very little is known about Elva's school years, but according to my grandmother Rose she was an exceptionally bright and confident child, impatient at times, and curious about the world. Eventually she reached that point where as a young teenage girl her education ended, and she watched her older brother and the boys of the neighborhood continue on to high school.

While other girls developed breasts and began cinching their waists with corsets, fashioning their hair into elaborate finger waves that framed their foreheads, and twisted buns that showed off their cheekbones and tapering necks, Elva was more interested in reading and in her Protestant faith. On weekends, she volunteered at the Sunday school. As the years progressed, Elva remained flat-chested, her sturdy body barrel-like, even under the most formidable whalebone contraptions, her hands sprouting from under her sleeves like Chinese gourds.

By the time she was in her early twenties, Elva and her family had moved to a working-class immigrant neighborhood on East Thirteenth Street off First Avenue on Manhattan's East Side. While her siblings had left home to start families of their own, there was Elva in her room, reading books and newspapers, ruminating over women's suffrage. Meanwhile, Benjamin and Sarah worried their youngest child would live with them forever.

When Elva met thirty-two-year-old Irish bachelor William Joseph Doran, it's not hard to imagine the elation in the Lisk household. At twenty-four years old, Elva was two years older than the national average age when most women married. She and her family would have heard "old maid" and "spinster" whispered in hushed tones within their social circle for years.

LITTLE IS KNOWN ABOUT Doran except that, according to United Methodist Church records, he was born in Athlone, Ireland, and had settled on the Lower East Side at 51 Henry Street, a neighborhood adjacent to the Chinese Quarter.

What is certain is that Doran entered during the Great Wave of European immigration that began in 1880 and continued to 1930—a period in which the U.S. began actively moving toward a comprehensive exclusionary approach to its borders. Just three months after passing the Chinese Exclusion Act, Congress approved the 1882 Immigration Act, targeting anyone "likely to become a public charge," including those who exhibited some sort of visible communicable disease or appeared to be a "convict, lunatic, idiot."

A year after Chinese Exclusion and the 1882 Immigration Act were passed, British scientist Sir Francis Galton coined the term "eugenics."

By the early twentieth century the eugenics movement, which shifted the focus from the selective breeding of agriculture and livestock to "improving" the human race, had taken hold on American immigration practices. But back in pre–Ellis Island 1888, when Doran arrived through customs at Castle Clinton at the tip of Manhattan (today's Battery Park), he would have largely escaped the kind of physical examination Dek Foon and other Chinese were subject to, unless someone had deemed him *likely to become a public charge.*

On a cool, rainy Sunday afternoon on May 26, 1895, the couple were married at Elva's local Methodist church on East Fourteenth Street.

There are just a few facts that we know about the wedding night, based on Lisk family lore, passed down by word of mouth from generation to generation, swirling at times elliptically around Elva's anatomy, but in my mind's eye, this is how I see it:

It's not hard to imagine Elva's nervousness that night.

She had never had a boyfriend and knew little about sex. While Doran washed up, Elva undressed in the semidarkness of their bedroom—peeling off her garments like so many layers of an onion—the outer dress, the whalebone corset, the cotton inner blouse and bloomers. She slipped into the white dressing gown her mother had made for the occasion, fingering the embroidery along the neckline. Like most Victorian women, Elva considered underwear scandalous, so the only thing between her bare bottom and the bed was this gown that Sarah had so expertly sewn. When Elva let down her hair, it fell in waves over her shoulders and down her back. It was so long she could sit on it.

What followed next would later be remembered as a series of flash impressions.

Doran placing the oil lamp on the bedside table, the lamplight casting long shadows behind him until he extinguished it.

His mouth suddenly against hers as he leaned over her, pushing against the covers.

Kissing him, like biting into a plump, veiny plum on a summer's day.

Doran's hands were moving underneath the curves of her backside, sparking a sensation like one of Edison's currents running down the length of her body.

Elva didn't want him to stop—her entire body was pulsating, electric. He moved down to the expanse of her hips, his breathing audible. Elva stretched her hands out across the bedspread, and was enjoying the feeling of being thoroughly alive, when a part of her rose up.

Doran pulled back, stunned, and somehow managed to light the lamp.

Elva would have struggled for what to say, feeling the terrible heat from Doran's gaze. He certainly wouldn't have looked like he was in any place to listen. Instead, I imagine him yelling in a hot rage.

Did Doran's hands ball into fists? Did he fight the urge to swing them, a right-handed hook straight into Elva's jaw?

Or maybe he grabbed her by the arms, leaving bruises across her skin the shape of his fingers, before finally letting go.

I believe Elva lay there, watching as Doran struggled to find his clothing, then, shoving himself back into his pants, leaving their room. She tracked his footsteps across the living room floorboards, to where he slammed the front door shut.

Doran hurled one word at her before he left. Although she tried to suppress it, it rang through Elva's ears and up through the network of synapses in her brain, hiding there, incubating over the course of the next couple of years, emerging every time she thought of him.

Monster.

WHEN DEK FOON MET Elva May Lisk one day at church, he was so taken by her, it was said forever after in our family that it was truly love at first sight.

It was seven years since her marriage to William Doran had ended so abruptly, and Elva had long since resigned herself to spinsterhood and living at home with Sarah and Benjamin on the East Side. Now at thirty-one years old, her potato-shaped face was beginning to get a certain hardening around the edges, and then there was the sudden appearance of small lines around her eyes whenever she smiled. She was accustomed to men not actually rejecting her so much as simply *not seeing her.*

Elva was so surprised that she didn't even look away. Instead she stared straight back at Dek, her pupils opening wide like an aperture, as if trying to take all of him in—this middle-aged Chinese man with hair still so thick and black it resembled a horse brush, and a generous mouth that broke out into an easy smile. Although his ears stuck out slightly, she liked the look of his square jaw and his rather lean, ermine quality reminiscent of a mink.

There was, of course, no chance that such a man was interested in her, an old maid, so she put it out of her mind at once.

Once the service ended, Elva stood up and was surprised to see the stranger talking to her friends, who were apparently their mutual friends. The wife of this couple waved to her, and was only too delighted to introduce them.

Neither Dek nor Elva would have been socially conditioned or raised by their respective cultural milieu to find the other the least bit attractive.

Back then, caricatures of Chinese men in the media fell into two categories: squinty, buck-toothed, braid-wearing laundrymen-laborers in soft slipper-like shoes, or sinister, evil predatory types who seduced white women into sexual slavery. White writers often harped upon their accented English and the tonal range of the regional dialects (*Singsongy,* they called it. *Musical!* we countered).

Based on the erroneous view that Sunday school teachers were especially vulnerable to the attentions of amorous Asian male students, many local churches were adamantly against missions for Chinese. But well considered long past her prime, with an exuberant teaching style and thick, masculine hands that easily broke chalk into clouds of dust whenever she was writing too vigorously at the blackboard, no one was thinking of Elva when they were writing about such fey, cinch-waisted Victorian beauties.

Long before they were officially introduced, Dek Foon had heard about the Sunday school teacher who taught evening English classes to the community.

Some said she was an *old maid.* A spinster. A self-declared single woman (*zi so neoi,* or *wong faa neoi*). Some whispered that Elva had been married before, but that it had never been consummated.

This did not bother Uncle Dek, himself a widower.

Dek was himself a full decade older. From his perspective, Elva was a wonderfully vital young woman.

As the weeks progressed, I like to think that Elva warmed to the kind, open expression of Dek's eyes and the almost overly formal way he was with her, as foreigners sometimes overcompensate, practicing his American manners of holding the door open *for a lady.* He didn't look like any man she had ever met before, although he dressed impeccably well, like the best senior members of their congregation.

THEN THERE WERE THE SMALL MOMENTS. Dek helping her bring out the plates and napkins for the after-service treats, or collecting bibles and placing them back into individual pews. Sometimes his hand was there at her elbow to guide her, even though she was nearly as tall as he was, as they headed downstairs to the meeting room.

Pretty soon, the advice from the church ladies came rolling in.

Chinese men make good husbands, one told her.

They bring home money and allow their wives to spend it.

They never get drunk.

Unlike heathen Chinese, these men never gamble, cheat, or smoke opium.

They might be small of stature, but the Lord blessed them with potency. Look at all the beautiful children Huie Kin and Louise had—nine, and the last two were twins!

Elva dismissed the talk as nonsense. All she knew was that it was hard not to notice Dek, slim in his suit, the skin of his long neck taut under its high white collar, quick with a joke and a helping hand, and consistently there every Sunday. How he stayed for the coffee hour at the meeting hall, and even helped her at the English lessons she taught for the newer Chinese, tutoring the others on the finer grammatical points of conversational English. Sometimes there was confusion in the class, over the meaning of a word or a euphemism or phrase, but there was Dek, whose English by this time was nearly impeccable, translating her instruction from English into Sayyup until the students' puzzled expressions transformed into looks of bright understanding.

She was soon to realize that mild-mannered, gentlemanly Dek was always engaged in something—Chinese civil rights, helping his countrymen, even the old bachelors, teaching them about God, and American society.

Did Elva know about how Chinese weren't allowed to become citizens? About the laws that essentially prohibited Chinese women from coming into America? (No, she hadn't been aware of these, although many of her friends had married Chinese ministers, and the more he told her, it did seem terribly unjust.)

Uncle Dek told her about the efforts of the League and Wong Chin Foo, and how they had lobbied Congress. The more Dek talked, the more fascinated she became, and she started wanting to know how she could help.

Although he and Joseph Singleton were in a successful banking and advertising firm on Pell Street, he still helped out his old laundry supplies boss whenever he could, combining business trips to Boston and Montreal. Both were good businesses, and he was teaching the particulars of it to Shim, his nephew, whose English was making great leaps through the help of the Sunday classes.

Did she want to see his drawings for the mechanical steam iron? (She did, and later, she even helped him find a lawyer to handle the patent application.)

He had lived in California, Hong Kong, and Canton (Guangzhou, he called it), and though some might refer to him as a *Chinaman*—a term that seemed derogatory to her—she would insist, *He is a Chinese Christian.*

The more he talked, the more it amused her, and the world through Dek's eyes had a charm and clarity she had not noticed before.

When he confided in her that his deceased wife was not a Christian, and how he prayed for her soul, and for his own son to convert and find the light, as his nephew who lived with him had, she told him that she would pray for both Wu Chow and the late Mrs. Ng Dek Foon as well.

Eventually, she allowed herself to attend the group dinner after services, where she began noticing that Dek always found a way to sit by her side. He was the first person to teach her how to use chopsticks (keeping the lower stick steady, and manipulating the top one with the same dexterity as wielding a pen); they ate a viscous soup made from swifts' nests, and savory dishes of meat and vegetables topped with a dark ebony-flecked sauce that held so much flavor that she was surprised to learn it was made from soybeans.

It would have been the first time she had eaten a fish that was served from head to tail with julienned ginger, soy sauce, garlic, and spring onions (that signature of my own family's meals in Chinatown, so many decades later). While she found some dishes odd, and others delectable, she found it all thrilling.

In this era, some of these quintessentially Chinese American restaurants were transforming from no-frills eateries catering to Chinatown's all-male community, where patrons might sneak the resident cat some scraps of food under the table in exchange for a pat on the head, to elegant Oriental restaurants that catered to merchants like Dek Foon, Singleton, and their business associates. Gone were the backless stools, the bare wooden tables, the floors strewn with scattered sawdust, replaced by all manner of *chinoiserie*—painted lanterns, silk hangings, ebony chairs. Now they served pineapple chicken, appetizers of candied ginger, tiny tart kumquats eaten whole, skin intact, a sweet-sour surprise in the mouth, and freshly peeled lychees in the summer months, with the black center pit that Elva had to spit out into a little plate. The tiny delicate teacup, so thimble-like in Elva's hand, was constantly refilled by Dek, even as he held court at their table. Even Shim sometimes joined them, nodding thoughtfully at his uncle's stories, trying not to interrupt.

Elva spent so much time helping out at the Chinese mission that her family was worried. *You're spending so much time with those Chinamen, you're going to turn into a Chinese!*

Despite herself, Elva May Lisk was falling in love.

As they grew closer, Dek Foon began to fret. Would Elva's family accept him or would they reject the union?

There were many things they might object to.

He was a widower with a teenage son back home.

He supported his live-in nephew, Shim.

But first and foremost for them, he knew, was the fact that he was Chinese. It was not that long ago that Singleton's marriage to a white teacher at their church made headlines as far away as Omaha, Nebraska.

But then one day, Elva suddenly grew distant.

She stopped attending the dinners, leaving as soon as services were over.

After the weekly evening class, she dashed off to catch the streetcar home, declining Dek's offer to walk with her and wait until it arrived.

Had he done or said anything to offend her? he wondered. Had someone said something? Had her family intervened? (Even from where

I sit, I can still feel my uncle's misery as he considered the prospect of losing her.)

Whatever it was, Dek was determined to find out. He couldn't let her simply slip away.

THAT SUNDAY, DEK SAT in a back pew, distractedly staring at the back of Elva's head.

The light from the stained-glass windows seemed to hover above her, playing about in the twist of her hair. As soon as services were over, he waited for Elva to exit her pew before approaching. *Would Miss Lisk have a moment to talk in private?*

Elva looked at him with a kind of happy-sadness in her eyes, but she agreed and followed him downstairs, where refreshments were being laid out in another room.

Miss Lisk, Dek began, *in these months of getting to know you I have been so impressed, not just with your dedication and kindness to my nephew and myself, but to our whole community. Maybe I'm being selfish, and I hope I am not offending you by saying, but in this short time that we have known each other, I have grown to care for you deeply.*

New York and this community have been good to me. I have enough to make a comfortable life for myself.

He took her hand.

I know it is a risk for you and your family. American society is unaccustomed to people like us. But I have deep feelings for you that I cannot turn off.

Ever since she met Dek, Elva Lisk had been wondering if this day would come. Although she had prayed about it at night before she went to sleep, and it was often on her mind when the first notes of dawn appeared streaming through her window, she simply didn't know what to say.

This is what she did know: she too had feelings for Dek. She could not have dreamed of a nicer, gentler man, a refined man, a true Christian. She didn't know what she would do if he rejected her like Doran had, and she didn't relish the idea of leaving him or this community, which she had invested in for the past seven years, just as she'd had to leave her last church in the aftermath of her marriage. But she could not risk what happened with Doran happening again.

Before you go any further, Elva said, *there is something you need to know.*

When she looked into his calm, brown, sympathetic eyes, she didn't know whether to be happy or sad that the day had finally come.

WHEN ELVA HAD RETURNED home to her parents' apartment on East Thirteenth Street that late spring day in 1895, she didn't want to tell anyone about what had happened on the wedding night, much less her parents. It was Sarah, who had dressed, clothed, and bathed Elva as a child, and who knew Elva better than anyone else, perhaps even more than Elva herself, who extracted the information from her. Sarah, who had a look about her face that Elva couldn't quite place (alarm? resignation? guilt?), sent Benjamin out to fetch the family doctor.

When the doctor arrived, he instructed Elva, in her bedroom, to take off her clothing. She was asked to lie on her bed naked, under nothing but a bedsheet.

Although Elva had known the doctor since the family had moved to the neighborhood when she was a child, she had never had cause to have her lower extremities examined. For a woman born and raised in the Victorian era, the exam would have been excruciating and humiliating, not to mention physically painful, given that she was still technically a virgin.

As she lay there, while the doctor bent over her, it's easy to imagine how angry she felt in that moment—angry at the doctor, Doran, and most of all, herself. Anger and hatred were easier emotions to contend with, even as the doctor felt his way under the bedsheet, than the pain and humiliation of having been left.

Did the doctor try to put her at ease while doing the pelvic exam, or was that too modern a convention? Did he contain himself as he felt inside Elva's vagina, smooth like a cul-de-sac, with no discernible cervix, no peekaboo womb or errant fallopian tubes? Did he express surprise or consternation upon uncovering what lay before him, an extra . . . what? No, not an unusually large, blushing labia, but a real-life miniature penis, one that could become aroused with certain thoughts or feelings, but which at that moment remained flaccid between his cold, clinical fingers.

After the examination, the doctor went into the living room and gave Sarah and Benjamin his prognosis.

Elva would never get her menses like other girls.

Elva would never be able to have children.

Doran may have called her a *monster*, but the doctor used another term, which circulated around the generations of her family forever afterward, and eventually reached my own ears when, after years of searching, I finally tracked down her siblings' descendants over a century later.

Hermaphrodite.

So now you know, Elva said.

Dek sat there, trying to collect his thoughts.

Coffee hour was over and several congregants were making their way back upstairs, looking curiously at them as they passed, waving their goodbyes.

Finally, Dek said, *What does hermaphrodite mean?*

I am equipped with both, Elva said. He had been married and had a son—surely she did not need to tell him twice.

And children?

Elva shook her head. *I have prayed for quite a long time about why God made me the way he did, but I have no answers.*

She stood up to go, but Dek grabbed her hand and beckoned her to remain seated.

I don't care about that, he said. He already had a son, plus Shim, who was like a son to him.

I hope you believe me when I say this, Miss Lisk, he said, looking into her eyes. It was as if he were finally seeing her, from her flyaway hair down to her sensible leather shoes.

All I want is you.

In 1902, Chinese Exclusion and the Geary Act were due to expire.

Vitriolic and racist arguments against Chinese immigration persisted on the floor of Congress. This would be a moment for deep entrenchment, not reform.

The final Senate vote was 76 to 1, in favor of extending the bill.

President Theodore Roosevelt signed it into perpetuity on April 29, 1902, and with that, Chinese Exclusion was made permanent throughout the land.

That summer, on July 22, Dek Foon and Elva May Lisk were married in Hartford, Connecticut.

Although her family couldn't believe they were marrying their daughter off to a Chinese, it was said that Sarah and Benjamin were happy that Elva had finally found someone who loved her.

As I read the Congressional Record for that period, wading through the highfalutin oratory conventions that were a carryover from the late nineteenth century, a heaviness descended onto my body, thick and viscous like tree resin.

My eye kept scanning the pages for politicians who spoke out against Exclusion, to find some solace in this tide of soaringly racist rhetoric, but by 1902, they were few and far between. The great sea of senators and congressmen were now in agreement about excluding Chinese, and the arguments were mainly tilted toward how to exclude those already living in the recently annexed Hawaii and the Philippines, and how to prevent Chinese sailors, working aboard U.S. vessels, from entering.

Senator George Frisbie Hoar, a Republican from Massachusetts, was the sole holdout against Exclusion. He had been opposed to it from his earliest days as a junior senator when legislation arose—the Fifteen Passenger Bill, in 1879—to ban entry of any ship carrying more than fifteen Chinese passengers, on the grounds that "it violates the fundamental principle announced in the Declaration of Independence upon which the whole institutions of this country are founded, and to which by our whole history the American people are pledged."

Out of seventy-seven senators, only Hoar stood up for us.

It is not simply Dek Foon that I am grieving for, or our family back then, but for the whole collective body of us living in America.

I find it difficult to swallow the racism laid bare in the voting record. Reading their testimonies makes me feel queasy, like I've eaten something that my entire body is rejecting. (There's a barnyard village Chinese term for uncontrollable defecation that comes to mind.)

I want to keep this rhetoric in the past—I do not want to breathe life into these men and their beliefs. I want it to stay safely back in the late nineteenth century or early twentieth century, where it can no longer hurt me or my family ever again.

I want my daughter to know none of this. I want to shield and protect her from it as much as possible.

But that is not possible.

As I have been writing this during the coronavirus pandemic, we have witnessed a U.S. president who repeatedly referred to COVID-19 as the "Kung flu" and the "China virus." This elected official blamed China to cover for his own inadequate response to the pandemic, and ushered in a wave of hate crimes scapegoating innocent Asian Americans, the likes of which we have never before seen in our lifetime.

There are GOP politicians who see all Chinese scientists and students as potential spies—*suspicious simply for being Chinese.* The most notable ones are themselves Latinos, and immigrants or children of immigrants, which tells us something about the complexities of this recrudescence today.

Anti-Chinese sentiment in this country in the form of anti-Asian attacks has made a roaring comeback in our time.

A friend—a sixty-eight-year-old retired teacher, with whom I joke around that we're "cousins," because we share the same last name and both our families come from Toisan—was sucker-punched in the face while she was standing outside a flower shop on Mulberry Street. She was knocked straight to the ground, while her much younger and larger assailant—a thirty-something white guy in shorts and white sneakers and built like a refrigerator—just walked away.

I had seen her just the weekend before at a crocheting circle, making yarn rosettes for a community art project to beautify Chinatown.

I watched the video of her assault on NBC News in shock, then immediately burst into tears.

Since then, it has only grown worse.

A Chinese American woman was pushed in front of a moving subway car to her death in Times Square.

Another, a young Korean American, was followed into her apartment building in Chinatown and stabbed to death in her own home, with her own kitchen knife, dying in the bathtub in a pool of her own blood.

A grandmotherly-aged Chinese woman in Queens was hit over the head with a rock while straightening up the sidewalk in front of her land-lord and friend's property, and placed into a coma before slipping into her death.

A Filipina in Yonkers was followed into an elevator by a lone man and punched in the head over a hundred times.

These random but very specific acts of violence fill me with both rage and fear.

I have friends, even the ones with several years of martial arts experience, who carry Tasers.

I've been traveling on the New York City subways independently since I was twelve, where I learned early on to keep an eye out for lecherous perverts, public masturbators, flashers, men with bad come-on lines, and drunkards who have tried to grab me.

But as a woman, I have never had to worry about being pushed to my death or punched to the ground, simply for my race.

These days, I only travel aboveground.

I carry a flashlight with me at all times, and I wear only shoes and clothing that I can run in, or dropkick someone in, if attacked.

I practice my squats and my daily push-ups on the ferry to my studio to strengthen my arms and my core, and I advise other Asians to do the same. (I even started a self-defense group, Sisters in Self-Defense, with artist Alison Kuo in order to help community members learn how to pro-tect themselves.)

Sometimes, it's like I can still hear Dek Foon's neighbors, 130 years later, boarding up their windows, hammering nails into plywood, tight-ening screws, adding additional padlocks to doors and entryways in an-ticipation of what is to come. As the realities of the bitter past and bitter present set in, I kept digging in my research for a better understanding of the origins of the denial of our rights.

I kept returning to the Naturalization Act of 1870—a Reconstruction-era piece of legislation passed just five months after the Fifteenth Amend-ment on citizens' voting rights and also, coincidentally, the same year that

Elva was born. While Charles Sumner of Massachusetts, a Republican and leading abolitionist, had proposed a naturalization act for all men—*regardless of race*—William Stewart, a senator from Nevada representing white miners and mining capitalists, who was decidedly anti-Chinese, enacted a filibuster to keep Asians out.

By the time the bill was passed, only white and freed African American men could naturalize.

Throughout the course of his career, Stewart, whose lumberjack beard went from dark brown to Kris Kringle white, made it his mission—starting with that naturalization filibuster a dozen years before the 1882 Exclusion Act—to ensure that Chinese immigrants never acquired citizenship and voting rights. "If it had not been for me, the Chinaman would be a voter before this time," he boasted in 1888.

Then, at the end of his career, after Chinese Exclusion was made permanent, Stewart said, "If they had been allowed to be naturalized and become voters, there probably never would have been any exclusion."

I was shocked. All this time when I learned about the Naturalization Act in school, I had simply thought we were forgotten, an afterthought. Now I knew it was entirely on purpose.

Every time I think about William Morris Stewart, I want to crack him like an egg.

WHEN DEK, SINGLETON, and the others learned that Chinese Exclusion had been made permanent, their dreams of becoming full-blown American citizens unraveled like tea leaves steeping in scalding water.

Dek and Elva settled down into married life, moving to the middle-class bedroom community of Bedford-Stuyvesant, Brooklyn, where there was space, and easy access to New York's Chinatown. They lived in walking distance to Singleton's Congregational church.

It could not have been easy for either of them. Although married before, Dek had lived the bachelor life for nearly two decades in America, and prior to being married to his first wife—which had been for only a short time before he needed to leave home in order to support them—he and his brother had gone to a boys' school in China from the time they were eight years old.

With the exception of the week she spent at her apartment with Doran, Elva had only ever lived in her parents' home. This was the first time she would keep her own household.

We know nothing about the wedding night, except that unlike the last time, the husband did not run screaming from the bedroom.

Much as Elva had a difficult time revealing the nature of her physicality to Dek, so do I have misgivings about revealing it now. In their day-to-day lives, no one in their social circle was privy to this information. Elva's secret was confined to her family, and between her and Dek.

I am hesitant to reveal it not only for some sense of wanting to protect my aunt's privacy—ridiculous, since she's long dead—but also to protect Uncle Dek.

Will you see him as just another emasculated Asian man?

Will you question Dek's sexuality?

Perhaps the better question is, how "straight" were Dek and Elva really behind closed doors?

As for Elva, even throughout the Roaring Twenties when hemlines shortened and silhouettes relaxed, she only ever presented as a modest Christian woman, wearing conservative ankle-length dresses with high necklines and the occasional bustle that were a full decade behind the times.

Sometimes, when I think about Elva, I'm reminded of Avalokiteshvara, the Buddhist bodhisattva of compassion. By the time Avalokiteshvara, a male, entered China in the first century CE with the spread of Buddhism, the shape-shifter bodhisattva, who hears the cries of human suffering, emerged as Guan Yin, the Goddess of Mercy. Even my grandparents' Christian-Buddhist household in Queens had a porcelain statue of Guan Yin, the most famous transgendered deity in the world.

Dek would have been very familiar with the trajectory of Guan Yin, and may have informed Elva about it.

But whether Elva would have been dismissive of this as *false idol worship*, or allowed herself to be intrigued by the possibilities of gender transformation, we will never know.

Although I have no proof, I suspect the two of them had a really fabulous sex life.

8

Dek Foon & Chin On

Ng-Doshim & Chin Families

伍 陳

In the late 1890s, Dek Foon and his band of brothers had learned about a nascent reform movement aimed at transitioning their homeland from an imperial dynastic system to a constitutional monarchy. Did Dek describe the Chinese Empire Reform movement to Elva as trying to institute the kind of government they had in Great Britain, as I do whenever I explain it to others? Its leader, Kang Youwei, sought to reinstate the young reform-minded Guangxu emperor and founded the Chinese Empire Reform Association, a.k.a. the Baohuanghui, or Protect the Emperor Society, sending out the call to the Chinese diaspora seeking their money and support.

Singleton and Dek returned to political activism, founding the New York chapter of the Chinese Reform Association. Singleton was elected its local president. They rented out an upstairs office across the street from the Chinese Consolidated Benevolent Association and On Leong headquarters, and announced their new organization by unfurling a flag—with two red stripes and three stars representing education, equality, and unity—out the window over Mott Street.

To spread the word, they launched *The Chinese Reform Weekly News*, one of the first Chinese-language newspapers in New York, as well as a series of banquet-style fundraisers to champion their causes—even if they couldn't vote themselves, they could socialize with politicians and try their best to move the needle. The lavish Chinese Delmonico, also called Mon Lay Won ("the length of ten thousand clouds"), with its round tables adorned with mother-of-pearl inlay and lacquered chairs, would become their go-to venue. This upscale restaurant, named after the famous Delmonico's steakhouse, was a lush second-floor affair in the heart of Chinatown. It catered to a high-end clientele, and could accommodate sizable dinner parties with musical accompaniment ("Chinese Orchestra, String Band and Songsters . . . We can make a 'Night in China' for you").

In November 1902, a day after Thanksgiving, they hosted local judges, New York Supreme Court justices, and politicians, including Congressman Henry Mayer Goldfogle, one of a handful of Jewish elected officials in Congress, and Judge Warren Foster, to a series of sumptuous multicourse meals there.

That night, according to the press, dinner consisted of bird's nest soup, shark fin soup, chicken stuffed with venison, and, capitalizing on the chop suey trend, chop suey with shiitake mushrooms (no pork or shellfish!). It was such a success that the next dinner was held in February of the following year, wherein a cub reporter from *The Sun* noted that freshly painted dragons adorned the walls. When Judge Foster invited Congressman Goldfogle to present a gift to cohost Joseph Singleton, *The Sun* made fun of Singleton's English ("I be cold indeed if I not be touched by this gleet. You genelosity gratefully accept. Land of libety hope some day to enjoy plivedges of Melican citizen.")

I'd like to rewind this and show you the scene as I see it.

Singleton, who was grieving the recent death of his wife, stood up from where he was modestly sitting on the sidelines. The present was revealed: a pastel portrait of Singleton himself, capturing his wiry likeness and trim, slightly droopy mustache. I can almost hear the appreciative gasps and applause as Singleton and Goldfogle shook hands. "I'd be cold indeed if I was not touched by this gift," Singleton said, holding the portrait, which would grace their family room. "Your generosity, I gratefully accept."

"In this land of Liberty," he continued, before the audience of local politicians, judges, and their wives, "I hope someday to enjoy the privileges of an American citizen."

As ever, Dek and his friends were tirelessly lobbying for Chinese equal rights.

"As president of the Reform Association in this country, I hope to induce my fellow countrymen to cut off their queues and superstitions, to show Americans we are *not* unworthy immigrants," he added, before taking a seat.

Were these banquets the first time such prominent Jewish politicians were invited by their Chinese neighbors to a fancy Chinese meal? Was this the beginning of Jewish New Yorkers frequenting Chinatown restaurants during the holiday season, laying the seeds for generations to come? Perhaps it was the first highly publicized event where so many prominent Jewish and Chinese folks, along with their spouses, partook of a high-end Chinese meal—with a modified menu for their Jewish guests (no treif)—but then, it most certainly was not the last.

That Easter Sunday of 1903 marked the first pogrom of the twentieth century—a bloody massacre in Kishinev, Russia. Over the course of the next couple of days, Jews in the city were brutally targeted by rampaging Christians invoking the blood libel—the erroneous charge that Jews used the blood of Christians for rituals—resulting in numerous rapes, assaults, and the deaths of forty-nine Jewish residents.

When news of the atrocities reached New York, the Jewish community put out a call for funds and launched a campaign for house-to-house collections. When Dek Foon and Singleton heard about the attacks, and saw in the newspapers the photographs of the victims, many of them children, they leapt at the chance to lend a hand.

ON THE FAIR EVENING OF MAY 11, 1903, a long line of Chinese and Jewish ticket holders clamored to get into the Chinese Theatre. The attendees, many of whom included Jewish women, according to Yiddish newspaper *Jewish World*, waited as long as half an hour along narrow, windy Doyers Street just to see the benefit performance, and in such numbers that police were forced to periodically push back the crowd. *The New York Times*, the Yiddish press, and numerous onlookers proclaimed the night was a first on so many fronts. The penchant for hyperbole was high ("Since the world began there hasn't been another such benefit performance").

Inside, host Guy Maine (Goi Mein in Yiddish), addressing the crowd in both Chinese and English, advocated for the common bonds of sympathy between Chinese and Jewish people. He was followed by Rabbi Joseph Zeef, who decried Russian cruelties, including a massacre of thousands of Chinese families only two years before, piquing the interest of many Jewish attendees. A representative from Congressman Goldfogle's office thanked the community for their philanthropic aid. "Let us extend a hand of welcome and hope that the Chinese may stand upon the broad platform of Americanism with us."

The Ten Lost Tribes—not a biblical reference, but a Chinese drama about oppression during the Ching dynasty—began. Onstage, the actors, an all-male crew of about forty performers, were decked out in lavish silks and headdresses. The staging was, according to custom, plain and devoid of props except for what the actors carried (a scroll, a sword) and a small orchestra sitting off to the side. A blue and white Zionist flag alongside the Chinese national flag with its dragon, claws outspread, presided over the stage.

The performance, about Chinese subjugation under Manchurian rule, was of particular salience to the southern Chinese in attendance. But while Dek Foon and the others sat rapt by the performances, it was an altogether mystifying affair to the majority of white audience members. According to one reporter from the *Jewish World*, many were more than a bit baffled by Chinese theater with its reliance on Chinese aesthetics and theatrical forms, its conventions of artifice and form ("the lead actress with a face as motionless as that of a statue"), and the gusto of the orchestra ("one has to hear how the Chinese orchestra scrapes and drums away behind the actors, drowning out their monologues"). The reporter observed, "To our ears it sounded, may our Chinese friends forgive us, very much like caterwauling."

Although unable to understand the dialogue or the meaning behind the songs, sung entirely in expressive Cantonese, the audience applauded politely, as the throng outside clamored to enter.

By many accounts, it was so stiflingly crowded in the theater that Maine had to frequently interrupt the performance to request audience members adhere to a half-hour time limit to allow others waiting outside an opportunity to attend. According to the press, the ticket-holding public entered in a steady stream throughout the entire set of performances—three in a row, after which the actors enjoyed a record number of curtain calls. Even if Jewish audience members were mystified by Chinese opera, they were appreciative of the volunteer efforts of the performers, or at least incredibly curious.

Afterward, a banquet dinner at their mainstay, the Chinese Delmonico, was thrown in honor of actress Bertha Kalich, the star of the nearby Thalia Theatre. Dark-haired, glamorous Kalich, often referred to as "the Jewish Bernhardt," and widely credited with introducing Jewish theater to American audiences, was at the apex of her career. Although her remarks are lost to history, Kalich's presence would have been a plum in the pudding for Dek Foon and the others.

Singleton addressed the attendees, saying that they had good sympathy and feeling for their Jewish neighbors, because of their own feelings of persecution by Russian and Manchurian authorities back home.

Richard Gottheil, first president of the Federation of American Zionists (the precursor to the Zionist Organization of America), was also in attendance. The federation had asked Jewish merchants throughout the city to donate a percentage of that day's earnings, Gottheil told reporters, and many had agreed to help. Wealthier Jews of New York City, like Emanuel Lehman and Daniel Guggenheim, organized their own relief fund.

All told, contributions for the Chinatown fundraiser totaled $282 for the relief efforts—about $8,000 by today's standards. Arnold Kohn, head of the Jewish relief committee, graciously addressed Dek Foon and friends: "Permit me to add my thanks and appreciation for your services in the cause of humanity and to assure you that your Chinese sympathy with the Jews marks an era in the history of civilization."

In truth, their greatest contribution was not solely the amount of money raised, but also the *news value* in their lending a hand.

Once this story of Chinese Reformers helping Jewish victims circulated in the press, folks from across the country, not to be outdone, began opening their coffers.

"The story about the Chinese giving over their theatre for the benefit of the fund . . . ," Kohn told *The New York Times* later that week, "seems to have awakened the conscience and the sympathy of the whole American people."

Donations came flooding in from individuals and churches across the country.

MOST WHITE AMERICANS BELIEVED that Chinese were "selfish" and insular—turning a blind eye to the system of Exclusion that their elected politicians had been cementing for decades. What appeared as ethnic insularity was a survival skill. This Chinatown fundraiser ran in direct opposition to popular misconceptions.

The story was so unusual in 1903 that the first Kishinev refugee to safely reach New York, Jacob Fishman, told reporters, "I have been told since coming that even the Chinese are helping my poor people."

I believe for Uncle Dek, the cause felt truly personal. He had escaped the hostile environment that forced so many of us out of the western states, and now, safely in New York, he was finally in a position to help others. Later that November, Dek's Chinese Empire Reform Association threw another banquet in honor of their Lower East Side politician friends, in what was quickly becoming a tradition.

To show their appreciation, the same crew of judges and politicians, including Judge Foster, Congressman Goldfogle, and Chinese Guild lawyer Colonel William Constantine Beecher, son of the abolitionist and social reformer Henry Ward Beecher, presented my uncle, Joseph Singleton, Guy Maine, and Jue Chue (the "J. P. Morgan of Chinatown") gold medals of honor. As part of the occasion, a Jewish actress, Florence Ceitland, delivered a toast in Cantonese, which was never transcribed by the English press that reported on it, but which was roundly applauded by the band of brothers and their friends, who were touched by the gesture.

Goldfogle and Beecher declared that they both welcomed the day when Chinese would be recognized as citizens with full rights of suffrage. I can almost feel Dek Foon's heart swelling at these words, even from over a century later as I read Goldfogle's remarks in *The Oregonian* from my studio on Mott Street, a stone's throw from the old Chinese Delmonico. When atrocities against Jews yet again erupted in Russia in the fall of 1905, Dek and his friends put on another benefit fundraiser that winter, again to a packed house, but this time *they* were the performers. Together, Uncle Dek and other members of the Chinese Reform Association were the principal actors in a Chinese opera version of "King David's Glory."

What I wouldn't give to see this performance, at Miner's Theatre on the Bowery, which was famous for giving bad acts "the hook" and where, a few years later, a young Eddie Cantor would make his stage debut, but very little remains in the way of English- or Yiddish-language coverage. The reporter for *The Sun* was not proficient in Chinese language or opera, and thought their interpretation odd ("King David in Chinese Garb: Weird Show for Russian Jews at Miner's").

To CELEBRATE HIS TWENTY-FIFTH YEAR as head of On Leong in 1902, Tom Lee threw a giant New Year's fete at the tong headquarters at 14 Mott Street. The guest list of over a hundred attendees included a bevy of Tammany Hall politicos, including the police commissioner, his deputies, the district attorney, and friends of Dek and Singleton, Judge Warren Foster and Judge Julius Mayer. Dinner began with the popping of thousands of firecrackers set off on Mott Gai, and guests were treated to an elaborate twenty-seven-course meal, during which Tom Lee toasted guests at each table, as if it were a wedding celebration.

Tom Lee's name may have been the one all over the English-language press, but the Chin brothers are shadowy presences throughout.

In those early years, when Uncle Dek and his Christian brethren were devoted to fighting for equal rights and aiding Kishinev pogrom victims, the Chin brothers had quickly risen through the ranks of On Leong with almost preternatural tenacity. Once established, they began making connections and deals that benefited themselves and Ying Chong, which was conveniently located on the same block as On Leong headquarters.

This period, in which the Chin brothers were busy lining their own pockets, was a happy time as my family recalls it, with business at Ying Chong flourishing. Their connections as On Leong merchants were proving profitable, extending their network out through the wider Chinese community, with demand for them to become the suppliers for other stores throughout New York and New Jersey.

But sadly for the On Leongs, all monopolies must eventually come to an end.

Back when Chin On was still finding his footing in the city, a new tong had arrived in town, and it was steadily gaining traction.

The Hip Sing Association, also known as the Workingman's Society, was often described back then as an underworld syndicate. Shut out from the ranks of On Leong, these new arrivals were hungry for what they saw as their piece of American opportunity. They saw a chance to challenge On Leong in its supremacy overseeing Chinatown's gambling parlors and opium dens, and quickly set up a presence on Pell Street, intent upon becoming as dominant as the "peaceful" merchants.

That year, several merchants on Mott Street informed the English-language press that the Hip Sings were a tong "organized for the sole purpose of levying blackmail." It was rumored that the New York branch, numbering around one hundred members, was composed of toughs for hire, who extorted money from shopkeepers and even popular actors from the Chinese Theatre. Anyone who refused risked the threat of violence. (Although I search for my family members at this press conference, which was reported on by *The New York Advertiser* and reprinted in *The Utica Observer*, I cannot find any of their names listed.)

When Hip Sing leaders gained the ear and sympathy of white Christian Reformers, the political lines were drawn. Tammany Hall, New York's powerful, incumbent political machine, backed On Leong, while the Reformers were on the side of Hip Sing, and no matter who was in charge—a Tammany Hall Democrat or a Reform Republican—whenever raids were necessary to show that the city was "doing something" about vice, the two tongs fed their white allies and police captains the addresses of their enemies' establishments.

August 1900 marked an uptick in violence, when a Hip Sing hatchet man was killed by On Leong agents in a rear tenement on Pell Street, only doors down from Uncle Dek and Singleton's banking office and within earshot of the Chin brothers' business. Police arrested five Chinese at the scene, who all turned out to be Hip Sing tong members, armed with pistols, knives, a wrist-bound piece of iron the size of a pear that swung by a cord, and an eighteen-inch-long iron bludgeon weighing five pounds.

In the summer of 1905, a group of Hip Sings lit a string of firecrackers into a standing-room-only opera performance at the Chinese Theatre on Doyers Street. The theater had long been considered neutral territory—a safe place for either faction to enjoy a performance. But as the crowd and actors turned toward the commotion, gunmen unleashed a string of bullets into the front row, killing four On Leong members.

Then, on Chinese New Year's in early 1906, Tom Lee's nephew and enforcer, the young, strapping Lee Toy, and three other On Leong members were gunned down while making social calls on Pell Street, lucky red envelope lai-see money for the neighborhood children still in their pockets. Lee Toy's death sparked a brand-new iteration of the Tong Wars, hitting business and tourism alike.

In his oral history, my grandfather Lung casts these violent periods as fights over territory—who owned Mott Street, Pell, or Doyers, and the right to run a gambling outfit and control prostitution—but soon the violence escalated between the two factions, ratcheting up to such a level as to concern all of Chinatown.

Tourists, whom Grandfather Lung deemed "rubberneckers," ate up stories of tong violence like moviegoers going through bags of popcorn, but only from the safety of newspaper headlines. Actual gunshots and murders were another story, and now folks were afraid to come to Chinatown. The Chinese consul and business leaders like Singleton and Dek Foon, desperate to bring back law and order, believed that the only way to effectively call a truce between both sides would be to get someone from outside the Chinese community. They called upon their friend Judge Warren Foster.

Both sides agreed to put down their weapons, to not shake down each other's establishments, and to dissuade their constituents from gambling.

To show their faith in the deal, each organization agreed to file a bond of $1,000.

LATER THAT MARCH, the Chinese Consolidated Benevolent Association and Dek and Singleton's Chinese Empire Reform Association threw a joint two-hundred-person banquet to honor Judge Foster's peace deal. Instead of the Chinese Delmonico, the event was held on Mott Street's newest restaurant, the sumptuous, balconied Port Arthur, with its pagoda-styled entrance just across the street from the Chinese Consolidated Benevolent Association and On Leong headquarters. At the door, each of the tong members was frisked by a city employee ("He found no guns," *The Sun* reported, "but he swears that he felt padding").

Uncle Dek circulated around the room, wearing the gold medal given to him four months before by Foster and friends. It was the size of a police badge, with his name etched at the top and sparkling diamonds festooning his initials. It must have glowed under the Chinese lanterns as he showed it off at the head table. A *Sun* reporter, referring to Dek Foon as "the laundry supply trust in the Quarter," captures this scene:

Serious, white-haired Colonel William Beecher, the Chinese Guild lawyer, asked, "Would you give me that medal, Mr. Dek?"

"Anything I got that I make myself or buy myself I will give to somebody. Anything that is given to me I will not give to somebody," said Dek Foon, smiling, *until the bosom of his dress shirt expanded.*

Then someone handed Uncle Dek a match. "Will you keep that for me then?"

Dek, in mock seriousness, said, "No one but I shall light anything with that match."

The first time I read this *Sun* article back in 2015, I dismissed this exchange as corny and avuncular. But this time, after so many years of sifting through English-language articles where Chinese Americans were vilified, made fun of for their accents, or rendered into mere statistics, I see it with more clarity.

These *are* corny old-man jokes, but the kind that are batted around by longtime friends who are truly comfortable with one another. This degree of comingling between the races, among the adult children of famous abolitionists, Tammany politicians and judges, and Chinese civic leaders and tong members, flies in the face of conventional wisdom about the time period.

During the eighteen-course meal of Chinese and American fare, Judge D. Cady Herrick, who had just come off an unsuccessful run for governor on the Democratic ticket and who was a regular at many of Dek Foon and Singleton's events, stood up to address the crowded dining room.

"I don't suppose that I'll get under indictment if I speak my mind about the Chinese. We, who are clamoring for the open door in China, should give the open door in America to the Chinese. When your ancestors and mine were naked, painted barbarians, their ancestors moved in silks and read books.

". . . When they do get into line with the nations of the world, then we must look to our own place. A people which wants peace must be prepared to fight for it. That is what China will learn to do. Our friends of the On Leong and Hip Sing tongs have illustrated that," Herrick said.

Then, indicating the table where tong members sat, with a sweep of his long arm, he continued, "They have shown that the New York Chinaman can fight at the drop of a hat."

The tong members in attendance smiled at being acknowledged, albeit sheepishly.

As much as I'd love to uncover this as a significant event where both sides of my family—Dek Foon and the Chin brothers—are present, it is most likely that my sauve great-grandfather Chin On and his older brothers were not seated at that table with their slightly chagrined associates. The hint comes from family documents that, only a few weeks later, place Chin On in San Francisco.

It was the early morning, April 18, 1906.

Great-Grandfather Chin On, an early riser, was in his accommodations in Chinatown and, according to family documents, awake and already dressed. He was probably in a dark, loose-fitting Chinese shirt jacket, as he was pictured in his official documents the month before. Like Dek Foon, he too had cut his queue years before and sported a short, Western hairstyle.

Suddenly, he heard a loud banging, and then the walls were shaking, as if someone were trying to bring the entire building down.

He went to the window. Outside, the landscape was changing before his eyes.

Walls and edifices crumbled like bedsheets. Soon, buildings were ablaze with fire, sending up plumes of black smoke.

Chin On knew that he had to get out.

As the banging continued and the ceiling plaster fell like snow with every new tremor, he threw the window wide open. He was three stories above street level, with a striped awning below him, and another just under that. If he played his cards right, he might be able to use them to break his fall. Was he feeling lucky?

All across the city, buildings were swaying and roads buckling underfoot. In another few hours, mothers attempting to make breakfast would unwittingly set fire to their homes, as chimneys caught fire and collapsed upon themselves. In the next few days, half of the city's residents would be homeless, carting their possessions on horse-drawn wagons, handcarts, baby carriages, and even children's toys, while many cooked meals on the streets.

Chin On had heard of these seismic earth-shaking events and how others had been buried under the crushing weight of walls and rooftops, and had decided long ago that if he was ever caught in one, he would seek the open air as quickly as possible. So when the house across the way began to tilt, and sway from side to side, Chin On climbed out the window, the sill shaking under his seat, his heels against the fabric of the awning, and without looking back, let go, taking in everything around him.

A mile and a half away, city hall was shape-shifting. The ornate walls and columns of the stately main building collapsed, as if held together by mere tacks, to reveal slipshod brickwork and sand-filled walls, which soon fell and transformed into rubble and dust, covering the street. Mere moments after the first tremors, years of work were undone, and only the building's steel frame remained, a naked birdcage through which one could see the sky.

Only the smaller Hall of Records appeared unmoved and impenetrable, the quiet little sister housing all the city municipal documents. The first of the structures built and completed in the early days of 1877, after the transcontinental railroad was up and running, it was in front of this ornate, domed building, on these very sandlots, where Denis Kearney first roused thousands of unemployed white men in shouting "The Chinese must go!" and pressuring city officials and industrialists to ban Chinese from municipal jobs and fire Chinese workers, helping to ignite the entire bloody apparatus of Exclusion.

Now, three decades later, behind the building's stone facade, below its many granite floors and marble staircases, beneath its basement and very foundation itself, built atop marsh and landfill, the city's gas and sewage pipes were bursting among the loamy sand, filling the basement, and then even the uppermost floors, with flammable gas.

It was only a matter of time before the city records—the marriage and death listings for San Franciscans, forty-niners, other miners, woodcutters, housewives, and children—and even the state and city flags, with the lumbering bear and the side-eyed phoenix, rising out of the fire, burst into flames.

The earthquake, which was felt as far north as Oregon and all the way to the south of Los Angeles, would be later assessed as the worst natural disaster in California history. Eighty percent of the city would be destroyed, and the death toll across the region would tally in the thousands.

But along with the pain, suffering, and loss of lives, another fissure appeared.

When the city hall birth records, inked so neatly by various clerks' hands in looped cursive, bound in leather books going as far back as the formation of the state itself, began to ignite—volumes upon volumes of records, smoldering in the flames—a great opening appeared in the wall of Chinese Exclusion, emerging through the smoke and blazing heat like light at the end of a train tunnel through the mighty Sierra Nevada, and everything for us, from that moment forward, changed.

PART THREE

1906–1914

9

Shim & Chun

Ng-Doshim Family

伍

My great-grandmother Cheung To Chun, or Chun Chun, as her family called her, grew up on the outskirts of the northern reaches of Hong Kong, in a richly green hillside village called Tin Yuen that clung to its traditions and roots ferociously, particularly during the height of monsoon season, when the skies blackened and the rain was so heavy it transformed footpaths into rivers and threatened to send their small mountain, with its low homes and curved rooftops, the chickens, pigs, and water buffalo, and all its residents, sliding down into the sea.

As Hakka, the other Chinese called them *guest people.*

Outsiders.

Strangers.

They mocked the Hakka women for their sun-kissed darker skin, for working in the fields with wide-brimmed, black-fringed rattan hats that vaguely resembled Victorian lampshades, for their fully formed, natural feet with the agile toes that could scale boulders and rocky outcrops, claw through dirt, and climb wet, slippery slopes (Hakka were often forced to live in the more reclusive, less accessible, less desirable parts of town).

Hakka women need their feet, her grandmother, her poa poa, said, *in case it is time to run.*

Others may have called them peasants and hillbillies, but Chun Chun wouldn't know that until much later—as far as she was concerned Hong Kong was Hakka territory. Chun, whose name meant Spring, and who was as lovely as a cluster of white narcissi nodding on a riverbank, knew from within her very bones that she came from a long line of sure-footed women who knew where they came from.

Hakka families let their girls grow wild and strong, Poa Poa said.

Originally they were northerners, just like the Cantonese who arrived only a few centuries before them, who, because of war, invasion, and social unrest, were forced to flee their homes in successive waves—first in the tenth, eleventh, and twelfth centuries, and then again in the seventeenth, under Manchurian rule. Hakka spread out across southern China, down through the storied coastal areas of Amoy (present-day Fujian and Xiamen) and throughout Guangdong Province. Too often they encountered hostile communities, who looked at them through narrowed eyes and questioned whether they were even Chinese (they were).

By the mid-nineteenth century, tensions were so high between Hakka and other Chinese in the South that by the time a young Christianized Hakka named Hung Sau Toon (Hong Xiuquan) arrived, proclaiming himself the brother of Jesus and a kind of second coming, it sparked the Tai Ping Rebellion—a relentless, brutal fourteen-year civil war that left between 30 million and 50 million dead—the bloodiest war of the century.

Much of the antagonism had settled down by the time Chun Chun was born in 1888, but it still lingered in the air like ash after a wildfire.

Chun was six years old when the earth split open beneath their feet like the cracked seeds of a giant melon. Where there were once roots and worms, everything receded and shriveled up, turning to dust. Chun Chun and her siblings felt like they were peering into the dark, open pores in the skin of the earth, large as platters, but the villagers were warning that deep down below, the earth was exhaling dark, noxious, invisible fumes.

It was certainly bad luck.

Only a month before, a cholera outbreak had spread from the western hilltop towns and fanned out across the fertile Pearl River Delta of Guangdong Province, leaving villagers—those lucky enough to survive—sickly and emaciated, begging for water. The bodies of the dying twitched long into the night, even after they were brought out onto the streets and deserted by families too poor to bury them. (Chun Chun's mother had at first blamed the village well, and refused to drag the water from it up to their house, instead preferring to collect rainwater from the roof, but this was different. There had been no rain for weeks. Finally, her mother gave in to Chun Chun's tears, her littlest sister pointing at her mouth, and then she and the entire family began humping the water, sloshing from their buckets, from the well again. But only boiled water and hot tea, Amah cautioned, setting the bucket down onto the floor.)

Then the rats began dying—nocturnal creatures emerging from their burrows in full daylight, coughing up blood along the footpath at the base of the village, the trail like a spray of painted blossoms. Chun Chun cried to see any animal in trouble, but her grandmother kicked the rodent away, and told her to save her tears for those who needed it most.

The earth's chi is killing them, Poa Poa told their father later that evening as they were eating dinner.

Nonsense, Baba said, scratching his ankle, covered in bites.

Chun Chun's grandmother didn't want to sleep downstairs anymore and they pestered Baba so much that he agreed that he and Uncle would sleep on the first floor, just to shut them up.

. . .

Soon, THEIR VIEW OF THE HARBOR, teeming with fast clippers, and junks with the wing of their sails like giant conch shells, that never lingered longer than a day or so, held the addition of something else: a large floating hospital ship.

As people started to fall sick, rumors spread about the gwai lo doctors.

Don't go to the hospitals.

They want our women and daughters.

They will make medicine from your eyeballs.

At first, the official colonial response had been lackadaisical. Many white doctors and bureaucrats initially believed that the strange disease afflicted "only Chinese . . . and rats," blaming the disease on the overcrowded and unsanitary conditions of the local residents. But when panicked workers all across Hong Kong began walking off the job—a mass exodus of able-bodied manual laborers humping it back to the mainland—and the swollen bodies of the dead began lining the streets, the government was forced to declare a state of emergency. By that time it was too late. Not two months later, there were close to 2,500 dead, and an epidemic of such magnitude that hospital and staff were stretched so thin that boatloads of patients had to be offshored to Canton, which itself was struggling to contain the plague.

A new depot, originally built to house pigs and other livestock, was hastily converted into a makeshift hospital. (They called it the pigsty.)

Government officials made house visits in the overcrowded Chinese area of Toy Ping San (Tai Ping Shan). Then they came knocking on every door in Chun's village, pushing their way into homes and collecting anyone who looked sick. They accused Uncle, who was napping in the back room, of having the sickness, which Chinese called syu yik or shu yi (rat illness, or the plague), and forced him out the door with other unfortunates and onto the ship. Poa Poa feared that Uncle would never return, since the sickness was considered a death sentence. But they let him go when it was obvious he wasn't ill, and he came back a few days later, fine, but malnourished.

The lo fan treated him well, but he couldn't say much about the food.

WORKERS ARRIVED AND SPRAYED down the walls with a disinfectant that assaulted nostril hairs like a thousand sharp knives, and made the family light-headed, but even so, people kept dying.

It was only when the rains finally started again that summer, filling the cracked earth, so that the land was awash in little eddies that overflowed and washed away the refuse and decaying rat carcasses down the hill, that everything changed.

They said the earth's chi had been restored.

Poa Poa, a devout Christian, who took Chun Chun and her siblings to church every Sunday, even while the plague raged on, was convinced that God could save them. She taught Chun Chun how to pray to Jesus and Mary, who was a little like Guan Yin, the Goddess of Mercy. (At home, they still kept an altar to Guan Yin and lit paper for the Kitchen God every New Year, because not only did old traditions die hard, but Poa Poa liked to cover all her bases.)

Despite the plague, smallpox, and cholera outbreaks, Chun Chun grew up fast and strong. She attended a missionary school where she excelled in math and Bible studies. She was a teenager when the syu yik entered its second decade, and Hong Kong officials and the medical community, concerned that the Chinese population wasn't being educated enough in Western ways, instituted more English-only schools—making them available to both boys and girls. Although most daughters were needed at home to help work in the fields, Poa Poa convinced Baba to allow Chun to continue her education.

Then the colonial government, concerned about the high mortality rate for Chinese women during childbirth, and the abhorrent custom of abandoning girl infants on mountainsides (doubly disturbing during a pandemic), hatched a plan with the London Missionary Society, housed at the local Nethersole Hospital, for a standard midwifery training program for Chinese women—the first of its kind.

Even before the program officially opened, word spread across the colonial territory to anyone who had an ambitious daughter to spare. A year after the launch, at sixteen years old, Chun threw her application into the pool. To her surprise and delight, she was one of six pupils accepted into the second year of the program.

She took a year of basic nursing training with head matron Jane Stewart, learning about anatomy and hygiene from a Western perspective. The next year, she apprenticed under Dr. Alice Sibree, Hong Kong's first European woman doctor, taking careful note of the tricky breech births and health complications like toxemia and preeclampsia, then, as now, the leading causes of maternal death.

In between her training, she helped out at the children's hospital and tended the little ones—the babies and grade-schoolers alike, who arrived with broken limbs and diseases that Chun and the other midwives patched up with clean white bandages, Western medicine, and new crutches.

When she was allowed to tend to the deliveries of local women, Chun traveled all across Hong Kong Island and throughout Kowloon on foot and by ferry, grateful for her ability to climb the steep hills of the island, even on days when the air was so hot and humid that soap melted, and when the monsoon season arrived, as it did every summer, and the rains soaked the foothills and muddied the roads, drenching her black nursing shoes.

Chun had several advantages as a young midwife. Not only was she patient and kind, and armed with excellent English and Cantonese skills, but she was bestowed with the kind of exquisite beauty that animals, babies, and laboring women alike immediately responded to and trusted. The kind of beauty that for children implies goodly wholesomeness, like a bowl of polished rice. It was the kind of universal beauty that transcends race and class, Hakka or Cantonese, colonial European or Chinese, and it was helpful in getting anxious fathers to run out and get her clean water and towels in preparation for the big push. Chun's unadulterated "natural" feet ensured that she could stand for hours, and travel great distances to the homes of rich and poor women alike. She was grateful every day that she was a Hakka and had escaped the horrific punishment of bound feet that was the sad fate of so many of the Cantonese women around her.

She entered homes in districts where the plague had wiped out sisters, aunts, and grandmothers, including the local poa poas who traditionally delivered the babies. She saw folks in dire need of midwifery services, folks who were still mistrustful of the government's interventions, until Miss Chun arrived like something out of a fairy tale and stepped over the threshold with her white frock, soft-soled Mary Janes, and nursing bag.

She tended to poor young and older women who lived in dark, overcrowded homes. She loved the women who squatted during labor, making for quick, easy births, admiring the ones who could practically catch the baby themselves, aiding them only with the merest snip of the cord with good regulation scissors. She guided others to keep their energy up until the baby was safely in their arms, some already latching as the mother pushed out the afterbirth. Chun instructed them and their surviving family members on the importance of cleanliness, sending neighbors down to the well for fresh water, and instructing the families to wash everything, and how to sterilize the bedding, the rags, the clothing, after the baby was born.

She treated the second and sometimes third wives of the richest men in Hong Kong, the young concubines who lived in lush, hillside households as complex as imperial palaces. These women, dressed in elaborate brocade silks from their tiny feet to the delicate woven knots at the base of their collarbones, and catered to by bevies of young moy moys, could labor only on their backs or their sides, because the practice of foot binding made bearing down on their feet excruciating. Even when one young woman insisted upon sitting up, instinctively knowing that gravity would help, Chun saw how painful it was for her to push, trying to bear down only upon her heels.

How many deaths Chun saw, nobody knows for certain. I can only imagine how she felt when a mother perished during labor, or a baby emerged in her hands stillborn and heavy like a blood clot, this woman who used to cry as a small girl whenever any animal died.

Chun logged long, uncertain hours, sometimes staying overnight, until the water broke, and the mother reached the point of full dilation. I can feel her joy at that moment when the baby's head first emerged, then the entire body, masterfully turning a breech, sometimes untangling the cord from the baby's neck. As she carried the crying infant to its mother, each birth to Chun was a minor miracle, that moment when life begins as a series of screaming cries and hiccups, legs extended and fingers splayed, as the infant takes its first crying breaths.

Afterward, she cleaned the babies and cut the cords, carefully recording the birth and gender for the government.

From the youngest, poorest mothers to the richest merchant husbands, everyone was anxious for sons.

Chun encountered families disappointed they'd had a girl—families who begged her to not register the birth to the government and turn a blind eye to the baby's fate.

As a nurse and a Christian, she could not in good conscience lie for them.

Once, a husband entered the room as she was recording the birth in her government book.

What is this that you won't help us? he said. *Surely you can understand what kind of situation we're in. We can't afford to feed another girl!*

Chun noted the rooms and the servants. *Sir, I've attended many births,* she said. *Every child is a gift from God. Be thankful your daughter is healthy.*

Why did I ever let you into my house? he yelled, his hands balled into fists. *Next time we'll use luk poa!*

She took her leave, thankful when she passed through their courtyard and high wall and finally reached the din of the streets.

Chun felt sorry for the child, but had to hope that this small, sacred intervention made a difference.

WHEN GREAT-GRANDFATHER SHIM arrived in New York City under Dek Foon's tutelage in late 1899 or early 1900, he was a shy, nervous young man eager to spread the word of God to anyone who would listen. He attended Guy Maine's Chinese school at St. Bartolomew's Church, and with Dek's encouragement, he applied to boarding school at Mount Hermon in western Massachusetts. In his application, Shim wrote in careful, looping script, "I am very glad that I have an opportunity to go to school, I would like [to] study to be a missionary, if possible."

His doctor evaluated him as an excitable subject with "a slight weakness of the eyes," which would later develop into severe myopia—a condition that we would all inherit down the line. I know that he was five foot seven and in otherwise good health, although the doctor noted, "he is a nervous subject, which would account for the [much accelerated] rate of pulse." The doctor listed it at 90 beats per minute.

Shim was accepted to the Mount Hermon School for Boys, where he studied arithmetic, rhetoric, and the Bible and attended chapel several times a week. From his academic record, we know, for instance, that he struggled with James Fenimore Cooper's *Last of the Mohicans* and did not sit for the exam. I want to say that he was a good student, given the fact that English was his second language, and that he had come to the country only a year before. Although he had cut his queue before entering Mount Hermon, he was shy, and disinterested in sports, and even back home had been considered something of a bookish "Mama's boy."

Despite his prep school education at Mount Hermon, and his considerable fluency, upon graduation and returning home to New York, Great-Grandfather Shim discovered that the only real business opportunities for a Chinese man were still confined to the community. Luckily, he had Dek Foon and his Christian network to support him. By 1907, in his late twenties and backed by Dek Foon's financing and guidance, by both Chinese and American standards Great-Grandfather Shim was doing well. He was a partner in the Quong King Long Company (Wide Prosperous Authority), his own laundry supply company founded with friends and the help of his uncle; it was partially modeled off Dek's old employer's business, with a twist—they were also manufacturers of laundry machines and Uncle Dek's steam press invention. Shim held a vested interest of $1,200 (over $31,000 today).

By our standards this may seem modest, but back then, most businesses in Chinatown were started by many partners kicking in small sums of money. It was common for these start-ups to have five or more partners in any given venture, and the larger family and regional associations helped promote cooperative lending among their constituents. Quong King Long bounced around the neighborhood for the first two years, from Pell Street and up and down Mott, before finally settling on 44 Mott.

SITTING AT HIS DESK at the *Chinese Reform News* one afternoon in February 1907, Shim peered over a tray of movable type through round spectacles. There were many pressures running a Chinese newspaper in an outpost like New York: he was not only editor in chief, writer, copy boy, transcriber, and typesetter all rolled into one, but he also needed to keep apace with the pulse of relevant news—Shim read at least three Chinese newspapers and five English newspapers daily. But perhaps the toughest, most frustrating part of the job was that there was never enough type for the article he wanted to write. This was the city's first Chinese-language newspaper, and the Chinese movable type—those little metal bits from which printing is done—that Shim so depended upon was a rarity in New York. The *News* had only seven thousand characters at its disposal, whereas, he told a *New York Sun* reporter, "no metropolitan Chinese paper would think of getting out the sheet with less than 30,000." Each time Shim tried to drum up a sentence, he often spent precious time poring over the limited type in the tray, searching for alternative characters.

At this rate, it might take another fifteen years of hard work selling subscriptions and garnering advertisements before he could even hope to obtain a complete working set.

By that time, they might not need the *Reform News*—perhaps China would already be a bright, new constitutional monarchy.

Earlier that day, Shim had received a letter from China. He tried to put it out of his mind, but it nagged at him.

He didn't mention the letter to Dek Foon until he arrived home. But his uncle already knew.

The subject of Shim's getting married had been the topic of several trans-Pacific exchanges between Dek and the family back home. The family's position was clear and unequivocal—Shim was now a rich Gold Mountain man, who could afford to support a wife and a family, and it was his filial duty to obey his parents' wishes. His mother had contacted a well-connected matchmaker who, through divination, word of mouth, and craftily worded interviews, had found him a suitable bride. She was a Toisanese girl from a neighboring village, who was quite a few years younger. Ordinarily this was not considered ideal—a Chinese marriage was considered greatly enhanced by the girl being slightly older and wiser than her husband. But now that Shim was pushing thirty, and *practically an old man*, in order to have any hope for continuing the family line, he would need to marry a young bride. And preferably one with bound feet that reflected his status as a rich man.

Shim's parents had pressured him with marriage prospects ever since he'd graduated from Mount Hermon, but he had always successfully put them off. He was just starting out in business, working and dealing with white manufacturers. There was also his political organizing toward the modernization of China. Couldn't they see how important that was?

Plus, he wanted to marry a Christian girl, someone who saw the light as he did, who could help spread the word through their community and save souls, and not some backwards country girl who would need the help of a moy moy to stand up or even go to the bathroom.

But the tone of his mother's latest letter was entirely different from past ones.

Don't be a useless rice bucket head, his mother said. She and his father should have done this before he left for Gum San.

Through the aid of a letter writer, she threatened that if Shim didn't come home at once to meet the girl, they would hold the *marry-the-rooster* ceremony without him.

It will be the most elaborate wedding the village has ever seen, she gloated. And she was going to use Shim's money to pay for it.

What's a marry-the-rooster *ceremony?* Elva would have asked, likely at the dinner table, the site of all good, juicy family conversation.

Dek Foon would have done the explaining, for it was all a bit too much for Shim. These were village rituals created during the Gold Rush days when men boarded ships to Gum San to find their fortune, and families worried they might never come home. *They found a poor girl, dressed her in the red bridal cheongsam, and married her to the rooster stand-in for the groom, which, more often than not, just pecked around the corners of the living room.*

Did Shim feel like he was going to be sick, and excuse himself to his room?

It's not hard to imagine that he would have slept fitfully.

MANY SINGLE MEN SHIM'S AGE visited prostitutes, mainly poor Irish women living in the Quarter, but as a Christian, that was not a possibility for him. When he first started working for his uncle, making his rounds delivering orders to the hand laundries they supplied around town, the younger laundrymen of his generation often made fun of him. They called him *Jesus*, or *Jesus in a Bowtie*. It became a kind of joke throughout the community, and it continued even now as he established himself as a well-known businessman.

Being called Jesus didn't bother Shim. He yearned to follow in the light of the Lord's path, and if being called Jesus reminded him and others of that mission, then he counted it as a blessing. Although the thought of marrying intimidated him, he believed that if that was his calling—and both Dek and Elva believed that he should marry—then he should consider the girl, especially if she was open to becoming a Christian.

Great-Grandfather Shim agreed to return home to meet the girl his mother wanted him to marry, but if he had any hopes of returning to New York after his trip, he first had to put his paperwork through with the Office of the Chinese Inspector, a process that, like getting married, he had put off as long as possible. He knew it would be excruciating. These were systematic attempts at corroboration, as in a criminal case. Only this was a case that would persist for the entire length of time Shim resided in America, and what was my great-grandfather's actual crime? Like in that physical exam he was required to submit to before entering Mount Hermon, his heart must have been racing the entire time—did it feel like it was going to leap up out of his throat like a fish, which he'd be forced to catch with his bare hands?

First and foremost, there was the securing of white witnesses.

Shim preferred doing things himself if he could, but in this case, he was forced to swallow his pride. The very next day, when John Holt, the stamp manufacturer from whom the *Reform News* purchased its type—the first Chinese characters Holt had ever produced—showed up at the store to drop off a case, Shim was excited to see him for more than just the new type.

He solicited Holt's help, as well as Robert Boon's, the paper dealer on whose pulpy news stock the newspaper was printed. (Added bonus: unlike Holt, who was German, Boon was an American citizen.)

It took me close to a year and a half of scouring the National Archives and Records Administration (NARA) sites in New York and the Bay Area, and of obsessive checking of Ancestry, with no luck uncovering Shim's file. Finally, I canvassed friends at the 1882 Foundation in DC, and someone knew a NARA volunteer in Seattle, who was aware of a hidden, nonpublic database for Chinese Exclusion files. She checked his name and its various spellings, and there it was—not in New York, his city of residence, but in Seattle, Washington. When I did finally lay eyes on Shim's file, after arriving at the Seattle NARA offices in spring of 2016, on the tail end of a book tour, I wanted to kiss every brittle, yellowing page. (I didn't, of course—kissing of archives is not allowed—but my heart felt as expansive as a hot air balloon the rest of the trip.)

From Shim's Chinese Exclusion file—which I am reading as a digital file from the comfort of my studio on Mott Street—I can see that Shim and his witnesses, including Howard O. Sing, another partner in the firm, were called into the Office of the Chinese Inspector in Charge on 17 State Street, just south of the Custom House. Shim's case was being handled by Albert B. Wiley, a particularly ornery "Chinese inspector"— a term synonymous with today's "immigration official" (none of the inspectors were, of course, Chinese). Wiley had served for many years in Malone, a small town in upstate New York just south of the Canadian border, with a new detention facility that locals dubbed the "Chinese jail." It was the only officially sanctioned immigration station for Chinese in the Northeast at that time—all legal Chinese immigration in the region had to pass through it. Although Dek Foon had been working at the New York Immigration Bureau for years as an interpreter for hire, Wiley was intent on not giving Shim any favors—even exceptional Chinese who were fluent in English and had gone to elite New England prep schools, whose uncles worked for the bureau, were not given free passes.

When Wiley learned that, in addition to being a principal stakeholder at Quong King Long, Shim was editor in chief of the *Chinese Reform News*, he immediately grew suspicious. Writing and editing news articles about political reform in China, including setting typeface for publication, all under the pressure of a weekly deadline, was in Wiley's mind *dangerously close to manual labor.* He quickly dismissed Shim's white witnesses—the stamp maker and the paper seller—on the basis that a newspaper didn't constitute a proper merchant business.

"Isn't it a fact that he [Wu Do Shim] gives the majority of his time to the *Chinese Reform News?*" Wiley demanded of Howard O. Sing, the treasurer of Shim's Quong King Long.

"He spends part of the time in our store and part of the time in the *Reform News,*" Sing replied.

"Doesn't he spend most of the time in the *Reform News?*"

"I guess about half the time," Sing said, not wanting to contradict Wiley.

"Do you know whether he has an interest in the *Chinese Reform News* or simply works there?"

"Simply works there."

"What does he do in the *Chinese Reform News?*"

Sing couldn't remember Shim's title, but he had certainly heard him complaining about the lack of Chinese typeface available, especially when trying to translate articles from English into Chinese. "Translator," he said.

SHIM SAT OUTSIDE WILEY'S OFFICE, trying to keep the panicky feeling in his stomach tamped down, but the fish was buoyant and swimming circles. It was bad enough that he had to go through this interrogation, but why did they have to include several of his business associates and friends?

One by one, Shim had watched the stamp maker and the paper supplier swiftly exit the office (they were dismissed so quickly that their testimony isn't even included in my great-grandfather's Chinese Exclusion file, only their names). But Sing had been in there for quite a while.

What the hell is going on in there? he may have wondered, before he could stop himself. Even in his head, Great-Grandfather famously refused to curse as a matter of principle and practice, because if it was in his inner thoughts, it might one day pop out of his mouth on the street, or worse, at home, in Dek and Elva's house, where it was strictly forbidden— a sign of poor upbringing, or *the devil*.

Sing emerged from the room, but there was no time to confer, as just then they called Shim's name.

He was told to stand against a measuring chart on the wall. (*5′8″ tall*.)

His face was scanned. (*Scar over right eyebrow.* How had Great-Grandfather gotten this scar? I wondered. Was it from riding his bicycle like me? But there's nothing in the record to reveal any hints.)

Frustratingly, the official record reveals nothing about what Wiley looked like.

After Shim was sworn in, the interrogation began:

Wiley started off by asking many of the same questions he'd asked Howard O. Sing. It must have been dull, mind-numbing work (which made for equally cross-eye-inducing, boring reading). *How long had he been a member of the firm?*

What was the amount of interest he had in the business?

What year was the firm organized?

Everything had to match up with what Sing had said or else there was no way they'd let Shim back into the country (or worse, he could be deported on the spot). At some point, I imagine Shim taking out a handkerchief to wipe away the tiny beads of sweat from his forehead.

"Through this time have you given your entire time to the firm?" Wiley asked.

"Not entire time, but part of it," Shim answered.

"What were you doing the rest of your time?"

"I spent the rest of my time in the *Chinese Reform News*."

"How much time do you suppose you devote to the conduct of the business at No. 44 Mott Street?"

"Just about half or something like that."

"Do you do any buying for the firm at 44 Mott Street?"

Shim said that he did.

"Do you buy goods from white men?"

Shim replied again in the affirmative.

"Can you get some white men who know you to be a member of that firm?"

"Sure, I can get some more if you want them," Shim said smoothly, although deep down inside, my great-grandfather was perspiring under his starched white collar and that fish was threatening to flap around the room.

Two more *white witnesses? Where was he going to get two* more *white witnesses?* He already owed Holt and Boon for the favor of coming down to State Street and vouching for him, and now he had to find *two more lo fan to speak on his behalf?*

Shim was positive that he was going to become ill. Right there, all over the slick government floors, while the fish made silvery somersaults in the arc of his vomit. Did he hear his mother's voice—not his real mother, who was already in bed, half a world away—but *the mother who resided in his head,* the ever-present mother, that indomitable village woman who was admonishing him to *stay focused* and *don't waste good food, otherwise she was going to scoop it up off the floor and feed it back to him with his favorite soup spoon?*

Shim was dismissed, but not before being ordered to bring his new witnesses into the office—within forty-eight hours.

Great-Grandfather clutched his hat and left the building.

Sing was waiting for him outside.

Bad luck, Sing said, shaking his head. *That dead dog has no heart.*

Stupid, decapitated head, my great-grandfather thought, in village dialect. If he actually said it out loud ("thlee yin hao"), it would have required nearly spitting out of the sides of his mouth.

A week and a half later, after five witnesses and many restless nights of sleep for Shim, Wiley filed his report to his boss, Harry R. Sisson, the top Chinese inspector in the New York bureau.

> *Sir:*
>
> *I return herewith the papers of WU DO SHIN, alleged merchant and member of the firm of Quong King Long and Co., of No. 44 Mott Street, this city, who desires to file papers in order that his status as a merchant may be determined prior to his intended visit to China.*
>
> *I have examined the applicant, the manager of the firm, and his two white witnesses, and copies of their sworn testimony are hereto attached. . . . These two witnesses were very positive in their identification of the applicant as a member of the above firm, having gained this knowledge from actual business relations with him . . . [one] stated that he had helped organize the firm, and that he had seen some very large checks and contracts drawn by the firm of Quong King Long and Co., and signed by this applicant.*

Even reading this, several times, and over a century later, fills me with rage.

After days of interviews and witnesses vouching for him, Great-Grandfather is still an *alleged* merchant at Quong King? What would Shim need to do in order to prove his legitimacy under the watchful eye of the law—provide quadruple the amount of white witnesses?

But I know, even ponying up one hundred white people necessary to speak on his behalf wouldn't make Shim any less suspicious. Even with his relatively privileged and exceptional background—prep school educated, literate, fluent in English, and dressed in the fashion of a prosperous American—being Chinese in America in 1907, during the third decade of Chinese Exclusion, he could never be seen as legitimate.

And could they even bother to spell his name right?

Wiley's report continued:

> *The firm of Quong King Long and Co., of 44 Mott Street, are dealers in laundry machinery and supplies, and have the appearance of doing a very good business. While it appears that Wu Do Shin has given part of his time to the management of the Chinese Reform News, my investigation shows that he is undoubtedly one of the leading members of the firm . . . and I believe that during the past year he has performed no manual labor except such as has been required of him in connection with the firm's business at No. 44 Mott Street, and in the management of the affairs of the Reform News. I would therefore recommend that his papers be vised.*
>
> > *Respectfully,*
> > *Albert B. Wiley*
> > *Chinese Inspector*

Even though Wiley had been a suspicious, paper-pushing bureaucrat throughout the entire process, the upshot was that Shim could travel to China freely without fear of being shut out upon his return.

Shim left for China on November 12, 1907, on board the expansive SS *Iyo Maru*, arriving in Hong Kong early the next month.

10

Shim & Chun

Ng-Doshim Family

伍

According to family lore, Chun was at church with her family one Sunday, when she looked up from her hymnal and caught a stranger staring at her. He was Chinese, but dressed like a foreigner, with close-cropped hair that was as thick as a horsehair brush, and a starched white collar that dug into his neck. He had at least the good sense to flush crimson and look away—pretending to be engrossed in the minister's closing benedictions.

She had only ever seen a lofan sporting such a collar, and couldn't tear her eyes away.

Flustered as he was, Chun thought he resembled a red and white lollipop.

After services, she noticed the man standing a few paces behind her, his hat between his hands, working up the nerve to talk.

. . .

SHIM HAD BEEN RESTING UP after the three-week trans-Atlantic journey from America, when he met Chun at church that Sunday. As the story in our family goes, one look at Chun—reciting over a hymnal, her eyes so perfectly symmetrical under the curve of her bangs that when she looked up, Shim felt like he was staring straight at the setting sun—and his family's plans for an arranged marriage to the village girl with the bound feet evaporated like morning dew on the leaves of unfurling tea bushes.

What had been planned as a short visit to Hong Kong before returning to our village to deal with his mother and her plans for his wedding, instead turned into weeks of courtship. Whenever Chun finished her shift at Nethersole Hospital, there was Shim, standing out front on the busy street with his bicycle, his starched white collar and bow tie, his hat

Chun, far right, and the Nethersole nurses, 1907

tilted to one side, offering her a ride. (He had learned to ride as a student at the green, rolling expanse of Mount Hermon, but the terrain in western Massachusetts was little preparation for the steep mountainous hills that formed the Mid-Levels of Hong Kong.)

Soon, Shim was dropping Chun off at various birthing appointments across the island several times a week. And before long, whenever she had to spend the night, he made sure to keep spare change in his pocket for the neighborhood children to run down to where he was staying on Connaught near the waterfront to tip him off when the baby arrived.

Whenever Chun stepped out of the home of the family she was tending, the next morning or afternoon, there was Shim waiting to take her to the Star Ferry.

Shim could not tell if the woozy light-headedness of nascent love that made his breath catch every time he saw Chun was partially a function of his own interrupted sleep as his hours began matching that of Nethersole's most in-demand midwife, or the warmth of Chun's strong, elegant hands when she switched from holding on to the bar under her seat to clutching his waist on a day when they hit a bump and she had to prevent herself from flying off the bike. (He turned to make sure she was all right, and in that moment staring into her eyes, he knew that he would do anything for her.)

Was it the many times they walked the esplanade together, Shim wheeling Chun's bag on the handlebars of his bicycle?

Although naturally quiet, Shim became a nonstop talker, inspired to tell her all about the marvels of the West—indoor plumbing, subways and streetcars, water flowing from every tap in every household, iceboxes. Some apartments, like theirs, even had their own private toilets.

He lived in Brooklyn, which until only recently had been its own city, with an aunt and uncle who were like parents to him—his aunt was a lofan who treated him like a son and made him giant birthday cakes that gave him a stomachache but he never refused because he did not want to disappoint her. He called her Mutzi, a variant of the German *Mutter*, and their Christian community of mixed Chinese and Westerners was long established and, from his point of view, warm and welcoming.

His aunt taught him all about American manners.

He ate with a fork and knife and ate butter on toast cut into long strips called "soldiers."

The Chinese American churches had picnics on a mountain called Bear, which they traveled to on a hired boat up the Hudson that looked just like the Star Ferry.

Do foreigners treat you the way they treat us here? Chun asked. Chinese people had no rights under British colonial rule. *Do they bring in outsiders from their colonies to police you?*

Shim considered it a moment. *We do not have rights in America yet, but we have been lobbying with local politicians in New York, just like the way merchants do here with English officials.*

My uncle and his friends are connected with high-ranking officials, he told her. Judges and congressmen, who were like members of Parliament.

Even now, there were Chinese cadets training under the aegis of the Chinese Reform Association and the Chinese Guild to enact change in Chinese governance.

He did not tell her about the suspicious looks and outright stares of hostility by the lofan when Elva and Dek Foon walked through their Brooklyn neighborhood. Shim had long ago grown used to being regarded suspiciously and, being naturally shy and reserved, some would say "guarded," took it in his turn. Even in Chinatown, where such mixed unions were relatively commonplace, some Chinese frowned upon them too. Dek Foon brushed it off in his optimistic way, but Shim knew that it bothered his aunt.

He had grown used to the eyes upon him as he and his uncle traveled from their bedroom community in Brooklyn to Chinatown. When one woman dropped her purse at his feet and Shim handed it back to her with *"Your handbag, m'lady,"* and a flourish, she'd nearly jumped out of her seat in surprise. He mentioned none of this to Chun, because after nearly a month in Hong Kong in her steady presence, the sharp edges of being treated with suspicion were blunted by a film of nostalgia. New York was *home*; this trip had made him realize that.

And he knew something else too—he wanted Chun to know all the great things about the West, because he yearned to take her there.

Watching her waving from the ferry as it pulled away toward Kowloon, shrinking smaller and smaller and out of sight, Shim knew he couldn't let her get away.

Quite simply, he was in love.

The prospect of Chun and Shim's marriage was a radical departure from Chinese norms, where matchmakers consulted birth charts and genealogy to ensure folks were not related—very important in a country where there were only one hundred surnames. For generations, such women were hired to ensure that the match on earth would shine as brightly as that determined by the heavens.

Shim's mother was adamantly opposed to the marriage. Shim may have been only a baby when the last of the Punti-Hakka wars ended, and didn't know firsthand any of the carnage, although countless villagers had died, but she remembered, and still very much believed that Hakka were the enemy.

Shim didn't care that Chun was Hakka, although he wasn't certain how she felt about his being Bun day, or Punti, meaning "locals" or "natives"—even though Cantonese had arrived only one or two centuries before the Hakka.

For her part, Chun was charmed by this older man who spoke American English and dressed like a foreigner. That they were both devout Christians was significant for each of them.

After so many years of living in New York, Shim was well beyond the point of merely obeying his mother out of filial duty. He was a modern twentieth-century Chinese living in America, and he knew that lovely, devoted Chun was the woman for him.

When Dek Foon's letter to Shim's family arrived at their village in Shun On, Shim's mother knew she was outmatched.

On March 16, 1908, thirty-year-old Shim married twenty-year-old Chun in a simple ceremony at their church.

That winter, as Chun, even more radiant in pregnancy, was about to enter her third trimester, Shim, who had taken on the more formal name of Do Shim or Doshim, signaling his role as a married man and provider, wrote the following letter to the Chinese inspector in Seattle.

Soy On Chong Co.
No. 119 Connaught Road
Hong Kong
Jan. 2, 1909

Chief Officer in Charge Enforcement Chinese Exclusion Laws,
Port of Seattle, Washington

Sir: In compliance with the above notification, delivered to me prior to my departure from the United States, you are informed that I intend to return thereto, through your port . . . on or about April or May, 1909.

I departed from the United States on the Steamship Iyo Maru which sailed from your port on Nov 12 1907.

I have filed with you the evidence required by law to support my claim of right to readmission. I am a merchant and member (or proprietor) of the store of Quong King Long Co. at New York NY in which my interest was, and still remains $1200.

I respectfully request that my claim be pre investigated, and that I may be notified before April or May 1909 at the above address, whether I will be permitted to reenter the United States, and, if so, upon what condition.

Respectfully,
W. Do Shim

Since I found it in the National Archives office in Seattle, I may have read this dozens of times. There's something about reading this form letter, filled out by Doshim's hand, knowing that he's transformed from a virginal businessman to a husband and soon-to-be-father that is simply heartbreaking. That last overly polite line requesting to be informed whether he'll be permitted to reenter and upon what condition, filled out in his clear, prep school script that looks so much like his daughter's, my grandmother's, handwriting, makes me feel indescribably anxious.

Suddenly, I'm the one walking on eggshells with my great-grandfather, trying to navigate the road underfoot without breaking anything.

February 10, 1909
Mr. H.R. Sisson,
Inspector in Charge,
New York, N.Y.

Sir:

I return herewith papers in the case of WU DO SHIN, an alleged merchant and member of the firm of Quong King Long and Co., No. 44 Mott Street, this city, who has signified his intention of returning to the United States via the port of Seattle, Washington.

I have examined the manager of the above firm and copy of his statement will be found attached to the papers, from which it will be noted that he states that the mercantile status of WU DO SHIN remains the same as at the time of his departure for China. I would

therefore recommend that this applicant be readmitted upon proper
identification.

Respectfully,
Albert B. Wiley
Chinese Inspector

That following spring, Chun gave birth to a healthy baby girl, surrounded by the midwives at Nethersole Hospital, who doted on both
mother and baby alike.

Doshim and Chun named the newborn Oi, meaning Love. The mul-
tipart ideogram with its many flourishes contains within its center the
word "heart," or sum (as in dim sum, "a little bit of heart"), but also
combined with the radical "good," it denotes "daughter," as in "my good-
hearted daughter." "Heart" itself, in its old, seal-script form, resembles a
mother cradling a baby in her arms, or two hands grasping the heart
center like a gift, rather like an Irish claddagh ring. When spoken aloud
it sounds like high-quality jade. Oi Oi was the perfect blend of Hakka
and Cantonese—the best of both worlds, no matter Shim's mother's
opinion.

Nobody would care about that in America, Chun knew. Her daughter
would grow into a sure-footed girl on Gold Mountain, as would all the
future Doshim children, if they were lucky enough to have more.

WHEN THE BORDERS SHUT against us, many, desperate to support their
families, came anyway.

Some arrived by train through Canada, on a railroad built by their
countrymen's hands, slipping out as the locomotives slowed down near
the border to make the rest of the way on foot.

Others came through the southern border from Mexico, swimming
across the Rio Grande, carrying large bundles of clothing, opium, and

razors. Many hiked the desert and survived off nothing but dried, desiccated horned toads rendered into a kind of jerky to last against the heat of the blazing desert sun.

Some came via steamships from Jamaica and the Caribbean, hidden in cargo crates packed with bananas, their bellies bloated with the fruit, leaving piles of decaying brown peels in their wake.

Still others entered hidden inside neat, satin-lined coffins—made in Canada, sold to the U.S.—like a line of sleek, luxury vehicles for the last journey to the other side.

Who among us wouldn't contemplate our own mortality in the seemingly endless hours spent in a dark, airless, body-sized box?

For most Chinese, folks who culturally avoided giving clocks on New Year's Day because the phrase for it sounded too similar to *paying respects at a funeral,* and the number four because it sounded too much like *death*—this particularly reliable method would have been completely anathema. Although no one knows how many cartloads of caskets slipped over the border this way in 1909, it was never going to be a popular choice.

For a long time, I had believed that Chun arrived in the U.S. packed in a cargo crate, like Maxine Hong Kingston's father in *China Men.*

Chun's beauty was legendary, and often touted in relief (as in, *My sister was beautiful, she resembled my mother—too bad I look like my father*). I imagined how magnificent she would have appeared, when the crate was finally opened with a crowbar by the smuggler on the other side, and Chun emerged naked like a dark-haired version of Botticelli's Venus, framed not by an iridescent shell but, instead, industrial cargo crates, sawdust falling like sea-foam from the soles of her bare feet.

This was before I realized Chun was a young mother traveling with an infant.

She would not have been naked, of course, that was my teenage imagination at work, nor would a twenty-one-year-old mother have entered the country stuffed in a crate with a baby, who could cry at any moment and alert the authorities.

It was only after I discovered Doshim's file in Seattle, Washington, in 2016, and had the opportunity to compare it to the 1910 Brooklyn census information, that their journey would come into focus.

Shim knew that getting Chun and baby Oi into America was a perilous proposition. Chinese Exclusion was in its third decade. Wives and dependents were not specifically mentioned in the Chinese Exclusion Act, and their fate at the border, whether on land or at the docks, was left entirely at the whim of immigration officials.

Returning through San Francisco with Chun and the baby was never going to be an option. A new detention center was being constructed on a lonely, barren island in the harbor—Angel Island—and now there was a surge of immigrants trying to get through before the restrictions became even more stringent.

Doshim, under Dek Foon's advisement, had chosen the Pacific Northwest as the safest place to land.

The family traveled across the Pacific in a first-class cabin, with stops for passengers and refueling along the way in Shanghai, Tokyo, and then lush Hawaii, Chun's favorite, so very much like Hong Kong but with volcanoes, and where the air smelled like pineapple. But it was there that Doshim received a surprising and cryptic cable from Dek Foon, telling the family to immediately debark the ship. His uncle had arranged passage for them on another international liner, this one headed to Vancouver, British Columbia.

In New York, in June 1909, the decomposing body of nineteen-year-old Elsie Sigel had been found in a trunk inside the apartment of Leon Ling, a waiter and Sunday school student. Ling, it was revealed in the newspapers, was Sigel's suspected paramour—and the search for him was underway. Sigel was the granddaughter of a Civil War general—her relationship with Leon Ling, a handsome Chinese restaurateur with a touch of the dandy, was fodder for journalists and the public.

A photograph of Ling, handsome, broad-shouldered, strapping in a well-tailored suit and tie (the press likened him to a "Chinese Don Juan"), circulated in newspapers across the nation. When a neighbor of Leon Ling was arrested as a suspect, *The New York Times* declared him "The Man the Whole World Is Seeking."

Sigel's murder, potentially at the hands of Ling, became larger than life—more than just another tragic homicide, this became a salacious cautionary tale of what could happen to young white women when they took up with Chinese men.

Sigel's father told reporters, "This should be a lesson to young girls not to mix with other than their own people."

The retribution against Chinese was swift.

In New York City, the local police chief vowed to "cleanse" Chinatown. They shut down the offices of both On Leong and Hip Sing, raided thirty-six gambling parlors, and drove out over a hundred "disorderly women" (white women they deemed prostitutes). This lasted for weeks. Business in Chinatown plummeted.

Vigilantes raided hand laundries across the city, terrorizing Chinese business owners and their employees, believing wild rumors that white women were being held hostage there.

Across the country, a nationwide dragnet was sparked. Police officers conducted raids and made arrests of Chinese in San Francisco, Boston, Pittsburg, Baltimore, DC, Manchester, New Hampshire, and Norfolk, Virginia, and as far away as Mexico and British Columbia, Canada. These suspects were subject to the "third degree," a new practice in policing of constant questioning and sleep deprivation that reminds me of those endless immigration interrogations of family members, only worse.

Lack of sleep *is* a form of torture.

Under this duress, two Chinese men—one in Pennsylvania, the other in Massachusetts—confessed. They were released when it was discovered they had nothing to do with the murder.

Chinese Exclusion was now in its twenty-seventh year, made per-

manent seven years before. Many in the community were becoming resigned to the fact that they might never be able to overturn it, despite
their best efforts to win the hearts and minds of reformers and local New
York politicos.

The Elsie Sigel murder just made it worse.

Officials all along the U.S. border, especially the ports, viewed any Chinese or Asian man as a potential murderer. Young, Americanized ones like
Ling, who spoke good English and wore Western clothing, were viewed
as especially dangerous.

The Chinese American community in New York was on edge.

Chinese Sunday schools across the city shut their doors and never
reopened.

Dek Foon and his friends, especially Guy Maine, were appalled. Leon
Ling had been a member of the Chinese Guild and trained as a cadet of
the Chinese Reform Association—he was supposed to be helping bring
about reform in the homeland, not bring disgrace upon them all. There
was even a picture of him in uniform on his home dresser, which the police found when they searched his apartment.

To be associated with Ling was a stain upon them all.

Under the aegis of the Oriental Club, they pledged a $500 reward for
Sigel's killer (around $14,600 today).

The Chinese embassy published a manifesto on imperial yellow paper,
and posted it in Chinatowns across the country: "For the body of a young
lady to be thus discovered in the lodgings of a Chinaman throws disgrace on the whole body of our people in this country."

The police captain in the heart of Chinatown mandated that *no Chinese
could leave the city* without his permission.

Chinese attempting to purchase rail or ship tickets were turned away
and refused passage.

The border was even more highly regulated as local police worked
with immigration officers. They grilled not just folks trying to leave, but
also any Americanized Chinese attempting to enter.

Doshim's Exclusion paperwork was in order for his own reentry, but when he left the country a year and a half before, he hadn't known he would be returning with Chun and the baby.

No one actually knew how long it would take for the uproar over the Sigel murder to finally settle, and now, Doshim was a liability for the family.

He could not stand to think of Chun and the baby getting stuck in the squalid conditions on the San Francisco wharf or being ferried from one dank steerage hold to another or languishing in the "Chinese jail" in Malone, New York, for months on end.

Trying to get into the U.S. was like attempting to step through an ever-shrinking keyhole, even for an elite merchant's wife and daughter like Chun and Oi.

In Canada, just like in the U.S., Chinese labor had been crucial in completing the railroad through the country's most rugged terrain. (Some men even had experience working on the U.S. transcontinental railroad.)

And just like here, once the Canadian Pacific rail was completed, Canada enacted its own versions of Exclusion. The innocuous-sounding Chinese Immigration Act of 1885 imposed a prohibitive "head tax," or a hefty fee on all Chinese immigrating into the country, which no other nationality or race had to pay). In 1923, the Canadian government would replace it with a Chinese Exclusion act that closely mirrored that of the United States. The one bit of luck was that the family was migrating within that crucial window.

Dek Foon carefully considered the dilemma from New York.

For several years now, Dek had been established as an interpreter for the New York branch of the Immigration Bureau investigating Chinese— as were his friends at the Chinese Reform Association, Guy Maine and Joseph Singleton. The consensus was that, given *the current difficulties with the authorities scrutinizing all westernized Chinese men at the border,* it was better for Doshim to separate from Chun and the baby, allowing them to slip through undetected.

The first problem was Doshim himself. Long gone were the nervous prep school boy mannerisms, the polite, deferential Chinese-ness—marriage had given him something of a backbone—and he was adamant against leaving Chun and the baby alone in a foreign country.

What kind of husband and father would abandon his family? What kind of man would do that? It was against everything that he stood for.

But once they landed in British Columbia, Doshim began hearing about the raids happening throughout Chinatowns across the U.S. He had picked up his old editor's habit of reading any newspaper he could get his hands on—both the Chinese and the English papers.

When local Vancouver police began raiding Chinese businesses in a desperate search for Leon Ling—harassing any Chinese who dressed in Western clothing—Doshim knew he had to act. If the authorities questioned him and gave him the third degree, the entire family would be at risk and might never be able to safely land in the U.S.

With promises for a happy reunion in New York, Doshim reluctantly left Chun and baby Oi and boarded the SS *Princess Victoria* on July 25 to Seattle, Washington.

THE OFFICIAL RECORD GOES dark here. It is like I am feeling my way through a secret tunnel with only a flashlight and my outstretched hands to orient me. I have to trust my gut and my foraging eyes to guide me to the truth.

New York was in the throes of languid late summer when Doshim arrived back in the city. Then, the verdant urban arbors shifted with the winds to yellow and vermilion red. By the time they were finally browning out and shedding their leaves entirely, Doshim had grown *worried to death.*

Doshim's entry to Seattle, 1909

Thanksgiving came and went.

Back in Vancouver, baby Oi, a mere beebee-ah when they reached the shores of British Columbia, had recently cut her milk teeth and was suddenly voicing her first utterances (did she say Baba or Dada, as most children do, even though Doshim was away?).

Finally, Chun sent word to New York that the beebee was sleeping through the night.

Dek Foon decided it was time.

In the last week of December, while the nation entered that slow yawn between Christmas and the New Year, mother and child made their way across country on the Canadian Pacific railroad. Doshim had the pair booked in first-class passage in their own private sleeper cabin, and from its window, Chun watched the landscape of forests, lakes, and mountains pass by in a blur before the land flattened out into wide, open prairie.

She marveled at the vastness of the Canadian landscape covered under a blanket of snow.

It was the first time she had ever seen snow—it rarely dipped below freezing in subtropical Hong Kong, and I like to imagine that she would have shivered slightly in her silk jik-sum jacket, only by now she was wearing Western clothing.

At first Chun felt like an imposter in such garments—Chinese women in Hong Kong wore looser-fitting Chinese tops and bottoms. She associated corsets and floor-length hemlines with colonial administrators, like the head of midwifery at Nethersole and the lovely Dr. Alice Sibree from the London Missionary Society.

But at Elva's suggestion, it was considered time that Chun became a proper American woman.

Back in Vancouver, Chun had received a box full of New York's finest undergarments, gloves, and silk stockings from her new aunt. She was fitted for ankle-length Victorian dresses (judging by one of her dresses passed down to me from Grandma Rose, she was a size 000 by today's standards) and her first corset, the lacing of which confounded her. One needed help to put it on, and it was so hard to breathe in.

As a Hakka woman, Chun had escaped the permanent injuries of foot binding only to confront the organ-shifting contraptions of women's clothing in the West.

To Chun, America was exemplified in the constrictions of a corset and a hard pair of leather shoes.

And there were so many layers.

They stayed on board the train as it neared the east coast, and prepared to cocoon themselves in that evening. They had their wool coats and blankets to keep them warm, but I think Chun would have preferred her sumptuous, padded silk jik-sum, which was cool to the touch yet insulating, and never scratchy.

Chun drew the curtains across the wide window, against the night sky. Those stars now emerging were the same ones shining down on Doshim hundreds of miles away in New York. She made sure to feed her daughter extra well, watching the beebee, now an eight-month-old, fall asleep, all arms and legs gone limp in her arms, but the mouth still working in ever-slowing cycles at her breast.

It's not hard to imagine Chun saying her prayers for an extra-long time. Oi Oi had been sleeping well throughout the night across the entire train journey, but if she hadn't, Chun had been instructed to stop off in Toronto or Montreal and wait until her sleep pattern shifted.

Now that they were nearer to the border, edging closer to upstate New York, Chun began to question their decision.

There is always a chance a child will cry out in the middle of the night—whether from a bad dream or a new tooth emerging or some other unseen phenomenon. Those cries could wake up not only everyone on board but alert an immigration officer, who would take one look at this young Chinese woman and her child and send them both "back to where they came from."

Chun had been guided by faith to leave her family and home behind when she married Doshim, putting her trust in their marriage, her own good judgment, and the Christian god she so ardently believed in, to guide her.

I wish I could say that this is the way Chun and Oi crossed the border, asleep, safely tucked away in a first-class cabin, but that is not the case.

Crossing over by sleeper train had been a common method of crossing the border in the first decade of Chinese Exclusion, but by 1891 it was no longer a safe loophole. (One night, two Chinese men woke up restless at three a.m., and stretched their legs after the train arrived at a bridge checkpoint, tipping off the night watchmen.) By 1903, six years before Chun and Doshim arrived in Canada, Canadian officials had started keeping a head count of every Chinese on board trans-Canadian-American trains, and wired the number ahead to sheriffs on the other side of the border.

Luckily, Dek Foon and Singleton had built a network of connections that extended throughout the Northeast corridor like a giant silken web.

I know only a few pieces of the puzzle, gathered from family legend and passed down through the generations.

Rather than attempt the rest of the journey alone, Chun and Oi traveled with a series of Christian missionary families who were returning home from the holidays.

When they finally arrived in Montreal, they disembarked the train.

Chun and Oi met up with another family, who planned to cross into the U.S. in a horse-drawn coach, at night.

It was close to New Year's and the border was quiet.

No one knows exactly if it was the continuous rocking of the vehicle, or the clomp clomp clomping of horses' hooves against the road, or because Chun had her daughter so well sleep-trained, but everyone, including the baby Oi, nestled in her mother's arms, slept most of the journey, even as their driver crossed the border.

When they woke up, Chun opened the curtains to a cold, sunny morning.

It was December 30, on the cusp of a new year and decade, and they were in America.

And for the first time since Doshim left them, Chun could really breathe.

OVER A HUNDRED YEARS LATER, I can almost taste my great-grandmother's fear of getting caught and being thrown into a "Chinese jail," of the humiliation of not being able to arrive legally, like any other wife of the period, simply because she was Chinese.

Her fear is metallic, and eclipsed only by my own rage.

I want to throttle the immigration officers like Wiley, whose first job was in Malone before getting promoted to the New York City office and turning the screws on my family members.

I'd like to grab all the politicians by the throat who voted in the Chinese Exclusion Act in 1882, and all its permutations in between, and pour in a dose of my family's truth, and all the suffering of all the other Chinese families that tried to make their way into America.

If I could climb back into 1909, and ease my great-grandmother's fears by whispering in her ear like a ghost from the future that she would be reunited safely with Doshim in New York, I would.

Instead, I visited Malone, New York, with my family, in late summer of 2018, seeking answers. I had just spent a week combing through a giant digital file on the Canadian head tax, searching in vain for Chun's name, before realizing that because they were "tourists," they may not have actually been made to pay.

I was following in the footsteps of Bruce Hall, author of *Tea That Burns*, and Jack Tchen of the Museum of Chinese in America (MOCA)— both of whom had visited the town's historical society decades before. I spent a few hours leafing through the slim files about the town's Chinese presence, but sadly, I'd already seen many of the materials in Hall's archives at MOCA in lower Manhattan.

Disappointed, I drove down Main Street later that afternoon. Just behind the courthouse buildings stood a ring of old depots and sheds that looked like they'd been around since the Exclusion era. But the Chinese detention center and the Malone jail where deportees were kept had been torn down long before, to make way for a parking lot for the new courthouse. I eased my car into that lot and parked.

I sat in my car, the ignition off, aware that under that layer of new asphalt, so shiny and black, lay a site of old misery and containment.

Back when Chun and the baby were attempting to enter the country, the total Chinese population in the detention house and jail could swell to over six hundred detainees in dismal, overcrowded conditions. (In 1903, a reporter for *Collier's Weekly* cited a single bathtub and a broken lavatory outfit for thirty Chinese male "prisoners.") And because the federal government paid the county two-thirds more than what the town spent for room and board, Malone actually made a profit off our immigration misery. I was so grateful that my young great-grandmother and her first-born child never got stuck here.

The golden afternoon darkened in small notes until it turned to twilight, when a car pulled up behind me—one of those giant SUVs—and cut its lights. I began to worry that folks were going to wonder what I was doing in my car for so long.

Even a century later, I'm still feeling the echoes of suspicions past, enveloping me like a cloak.

I was just about to turn on the ignition, when another almost identical-looking SUV pulled up into the lot.

Now I really have to go, I thought, turning the key.

I heard a car door open. In my rearview mirror, I caught a glimpse of a kid's backpack and sneakers before she disappeared into the other car, the sound of a door slamming shut.

Before I even had a chance to turn on my lights, both cars had driven away.

It took me a moment to realize what had just happened.

A drop-off.

Another child of divorce toggling between two parents, neither of whom got out of their respective cars, or even rolled down their windows to talk to one another. (That the designated exchange place was the courthouse lot revealed the acrimonious nature of the split.)

Would that kid grow up wanting to know everything like I did? Pestering everyone about what happened until the adults grew weary and tired of such questions? ("Don't you ever get tired of asking questions?" my father asked me years before. "Why do you need to ask so many questions, the past is in the past," my grandmother Rose would say. It was the only thing they ever seemed to have in common, aside from me.)

I had always been told that it was easier for Great-Grandmother to get through via Canada because as a Hong Kong citizen, she was a subject of the British crown, and allowed to be there.

Dek Foon and Wu Chow, 1910

I never once thought to ask my grandmother why her mother, the wife of a Chinese merchant, would need to sneak across the border like a criminal (*no criminals, paupers, insane, or Chinese*).

Exclusion was the unspoken premise like a background painted by the hand of an unseen force that I now knew was all too human and all too powerful.

Under a darkening sky, I drove back through the streets of Malone, back to my motel where my own husband and daughter were awaiting me.

Two months after successfully getting Chun and Oi safely into America, where everyone was living together as a blended, intergenerational family in Dek and Elva's Brooklyn apartment, it was decided that it was high time for Dek to bring his one and only son, Wu Chow, to America.

It was the realization of a long-held dream.

Dek had only ever seen intermittent photographs of his son as he was growing up, along with letters written in the flowery style of nineteenth-century Chinese prose conventions, politely asking for more money. He always sent along more than the requested amount.

Bringing Doshim's family over was a masterful feat that emboldened Dek, and Doshim was determined to help out. But as difficult as it was navigating Chun and a baby past the gates of U.S. immigration in 1909, getting Dek's son in was perhaps even more challenging.

Wu Chow, a pampered pretty boy who grew up in a boarding school in Guangdong Province, who knew his father only via the checks he sent, was no longer a minor. At twenty-six, Chow was now a handsome, reed-like man with the long, thin face and hands of a scholar. Although he had taken the imperial exams and had passed well enough to become a teacher in their village, he spent most of his career teaching a year here or there at various schools, coupled with doing errands for his rich father—including delivering mail and remittances from America. Luckily, he was married to a level-headed woman, and raising a young son back home in their village.

At forty-eight, trim, and financially successful with his own joint businesses with Doshim and Singleton, Dek Foon knew that he had to plan for the future. He was thankful that he could keep Elva happily situated, but now Chow needed to become self-sufficient and not continue to be a *good-for-nothing bucket head*. Toisan had a reputation as being full of *lazy villages* for all the remittance money coming back from the Americas. If Dek could get his son over, he knew that he could be the kind of good Christian father and role model that Chow so desperately needed, even if, so far, Dek felt he was a poor one compared to Singleton or Huie Kin, who were each busy supporting a large brood of beautiful biracial children.

Dek Foon considered Chow's situation from all angles. They hatched a plan to use Dek Foon's status, not as a merchant, or a banker, but as an interpreter working with the New York Immigration Bureau.

While Dek and Doshim worked on bolstering Wu Chow's case file—collecting white witnesses to speak on Dek's behalf, even though everyone at the bureau knew that he had a son—Elva continued teaching Chun lessons in Americanism.

Elva, who believed that *cleanliness was next to godliness*, liked to keep a tidy house. She flew into rages if beds were not made and if messes weren't immediately cleaned up. Just-washed dishes had to be dried carefully before being put back into cupboards. Luckily Chun, trained under missionaries and the Florence Nightingale era of nursing—white badges, white frocks—was used to a strict cleanliness regimen. Even if it wasn't her nature to bow down to the tyranny of the household, life was smoother when they kept her aunt happy. Plus, Elva doted on the beebee, whom they called Oilily or Lily, in honor of Elva's beloved sister.

Once, after Elva had put the toddler down for a nap, Chun asked her, *Aunt, why did you and Uncle not have any children?*

Elva paused. Did she yearn to share her secret with someone other than Dek and her family? To this young mother who was becoming like a daughter to her?

It would have been nice, Elva said.

Perhaps it is not too late, Chun said, knowing her aunt was somewhere in her late thirties.

Chun enjoyed their daily afternoon walks throughout their Bedford-Stuyvesant neighborhood, a bedroom community of mainly middle-class German and Irish families, taking turns pushing Oi in her stroller. Occasionally, they drew stares as they traversed Fulton Street, but mostly folks left them alone and their walks out of the apartment kept her from focusing on her own loneliness.

While their church community of Chinese and white parishioners was largely accommodating of Chun, there were so few Chinese women to be friends with or confide in. While she was grateful she had Elva, she still yearned for the company of other women who could speak her language and understand her frame of reference—the challenges of both child-rearing and living with a husband who was a decade older, and who had spent so much of his time in America. (Among the things she missed, aside from her friends and her family, was the food—she *really* missed the food in Hong Kong.)

She did not confide in Elva about any of this, for fear of making her aunt feel bad.

Instead, she resigned herself to sewing dresses with bows for Oilily and helping Elva make their home a temple of cleanliness of which even the head nurse of Chun's midwifery school would have been proud.

My grandmother Rose once told me the following story:

One day, Aunt Elva and Great-Grandmother Chun went shopping. Chun was pregnant again, and they needed fabric to make maternity clothing to accommodate her rapidly expanding belly. Chun, pushing Oilily around in her pram, paused by something she liked, where the salesclerk was tidying up.

But when Chun made inquiries about the price, the clerk frowned. With pursed lips, she stood up and walked away.

Chun thought perhaps she hadn't spoken loudly enough. Maybe it was her British accent that the woman couldn't follow? Certainly, she had a hard time understanding many Americans, especially New Yorkers with their polyglot accents.

She followed the clerk down to the other end of the store, pushing the pram, and repeated her request, slower this time. She tried to smile, but Oilily was squirming, wanting to get out.

This time the clerk glared at her. *We don't have anything for the likes of you.*

When Elva appeared, carrying an armload of goods pressed close to her bosom, she was surprised to find Chun standing before the clerk, clearly upset, her generous mouth a tight line.

The salesperson regarded Elva. *What right does she have to come into our store?*

Elva watched the woman's back as she walked away.

What just happened? she asked.

Chun looked down, unsure of what to say. She was used to such treatment by colonials in Hong Kong, but to articulate this to her aunt was embarrassing—and seemed, somehow, impolite.

*Chun and Shim, with Oilily
and baby Normon, 1911*

It's nothing, Chun said, trying to smile a little, unable to meet her gaze.

Elva, who knew firsthand what it meant to be shunned, marched toward the front of the shop.

As they neared the cashier, Elva dumped all the goods she was going to purchase onto the counter where the clerk and the owner were ringing up sales for another customer.

Elva said, in a voice loud enough for even the paying customers to hear, *We are never coming here again!*

LATER THAT SPRING, Dek Foon's son, Ng Wu Chow, who had married the sensible Miss Mah, packed his bags and left Shun On, their rural village in Toisan, for Hong Kong. It was early June when he boarded the SS *Empress of Japan*, setting sail across the great Pacific for Canada.

Although not much is known about Wu Chow's life at this point, it's not difficult to imagine his nervousness about meeting his father for the first time as an adult. Like me, he had to have been curious about this man his entire life. In a funny coincidence, he was the same age that I was when I met my father, but the similarities end there. Chow had the advantages of being male, and financially supported by his father throughout his life. Dek Foon had not left for unknown reasons—he had left to provide for the family.

Although once his mother died, Wu Chow must have wondered why his father had never come back to see him. No explanation about international laws and legal red tape concerning a country an ocean away can really ever adequately address for a child the wound of a missing father.

ON JULY 4, after nearly a month at sea and making that same Canadian Pacific railroad trip that Chun and the baby had taken a mere seven months before, Wu Chow arrived in Boston Harbor on the SS *Halifax*, traveling along the Eastern Seaboard from Canada. But they wouldn't release him, and his journey navigating the byzantine labyrinth of the Chinese Exclusion Act had only just begun—his father came in from New York to lobby for his release.

11

Yulan & Chin On

Chin Family

O ne morning, soon after I moved into the building, I was lugging my packages up the back staircase. The last flight to our
apartment was always a killer, and as I rounded the corner, my
breathing was heavy with exertion.

I slowed down as I reached our floor, trying to catch my breath, my
gaze wandering down the vanishing point of the hallway. The overhead
light shimmered across the terrazzo flooring like shallow pools of water,
when suddenly, it was as if one of the doors unlocked, and a woman
emerged. She was short, round, middle-aged, dressed in a housedress and
slippers, and in a rush. And then, a man's shouts, before the door slammed
shut behind her.

The woman was breathing heavily, out of breath, not so much like me
out of exertion, I sensed, but from animal fear.

She lunged toward the apartment directly across the hall. In one motion, she grabbed the door handle, twisted it, and flung herself inside.

By the time I realized that the woman had run out of my great-grandparents' apartment, she was gone.

I'm not someone who can't distinguish between what's happening in the here and now, and what is an echo replaying like a tape loop from the past.

I stood in front of the apartment into which the woman had disappeared.

It looked like any other door on the floor, with a dark green coat of paint that in the summer makes it stick to the doorframe. But there was something special about this apartment.

It was my Chin grandparents' apartment, where Lung, the grandfather I never met, had lived most of his life, and where Stanley was born. The only interior view of it that I had was an illustration from Carl Glick's *Shake Hands with the Dragon*—where Lung was pictured cradling my father as a newborn, seated in a Morris chair, surrounded by his family.

WHEN I FIRST MET MY FATHER, he of the bounding footsteps, that day so long ago on Pell Street, I found him to be initially welcoming. But even as I entered the fold of his life—birthday parties in Chinatown and Queens, meals with his ex-wives and girlfriends, shooting pool in the basement of his house in a tony part of Queens—my father would never acknowledge that having walked out on us was wrong.

Watching him compartmentalize anything that he found unpleasant, including how he treated my mother and me, was tantamount to watching the struggles of my childhood be erased—my father's not being there defined me, for better or worse. His denial was unbearable, so I did the only thing I could think of—I wrote about it.

My essay, "The Missing," about being raised by a single mother and growing up without him, was published in an anthology that I also edited when I was in my twenties, *Split*, about my generation—us former kids of divorce.

Although I heard through the grapevine that they were upset I had written about them, I didn't hear from Stanley or my immediate Chin family afterward. I never did. Not in the four years I was in graduate school in California, not even when I returned home, after having landed my job as a creative writing professor at a local branch of the City University of New York. Although I called a few times, my messages were never returned.

Then, many years later, after I'd become a professor, a wife, and a mother, a series of events occurred in 2014 and 2015 that a gambler might liken to a perfect winning hand: I was introduced to Jack Tchen, the cofounder of the Chinatown History Project (the precursor to the Museum of Chinese in America), and I was finally able to get ahold of my grandfather Lung's oral history.

That fall of 2014, I attended the *Chinese American: Exclusion/Inclusion* exhibit at the New-York Historical Society with my husband and toddler daughter.

In the front room, there was information on Wong Chin Foo, and Uncle Dek Foon's Chinese Equal Rights League.

In another was a replica of the barracks on Angel Island, where my father's side had been detained.

And then, on a back wall of the exhibit, I saw an image of my great-grandfather Chin On, Stanley's grandfather.

> Name: Chin On
> Age: 40
> Height: 5 ft, 7¼ inches
> Occupation: Merchant, New York, New York
> Admitted as: Merchant . . . S.S. Siberia, June 13, 1914
> Physical marks and peculiarities: Mole on right eyebrow

It was his Chinese Exclusion Act identity paper.

· · ·

THE SUMMER OF 2015, my family and I flew out to California for our first cross-country road trip, and I visited the National Archives and Records Administration offices in San Bruno to look for the Chinese Exclusion files for my Chin side. I had already seen some from the New York NARA office, but the early files were still out in the Bay Area. Although I could have called up the files and had them scanned for me remotely, I needed to see these documents with my own eyes.

One of the results of the 1906 earthquake and fire—one of the deadliest in American history—was that Chinese now had a new way of navigating the Exclusion laws. Many started claiming that they either were born here or were children of native-born Americans, and because the city birth records had gone up in flames, officials could not prove otherwise. Instead, government inspectors engaged in lengthy interrogations, and kept extensive files on Chinese immigrants, meticulously trying to catch any inconsistencies in testimony, and tracking their whereabouts as they came and left the country, decades before passports were universally necessary for anyone trying to enter.

My Chin side was different. Whereas others had to lie about who they were, Great-Grandfather Chin On was able to establish himself in the store, after his illicit border crossing, because in that window of time, businessmen were an exempted class, along with students. Presumably, it would be easier to get his wife and the boys in as well, but they would have to go through the new facilities at Angel Island—a detention center on an isolated island where misery was carved into the walls in the form of Chinese poetry.

The NARA offices were freezing—despite my jacket and long sleeves, I was shivering as I read through several Chin family files. There was one for my grandfather Lung, a large-eyed seven-year-old, and his little brother, Jack (a six-year-old with pillowy cheeks), who was listed as "Duke" on the ship's manifest. In their ID photos, they sport the same square hairline, cut by their mother's hand, and are even wearing the same suit. But whereas Lung looks directly into the camera like a future pugilist, and is listed as having a "scar below left ear," little Jack is perfect, with no physical imperfections or even a visible mole or beauty mark that the inspector can find, staring wistfully outside of the frame. There was a thicker file for Chin On, their father.

It took me a few tries to locate his wife, Yulan, my great-grandmother, because I had requested the file for "Chin Shee," or "Mrs. Chin." My newbie mistake was in forgetting that Chinese women kept their maiden names—a practice that may seem surprisingly modern to us now, but which was a traditional Chinese custom. I finally found her listed as "Lee Shee," or "Mrs. Lee."

I opened the file, and found some of the earliest photographs of Great-Grandmother Yulan that I had ever seen.

In the first, taken in China in 1913, she is wearing her hair in the old Ching dynasty fashion—twisted into a low bun—high forehead and the right side of her face illuminated in the studio light. She is thirty-three

Yulan, 1913

years old, and pretty. Her expression is open, hopeful—her husband is coming home and wants to bring them to America.

She is one of the lucky ones—many husbands on Gold Mountain never attempt to bring their families over. (Does she ever wonder *why*? Why more Chinese men did not bring their families over to America?) She has been told to stare at a spot on the wall behind the photographer's shoulder. She is standing still, doing her best to be accommodating.

I flip the page. The next picture was taken at Angel Island the following year, after they had landed—although sometimes called the "Ellis Island of the West," Angel Island was more like Alcatraz than a welcome center. Yulan is ordered to stand in front of a wall, upon which hang a series of flip numbers (#1436), corresponding to their cataloging system for Chinese.

Great-Grandmother is told: *Look forward.*

Freeze.

Turn to the side.

Freeze.

The bulb flashes before her eyes. One could be forgiven for mistaking these for mug shots.

It is here in her file that I learn not only her exact age but also that she is nearly eight months pregnant.

She has endured a month at sea in her third trimester.

Although she is a merchant's wife, Yulan and her two young sons have been detained in this complex, separated from her husband, for over a week, with no indication of if, or when, they will finally be released.

The exposure is overly bright, washing out her hair, combed into a neat bun at the nape of her neck, obscured by the high mandarin collar of her jacket, and blurring her features, so that only the eyes, nose, and her unsmiling mouth are prominent.

She has dark circles under her eyes.

Between the subpar food and seasickness on the long ship journey over, and now the slop they feed them here, instead of gaining weight,

Form 2512

Angel Island, Cal. _____, 191___.

Chinese Inspector in Charge,

    Angel Island, Cal.

Sir:

    I request that the photographer make _____ life* photograph of
                                                          copy

applicant in case No. _13486_ s.s, _Siberia_

arriving _6/13/14_ 8-4 191 ___, to complete the record.

                                       Inspector.

                                191___.

                           quest O. K.

                    se Inspector in Charge.

Received the above photograph this _____ day of _____ 191___.

                                      Inspector.

    *Cross off copy or life, and insert number of photographs desired.

            (TO BE MADE IN DUPLICATE.)

Yulan, 1914

Yulan has been shedding pounds. Modern obstetricians would be appalled. In fact, she is carrying so far below weight that the medical examiner believes she is only in her second trimester, but she's a good two months further along than he suspects.

She looks like she wants to murder someone.

It had been a long journey even before they crossed the Pacific.

Lee Yulan, otherwise known as Yook Lan, was born at the tail end of China's last dynasty. She was named for the beguiling Chinese magnolia that blossomed forth from nude branches at the first touch of spring throughout her village and across much of southern and central China. *Yulania*, a majestic white and pink bloom that for centuries had been hidden behind monastery walls, until it was offered as a gift to the Tang dynasty emperor, and later introduced to the West by a besotted white monk, who, risking punishment of death, smuggled the living plant out where it would eventually hybridize with magnolias brought over from the Americas. *Yuklan*, which village girls across the region slept with, nestled near their headrests, so that they could bloom as beautifully as the flora itself.

Yulan grew up in a small fishing village within the city of Kwong Hoy, a port whose very name indicated the wide, open sea. An ancient city along the Maritime Silk Road, Kwong Hoy had for centuries been plagued by pirates, bandits, and warlords, and Yulan's people learned to navigate each successive invasion with the weary preparedness of true survivors— locking doors and shutting windows, tossing the most prized family possessions into bags that seemed perpetually prepacked, fleeing for their lives toward the safety of the mountains. To foil pirate raids, the emperor himself sometimes mandated they leave, and so Yulan's ancestors stayed inland for decades. Although they could have chosen to permanently settle near the county capital, Yulan's family returned each time, drawn back by the lure and bounty of the sea.

Yulan was her father's, Lee Woon Jung's, only daughter, and from him Lan Lan, as they called her, learned to shuck mussels from their shells and to haggle with the fishermen who sold them piles of shad, bluefish, octopus, and yellow croaker, the fish that she loved the best. She had grown up watching from a distance how the croaker leapt into the air, shimmering silver and gold in the sunlight, before plunging back into the sea.

Although not a rich man, Lee Woon Jung was proud that none of his children had ever perished from hunger. Living in Kwong Hoy meant there might be bandits, warlords, or barbarian Japanese and Austronesian pirates who attacked their coastal village, raiding food supplies and killing old and young alike, but the cycles of drought and famine that plagued the hilly region were for inlanders.

Live by the sea and you will never go hungry, he told Lan Lan, teaching her how to gather clams and mussels by rooting around with their feet in the salty silt flats near their village, and pulling them up with their toes.

Her parents taught her to salt and dry the yellow croaker in the hot sun outside their home for the local specialty known as ham yue. It took weeks to cure, but ham yue was a necessary part of their income and diet—the fish that didn't sell by the end of the day was transformed into ham yue. It appeared in nearly every meal throughout the winter months, especially when food was scarce. Salted fish was mixed with ground pork and sliced ginger, then steamed in a clay pot over rice. When she and her mother lifted the lid, the steam rose up into their faces in white clouds like a savory sauna.

She was short—only four foot ten or four foot eleven inches, depending upon who was doing the measuring—with a tendency to speak her mind and a stubborn set of chin that some said was *unlucky*. These tendencies had gotten her hit many times throughout her childhood by her mother, who called her *ungrateful* and *worthless* and cursed the day she was born.

While the standard of beauty was for girls to resemble fair-skinned northerners, Yulan's skin retained a golden quality to it, even through the mild winter months in their semitropical coastal village. From the time she was a young child, looking at her was like seeing the warm glow of the sun on the watery horizon.

According to family lore, when Yulan was just three years old, her mother wanted to bind her feet with wrapping to permanently alter them into coveted *lily feet*. Although you could hear the cries of girls whose feet were bound ringing throughout the village, and this permanent injury meant that every step they took was accompanied by a feeling like being stabbed by cascading knives, her mother called them *the lucky ones, who would land a good husband*.

Baba forbade it, despite her mother's entreaties, which went from pleading to straight-out demands. *Who would marry her if they didn't? Did he want to doom their family by being saddled with a worthless daughter forever?*

But Baba, who had worked his way up from being a fisherman to becoming the middleman fishmonger—buying live fish from his fishermen friends and selling them at market to the local restaurants and residents on the wharf—to finally opening a small restaurant himself, was adamant. Not only couldn't they afford to raise a daughter who couldn't work, but what if pirates attacked the city? What if another conflict with the Hakka erupted again—how would she be able to run? (Just like Chun's family in Hong Kong, Yulan's father was also steadfastly practical.)

Of the children who hadn't died of tuberculosis, cholera, or the plague, the only surviving ones left were the boys and Lan Lan.

Lan Lan knew she would live and die by the sea, although she never voiced these thoughts. Even as a child, she was old enough to know that talking about death was heavily frowned upon—*bad luck*.

Yulan was bright and quick, and grew into a resourceful young teenager. She managed to elude her mother's intentions to sell her as a moy moy to a rich family—life as an indentured servant until it was time to get married off was not for her—but even for all her natural abilities, she was still just a fishmonger's daughter, living in Toisan in an era when so many men had journeyed to Gold Mountain, surrounded by many tiny-footed contemporaries competing for the small pool of eligible prospects. Her chances for landing a suitable partner were growing bleak.

She was twenty-six when the matchmaker told them about Chin Lin On, a Gold Mountain man, living in a city called Mott Street.

CHIN LIN ON, OR CHIN ON, as he was called for most of his life, was the third son of Sifu Chin, the now deceased, but still revered, kung fu master whose martial arts school provided bodyguard protection from local warlords and guaranteed safe passage from Kwong Hoy all the way to the nation's capital. Although he had passed the imperial exams, Chin On had chosen some years before to join his brothers in America. Now he was back home for a visit, and looking for a wife.

There was a village saying that Yulan's family knew well: *Never let your daughter marry a Gold Mountain man.*

Mr. Lee was inclined to pass. If he let Yulan marry this man, she might as well be a widow for all that she would know of her husband. (For some families that was enough. The Four Counties area was filled with rich "lazy villages" where the wives raised the children like single mothers with a trust fund.)

There were other reasons to hesitate.

Based on his Chinese Exclusion file, which I first unearthed in New York, and then also in San Bruno, California, Great-Grandfather Chin On had been married before; he was a widower with two children—children who would have to be provided for and, being old enough to remember their mother, would have her imprint heavily upon them.

But despite these challenges, Yulan was intrigued. A third son in a big family full of boys was not considered much of a catch, but neither, she knew, was she. At twenty-six, she was over the hill by societal standards.

In late imperial China, it was unlikely that she would ever get such a chance again. She said yes.

ON THE DAY OF HER WEDDING, Yulan arrived at the village of the third Chin son in a sedan rickshaw provided by his family. Ow Bein, on the northern outskirts of Kwong Hoy, was so close she could have walked herself, and that was much remarked upon when the other Chin women saw her taking her first steps into the ancestral home. Chin wives were tall and willowy, and who themselves had the "lily" feet that Yulan's mother so admired.

I imagine that in that moment, Yulan heard none of their remarks, only murmurs as she was led into the room, her face hidden behind the red silk cloth like a present. The world was nothing but a noisy, scarlet screen with her at its center.

She was bade to sit on a wooden chair.

She was nervous, so she did as she was told.

If her breath had been visible, Yulan imagined her new husband, who had only recently returned from Gold Mountain, would see only thick, white clouds shaped like Buddhist flowers obscuring all her features, except her eyes.

The red world retreated with the removal of the cloth, and Yulan came face-to-face with a tall, lean, impossibly handsome man with the close-shorn hair of a foreigner, staring at her with curious, calculating eyes. Did she catch a glimpse of approval in his expression? Or a glint like forged metal in his eyes?

There wasn't anything else she could think of to do, so Yulan allowed Chin On to take her by the hand, and stepped forward.

ACCORDING TO LUNG, the couple lived in a small, ramshackle hut with a bare earth floor—the second house in the fifth row of the Chin village, the worst of the family homes. Every day, before she got pregnant, while her husband went to town to "do business" (including meeting clients while playing fan tan and Chinese poker), Yulan made her way past the fancier, spacious brick houses of the older brothers, now in Gum San 金山, carrying two large wooden pails. Her sisters-in-law sat with their bound, naked lily feet propped up on cushions, sneering as she carried the water from the well to her hut.

How did a peasant marry into our great family? they called out, while the moy moys ran painted fans across them in the summer heat.

Perhaps Yulan could have tolerated this better if Chin On had been more supportive, but one day, after only a few years of marriage, her husband was called to return to New York to attend to his business affairs—packing his bags and boarding the next boat out to Gum San.

Yulan spent the next five years doing the double-duty, backbreaking labor that her relations took for granted. In addition to taking care of the many children in their blended family, she tended to the pigs and the chickens that lived outside their shack, and worked the fields, sowing seeds, pulling weeds, then harvesting fruit and vegetables. Certain days of the year, she foraged, gathering the tall grass in the mint family they called *sin toe* (xiancao) every summer, lugging armloads back home by lunchtime, then rendering it into cooling grass jelly that the children loved during the hottest days—topped with a clear, simple syrup—slurping it all down with wooden spoons.

Some mornings, Yulan hiked into the mountains to gather tea leaves from trees that clung to the hillsides. She was petite but strong, and could climb even the tallest arbors to their highest branches, even with a child strapped to her back, but these tea trees were short and spindly, almost like bushes, and would bend even under her own weight. Once she gathered a bagful, or when the tree seemed to have had enough of her picking fingers, she made her way back down to the village. Under the hot afternoon sun, she laid the foliage out to dry on bamboo trays, until they shriveled and curled into themselves like bugs; later, she admired how they unfurled again, steeping in boiling water, creating a sweet cha prized for its ability to keep you hydrated, even on the *so hot you could die* days.

Each morning, she poured the tea into a gourd, slung it over her shoulder, and entered the field with a spade or hoe. By noon, when exertion and the full glory of the sun finally forced her to take a break, Yulan took sips between the rows of elephant-ear taro leaves—some as tall as her waist—wiped her mouth, and then, miraculously, did it all over again.

Was she thankful that her mother did not break her feet, when she rotated the crops from taro to sweet potatoes, or pulled the weeds clear of her winter melons, round as globes? Or when she climbed the hills and cleared the family gravesites, leaving offerings to the ancestors every spring?

Perhaps there were times that Yulan wished her father had never intervened on her behalf. If her mother had had her way, she would have been one of the feet-up-on-the-stool aunties eating watermelon seeds in a nice brick house, spitting the hard shells onto the floor for the servants to sweep up.

Because food was in short supply and the children devoured mostly everything—they were growing tall like Chin On and ravenous, so there were barely any leftovers—Yulan had to feed the livestock with scraps that her father shuttled over from his restaurant in town. She scrimped and saved and tried to feed everyone—Chin On's older children and their young ones too—off what they grew and the meager allowance that her husband sent home every Chinese New Year.

He must be barely scraping by to only send home so little money, Yulan thought, trying to budget out her lowly $200 per year (the equivalent of slightly over $5,000 today). *My poor, arrogant, useless husband.*

She was determined not to complain. Chin On was proud and haughty, and she would not have wanted him to be diminished in the villagers' eyes. She also knew better than to inform her husband's mother or the other Chin wives. Even if they knew, they probably would have used it to further humiliate her.

So instead of complaining or confiding in anyone, Yulan diverted her focus elsewhere.

THE DAY THAT CHIN ON LEFT, they had walked down to the waterfront, an area that Yulan visited with her family every day in her childhood. She and her husband headed up the hill and approached a giant boulder. It was several times the height of the tallest man in the village, and inscribed with four characters: "No Waves, Sea Forever." An unknown artisan had carved these words hundreds of years before, after villagers had successfully put down a significant pirate invasion.

No waves in this sea forever, was the implicit meaning.

It was both a wish, and a promise.

Now the forever sea was going to take her husband away from her, as so many of the Gold Mountain fathers and uncles had left their families behind, for generations.

She knew to expect this, but even so, it was not easy. She had grown to love him, his gruffness during the day, his fondness for classical poetry, how tender he was at night—she would even miss his snoring, which was so epic that on some nights she could swear that it made the roof of their shack rattle. Many said that Gold Mountain men all visited prostitutes (*visiting the phoenix* or the *chicken*), and she wondered how many women Chin On knew, or worse, if there was one with whom he had a special relationship, who might separate them as effectively as the American laws and their struggle for money.

And now she was pregnant again only a few months in and her belly already jutting out, and the whole village was speculating over its gender.

Chin On promised that in the future he would send for them. But how could she really know for sure?

With each successive year that he was away, Yulan wondered when her husband would return. Would he really bring them all to America?

According to Grandfather Lung, Yulan had heard about the suffragists in the West, who had been calling for women's equality and the right to vote. They gathered en masse, carrying banners, marching down streets.

"I like that," she thought, turning over the earth with her spade.

LUNG, WHOSE NAME MEANT DRAGON, the luckiest sign in the Chinese zodiac, grew up in the Chin kung fu school. He had never met his yeh yeh, who had died long before he was born, but every day, after school, he and his younger brother studied the Southern White Crane style of fighting our family were the local experts of—a close-combat style involving a series of rapid jabs and quick strikes, and an intimate knowledge of anatomy and the body's most vulnerable spots: eyes, throat, groin, knees. Us lanky Chins, with our long, wiry arms and limbs, seemed particularly well suited to it.

His grandfather's master had been a second-generation crane fighter who had studied under its originator, Fang Cat Noeng, a.k.a. Fang Qiniang, the daughter of a Shaolin disciple who had been trained in martial arts.

There are many versions of this story.

In one, Miss Fang was at home combing her long hair, when she noticed a crane alight on a tree branch outside her window.

In others, she was outside drying grain in the courtyard outside their home, when the crane flew down from the roof and tried to steal some.

Either way, Fang grabbed a bamboo pole and tried to scare the bird off, but the crane refused to budge. It easily batted her pole away with its huge outspread wing, and then again with its long thrusting beak.

Before long, after much thrust and parry, attack and counterattack, which grew into a course of several insightful "lessons" spread across daily and weekly visits by the crane, Fang Cat Noeng gave birth to an entirely new style of kung fu—a style some say was particularly ideal for women, given its emphasis on nuance, speed, and tactical strikes.

In the spirit of kung fu lineages, Lung counted himself and his father and his father's father as descendants of Fang Cat Noeng.

While he was fascinated by his lineage, Lung was interested in his father most of all. Ever since he was very small, Lung looked for Chin On in the likenesses of other family members.

Since the older uncles were also away in Gum San, he searched in the faces of his younger uncles, and his cousins, but all he saw were the individuals themselves.

Many laughed when they noticed the little one staring at them so intently. They said, *You look just like your baba.*

A clever and winning boy, wiry, strong, and seldom shy, Lung Chin was adored and doted upon by his grandmother—his poa poa—and the aunties of the family. It would take him years before he understood why they were so unkind to his mother, whose status, though raised by giving birth to a son, was still looked upon derisively.

Every afternoon after martial arts practice, Poa Poa invited Lung and his younger brother into her big, roomy house where she had lived for decades, long after their grandfather died, and regaled them with stories of their illustrious ancestors. She sat on her big lacquered chair with her feet elevated on a cushioned stool, while the servant poured them tea, allowing the boys to sit with her.

There was Duke Chin Gwan Hing (Junqing), a high-ranking scholar in the imperial palace, who lived in an era in which scholars were so revered that whenever they traveled outside the palace gates, they did so seated in palanquins, like princes. In a bad bit of historical luck, the duke resided in the capital under the Mongol ruler in the fourteenth century, a precarious time for Chinese bureaucrats. When the duke was stripped of his imperial ranking and sent fleeing for his life, he escaped the palace aided by his favorite guard dog, a black-tongued *bear dog*, or Chow.

The loyal canine led him to a rushing river, where they soon came upon a water buffalo, dozing in the mud. Seizing the opportunity, our deposed duke jumped on the back of the ox-like animal—an amazing feat as palace scholars were not known for their physical agility, and at upwards of two thousand pounds a water buffalo can easily gut a human.

With the Chow leading the way, the motley crew crossed the river to safety.

To honor these noble creatures, Lung's grandmother told him, wizened finger pointing for emphasis, *our family refrains from eating dogs or water buffalo, even in times of drought and famine.*

Gwan Hing's son Chin Dai (Chen Da) grew up to avenge his father's honor by leading an army against the khan, and driving the Mongols out of China. For his efforts, the emperor of the recently established Ming dynasty bestowed upon Chin Dai and his male descendants the official title of Ming general—creating a new class of military nobility, rather like the samurai in feudal Japan.

Lung marveled at these tales told to him by his grandmother every afternoon.

While most Chins from the North fled to Guangdong Province in the late twelfth century, escaping a bloody purge during the Song dynasty, our Chin family came to the South a few centuries later, to the seaside village of Kwong Hoy in 1427, at the behest of the emperor himself. General Chin Dai's son Bin and his family were sent to protect the region against pirates in the South China Sea.

The next Chin general to the post was Zhi, or Wencong, a tall, barrel-chested man with a long, curly beard who put down insurrections against the emperor in the 1440s and 1450s. Once, when Canton was under siege for three months by a particularly fearless rebel, killing civilians and military alike, General Chin Wencong decimated the enemy and their chariots with all manner of fire-weaponry—flaming bricks, flaming arrows, and a kind of early Molotov cocktail, *lit jars of fire.*

Wencong was ruthless in battle—*he and his men beheaded thousands of enemies and captured twice that amount,* said Lung's poa poa. But he was also a bit of a healer, adding to a growing list of Chinese materia medica, compounding his own medicines, even garnering a reputation as a master of leechcraft, as was the fashion of the day.

Lung learned about his ancestor Sheng, Wencong's great-great-grandson, who was nearly killed as an infant by his stepmother, the first wife. When she realized the lowly concubine had given birth to a son, she ordered a servant to slip the newborn into a cave in the hills without anyone noticing. But when an old woman traversing the countryside heard a baby's cries from inside the cave, word was sent back to the general.

Sheng, the newborn, was discovered half-buried in dirt by termites.

Luckily, he survived. (To punish the first wife into perpetuity, her name is erased from our genealogy books.)

But by far Lung's favorite stories were of Sheng's grandson, the tall (*long-strided*), swashbuckling general Chin Kai Ming.

Young Lung learned that we came from a family who tried to murder each other, as well as hearty survivors.

Tell me about Kai Ming, he begged his poa poa. *Tell me about his uncle and how he foiled his assassination attempt.*

Kai Ming's life span, circa 1579–1644, according to our Chin family genealogy, was solidly in the later Ming dynasty era, but in Lung's imagination, this swashbuckling ancestor leapt between several centuries—and was both a prodigious lover and a fighter.

When Kai Ming, whose name means Brightness and "Venus in the eastern skies before dawn," was a teenager, his father died while traveling in another province. He was raised by his mother and grandfather Sheng, at that point a long-retired yeh yeh, until he could inherit his rightful position as general.

He tenaciously survived not one but two assassination attempts by an uncle who wanted the military title for himself, and was so big-hearted that he even forgave him.

After acing the imperial military entrance exams, Kai Ming became a young general who led an army that wiped out bandits in the mountains and valleys of Guizhou Province, and forced out invaders from Canton. In the winter of 1636, he even battled Li Zicheng, a charismatic Robin Hood–like leader, who arose from poverty and gained popularity for attacking the excesses of the imperial court.

Kai Ming and his army chased Li some one thousand miles across the mountains of Sichuan Province, home of giant pandas and tongue-numbing Sichuan peppercorns. As the story goes, Kai Ming and his men were so committed to putting down the insurgency that they slept in their battle armor for three weeks straight. After a month of fighting, they defeated Li, who was forced to retreat into the mountains.

For this, the emperor himself promoted Kai Ming to general of Sichuan Province, Fujian Province, and later general of Canton. Towns erected Kai Ming halls and temples, lighting incense and painted paper, representing money and good fortune, in his honor. (Li Zicheng would later return to upend the entire Ming dynasty, but that wouldn't be for several more years to come.)

For young Lung, in the absence of his father, Kai Ming's noble figure rose like a conifer.

EARLY IN THE SUMMER OF 1913, as the lychees grew fat and reddened on the edges of their branches and the grapevines stretched out their leaves and young tendrils, Yulan received a message from her husband in Gum San, and along with it, a surprising sum of money. She dismissed the messenger in a bit of shock.

It was two years after Dr. Sun Yat Sen established China as a new republic, and change was afoot. The cruel practice of binding young girls' feet was outlawed, and so was the mandatory queue. Now, in the Chin household, with the news from America, the entire household was in a frenzy, and everyone was ordered to pack as quickly as possible.

Within the week, Yulan had sold the pigs and chickens for a tidy sum, and moved herself and her children out of the dusty Chin family village and into a house in the center of town. (*Good riddance,* Yulan must have thought, to finally leave the one-room shack and her in-laws behind.)

Their new rental was near the main artery of Kwong Hoy, and within the stone walls of the city limits. Although it was only a humble former dried herbs store, with no furniture except for some low stools, the feeling within the household was jubilant—it was so grand in comparison to the old hut. Lung and his siblings spent hours exploring the back rooms—finding a chest, rummaging through it in search of coins. The little ones were so excited they never asked why they had moved to the center of town, although I suspect the older siblings knew.

Here they saw their mother's family almost daily—having meals in their grandfather's restaurant and at his home in Sai Gwan, Yulan's old village only a short walk to the sea.

ONE LANGUID AFTERNOON IN late summer, as the light was liquid and golden, the door suddenly opened with a flourish, and the tall figure of a man in silhouette filled the doorframe.

Lung blinked as the stranger strode into the room.

For a moment, it was as if General Kai Ming himself jumped down from his horse and came striding into their home.

Baba was home from Gold Mountain.

The only ones who recognized him were Lung's older brother and sister and Yulan herself, who dried her hands, coming away from the stove.

Lung stood up and looked at this man, uncharacteristically shyly, the younger ones watching to take his lead.

For years he had wondered about his father. Everyone said he looked just like him, but was it really true? *How else was he like him, this man who had left when Lung was a toddler?*

When Lung practiced kung fu at their school, the teachers took special interest in him as the grandson of the master, and the son of Chin On.

Lung learned chi gong (qi gong) in a martial way—not like I do it, as a form of moving meditation to stay warm on a cold early morning ferry ride to my studio, but by holding warrior stances for unfathomable periods of time to build strength and endurance. So many afternoons, Lung stood in horse stance, the basic wide-legged posture that is like straddling a horse, for several minutes, until his small legs were flushed with heat and quivering like the military flag that is a component of the characters of our surname (陳).

Although Chin On was wearing a well-fitted Western suit, Lung could tell that his father's legs would not quiver as his did.

He looked up at this tall father, who seemed to dwarf everyone in the room, including their petite mama.

Chin On, not the type to squat down to the eye level of a child, had a look upon his face like he might smile at any moment, but chose not to. He produced a tin of cookies from his pocket, and then all pretense of politeness broke down.

I want, I want—they crowded around their father, arms reaching out to touch him.

Many things had happened in the six years that Chin On had been away on Gum San.

Dr. Sun Yat Sen was currently in exile, and the novice republic and its Nationalist government were on shaky ground. Local warlords and roving bands of thieves and bandits who had flourished under the long, slow decline of the Ching dynasty took advantage of the ensuing chaos. In our town, the Chin family protection business thrived under such conditions, but who wanted to be a hired bodyguard forever?

Chin On and his brothers had done well in Gum San. In New York, they were more powerful and wealthy than they could have ever imagined (their baba had "made it," the family recalls), to such an extent that even Yulan couldn't quite comprehend.

In addition to their lucrative business as importers of Chinese dried goods and porcelain, which served not only the Chinese Quarter but also the Chinese community throughout the tristate area, they leveraged their rank as officers in the On Leong tong to their advantage.

On Leong offered a feeling of kinship, alliances, and business connections for its members, and had its fingers in every pie in Chinatown—including the gambling networks that Huie Kin and Dek Foon's band of Christian brothers had tried so hard to shut down decades before. It collected a fee from every Chinatown business that was a member, and provided protection from police raids.

And by protection, I mean actual tip-offs from within the police department as to the time and location of planned raids.

On Leong even provided stooges willing to get arrested in place of owners and staff, so that after the raids and roundups, the gamblers and the house could return as quickly as possible to business as usual.

It was a very efficient machine.

Even law enforcement looked good for having made so many arrests.

But once the Hip Sing tong began elbowing its way into On Leong territory, life in New York had become increasingly more dangerous for Chin On. Although he and his brothers were martial arts masters, who could take on almost anyone one-on-one, in any saloon or gambling den in America, none of them had the time to keep an eye out every time a contract was placed on their heads.

Chin On needed a lieutenant. A hatchet man. A bodyguard.

He needed a fighter he could trust.

Someone who couldn't be bought.

So it was with these twin goals of family and protection in mind that Chin On returned to sleepy, semitropical Kwong Hoy.

THAT EVENING, YULAN LAID down a special feast celebrating Chin On's return, splurging on a giant platter of crabs, which she set—stir-fried and steaming—in the center of the table. Hong, the oldest brother, from wife number one, was a boisterous, energetic seventeen-year-old used to getting his way. He grabbed a crab leg—the largest one at the top of the heap—the *Dad-sized* crab leg.

In his eagerness, Hong upset the table, and suddenly the table legs were pointing to the ceiling and dinner was in heaps on the floor—crabs containing unctuous orange eggs, pools of vinegar, fluffy mounds of rice topped by piles of verdant, sautéed water spinach.

Yulan was on her knees, instinctively trying to salvage the food that would have lasted them several meals, plus leftovers for the pigs (habits from so many years of scrimping and saving and tending to the livestock were hard to part with). She knew only too well how angry her husband became if anything was wasted.

Hong's expression was a frozen mix of elation and dismay, one hand still clutching the big crab leg. Chin On looked pained.

In his great grab, Hong upset not only the dinner but the family order—by custom, the father had first pick, and no one was supposed to even make a move toward the food until Chin On finished filling his rice bowl, and then only after he indicated it was okay to start.

Hong lowered his head, resigned for the imminent beating.

Chin On cleared his throat. "Never mind. We'll go to Yeut Sun."

Yeut Sun, the best restaurant in Kwong Hoy.

Now, their father was a very strict man, as Jack would later recall in his memoirs—a single, long letter to his descendants that I was able to get ahold of once I began interviewing extended family members. But that night was different. That night, Chin On could afford to be generous.

Suddenly, everyone was elated and on their feet. Hong, relieved at not getting a beating, righted the table. Lung and Jack, relieved at not having to witness his humiliation, helped too.

Only Yulan seemed confused, carrying the plates back to the kitchen. What was responsible for all of this excessive generosity?

Dinner at the restaurant was a homecoming of sorts—old friends and neighbors, cousins, and school chums greeted Chin On, wanting some of that Gold Mountain luck to rub off on them. The children, who had never eaten out at a restaurant besides their grandfather Lee Woon Jung's, had never had it so good. While Chin On ordered dish after dish, inviting friends to sit down with them, the family dug into the feast, and Yulan began mentally tallying up what each dish was costing them.

The price of dinner at Kwong Hoy's best eating establishment would have seemed astronomical on her budget of $200 a year. With each additional dish that Chin On ordered, the figure in her head kept tallying upward like a cash register, even as her husband invited others to join them. The food arrived in overflowing heaps, which were quickly drained empty, even down to the sauce, and then replaced again and again by the waitstaff.

Her husband certainly seemed to love playing at being the *Big Gold Mountain Man.*

She watched him sitting at the center of attention, beaming, flushed from the excitement and alcohol. Perhaps the rumors were true—Chin On *had* made it and they really *were* rich. Moving into town fit that image, unlike the old family shack. And that was the thing of it. What he had said in his message was even more true than what she had realized at the time, so eager was she to leave the Chin village and the scrutiny of those petty Chin wives.

Yulan and the children could no longer stay in the old village for their own safety.

Chin On was so wealthy that they would have been at risk for being abducted and held for ransom.

They were lucky to have gotten out when they did.

But if they were so rich, she wondered, surrounded by the rapidly emptying plates and disappearing platters of food, a nagging thought gnawed at her. *Why had he sent her so little money all these years?*

. . .

ALONG WITH THE ARRIVAL of their father came new things:

Toothbrushes and starchy toothpaste.

Chewing gum and cookies sweeter than oranges.

And a certain odor that clung to the walls like heavy syrup.

"What is that?" Lung asked Yulan, one evening as Chin On and his friends gathered around the dining table, now littered with small paraphernalia.

Someone lit a match and offered a long pipe to Chin On, who took it, bending his head so that the mouthpiece was obscured from view.

Soon the smell permeated the whole room, even the back where Lung and Yulan were sitting, watching.

Yulan frowned, the small lines around her mouth deepening. "It's bad," she finally said. (*Mm'ho. No good.*)

In Chinese, opium is called yen, and when the habit of smoking opium entered English parlance, it became a verb, meaning to have a deep craving for something.

The scent lingered long into the night, long after Lung and the others were put to bed.

Later, after the men left, Chin On remained, laid out on the matting.

Yulan wondered if he wanted to have her again, in that way, even though she suspected that she was already pregnant, her menstrual cycle having gone missing for some weeks now. She sat near him and waited, but Chin On's face was a mask as smooth and elegant as a vase, and pretty soon he was loudly snoring.

Yulan began collecting the opium pipe, and the entire works, the residue slow and sticky like tree resin, when Chin On suddenly grabbed her by the wrist. *Leave it.*

I don't like you doing this in front of the children, she said.

Did his grip become a tightening vise, so that her breath caught and she cried out in surprise, the pain sharp and searing, until she released everything in her hands?

Did he hit her? If it wasn't for the mitigating circumstances of the opiate, it's likely that he would have hit her. Chin On's rage would become legendary in the family lore, but Yulan was experiencing it for the first time in a very long while.

Even under the calming presence of opium, Chin On didn't like anyone, especially a wife, telling him what to do.

Whatever happened that night, she felt the pressure of his fingers against her wrists, long after the bruises disappeared.

Yulan never questioned him about smoking opium in the house again.

ONE DAY, A FEW WEEKS into his trip, Chin On visited a gambling joint he had heard about in the center of town. A group of men were huddled in front of a fan tan table, placing their bets.

"Hey, hey, hey, don't just stand there, come join in on the action," the dealer called out to him.

Since there was very little action that he didn't like, Chin On took a closer look.

He was about to throw down a few coins onto the table, when a tall, strapping young man walked by.

"Don't gamble at that table," the young man said, under his breath. "That guy's a cheat."

Chin On looked at the dealer, whose hands were moving quickly but whose eyes were always on the players, his mouth constantly yammering. Great-Grandfather's instincts told him the youth was right, so he kept his hands in his pockets and continued on his way.

Later, at the end of the day, Chin On stopped at the butcher's, where a fine display of pork and chicken cuts caught his eye.

A tall youth hauling a giant pig across his meaty shoulders laid it down. It was same man who had tipped him off. He appeared to be a similar age as Chin On's eldest son.

"Aren't you the boy from earlier today?" Chin On asked. "You saved me a lot of money."

The young man nodded. His name was Wong, and he had just come back from the war, fighting for China's independence as a republic.

"Do you know kung fu?" Chin On asked.

Young Wong shook his head. "I'm the butcher's son, I never had time to learn.

"But in the army I learned to shoot," he said, cocking his finger and making the motion like he was pulling a trigger. He was the best shot in his regiment, at least in his estimation.

"I can do this," Wong added, picking up his cleaver. He threw it toward a tree several yards away, as easily as a fisherman casts a line.

From the sound of the cleaver whizzing through the air past his ear alone, Chin On knew that it was a good throw.

The blade landed squarely in the trunk of the tree, splitting the bark like the seam of a zipper.

Chin On would later recount this very moment when he realized, *This is the man for me.*

12

Angel Island

—

Chin Family

T he family and their belongings first traveled by rickshaw to a
ship bound for Hong Kong.

In the British colony, they stayed at the house of a rich im-
port/exporter, Mr. Chin Kung Cheong, a.k.a. K. C. Chin, who kept a
flashy Aston Martin in the front garden. This Mr. Chin, another Kwong
Hoy native, had moved to the big city as a boy and was now sole owner of
Yuen Sing, located on Hong Kong's busy waterfront on Connaught Road.

K. C. Chin traded Chinese goods and supplies throughout the world,
and in 1914 was one of the few Chinese in all of Hong Kong wealthy
enough to own a car. According to Uncle Jack, the rumors were that he
was greatly indebted to Chin On for helping to close a big deal that had
set him up for life; other family members point to the fact that K. C.
Chin was an early supplier to the Chin family store on Mott Street. To

Chin On ID papers, 1914

return the favor, K. C. Chin was only too happy to show his gratitude by hosting Chin On and his family until they were ready to board their ship.

Although Yulan and the boys were still country bumpkins *walking around with cow dung on their big toes,* they traveled around town in rickshaws like colonists, noting the towering Sikh officers that the British put into place as law enforcers, and encountering whites for the first time in their lives. (*How was it possible,* seven-year-old Lung marveled while staring up at a Russian, *for blue-eyed people to actually* see *through those corneas?*)

They boarded the SS *Siberia,* a giant steamship owned by the Pacific Mail Steamship Company—the same shipping company that had been running Chinese passengers across the Pacific since Dek Foon's time—in the middle of the night, because the ship was due to set sail at two a.m. with the tide. The deck of the *Siberia* was ablaze with flickering gas lamps.

Jack, the youngest son and five years old at the time, later recalled the hissing of the oil lamps that lit the steamship, and the grotesque light and shadows they cast as the family boarded.

Instead of checking them in to a first- or second-class cabin, Chin On had booked the family in a cabin in steerage.

SS Siberia

We entered a large common room, along the sides were mats—bamboo, cane, rugs, or plain blankets. . . .

In the center were groups of people of three or four, some had wicker chairs, some stood, all talking and gesturing.

There was a group of people making a semi-circle around a man who was speaking in a loud voice about the injustice of something or another that I could not understand.

Inside their cabin, the hanging lamps swung, and the shadows of the boys' bunk beds lurched with the rocking of the ship. (Jack recollected this as part of their journey out of the mainland, but it was likely this was the beginning of their trans-Pacific travel.)

Why did Chin On book them in steerage—was it because he was cheap or because he knew they would prefer to travel in the company of other Asians? Perhaps it was both, but certainly, it gave him greater access to the common room where he could gamble his time away on any of the endless games that started up once the ship set sail.

. . .

FOR LUNG AND JACK, the voyage over was nothing short of a marvelous adventure.

They made friends with a Japanese family in the neighboring cabin.

They hung around the ship's massive, steamy kitchen. Before Lung met the Chinese cooks and charmed them into giving him snacks, he stole oranges, dried shrimp, and cooked chicken gizzards whenever their backs were turned. (*If you want power, sidle up to a judge,* went the Chinese adage. *If you want to eat, sidle up to a cook.*)

After they gave him a thick-skinned American orange, Lung ferried it downstairs, weaving between the tables of gamblers, the journeymen laborers, the addicts sleeping through the journey with opium-soaked linen cloth wadded in their mouths.

He shared it with his mother, who never left the cabin, and had trouble keeping any food down.

In Yokohama, the Japanese family departed, gifting them the rest of their fresh fruit and baked goods.

Once, when they were crossing the Bering Sea, a choppy, dangerous leg of the journey, Lung and Jack climbed to the upper deck at the back of the boat. It was rumored that the ship was carrying a cargo of goldfish, which, like them, was destined for America. It was raining and the brothers wore high-collared, Sun Yat Sen–style jackets that their mother had fashioned from a coarse linen made from flax that grew throughout their province. While the rain beat upon the deck flooring, now slick with water, Lung and Jack arrived to find the goldfish flapping against the hard deck.

As the boys rushed to save them—tiny, lucky goldfish—Lung suddenly remembered a story his grandmother had told him.

Once, when Kai Ming and his men were weary from battle after fighting in a faraway mountainous province, they camped out by a pond. The water was resplendent with golden yellow and orange carp, swimming in large circles, diaphanous fins trailing like wings.

Kai Ming's soldiers caught many fish, and that night they had a feast.

But the next morning, the soldiers were gravely ill—so ill that many struggled to stand, and most had lost their voices.

Kai Ming, who had not joined in the meal, was worried.

That evening he had a dream that he was visited by Guan Yu, the red-faced, long-bearded God of War and Wealth—revered by soldiers, gamblers, students, and police officers alike.

These are immortal carps, the God of War thundered. *Anyone who eats them shall die!*

But you are these men's general, and you are loyal to the emperor, he said. *You are forgiven if you refrain from eating dogs and water buffalo. Tomorrow, all will recover and you can continue your fight.*

When Kai Ming's troops miraculously recovered, and they were able to successfully defeat their enemy's troops, the general ordered all his descendants to avoid eating such noble creatures.

Lung, who believed these stories with all the ardor of a young boy's heart, raced across the slippery deck of the SS *Siberia* to save as many goldfish as he could.

With the small quivering fish flapping in their hands, the boys tried to get them back into the tank, one by one.

Goldfish were *lucky*—a symbol of abundance and wealth—and with every rescue, Lung felt a small sense of heroic relief, like a miniature Kai Ming on his journey to America.

BETWEEN THE SHIP'S MOTION, the lurching walls of the cabin, and her own morning sickness, Yulan largely stayed in bed. Steerage's gloomy darkness meant they were deprived of any sense of day or night, and for the entirety of the journey, for the first time in her life the fishmonger's daughter never saw daylight or the sea.

Yulan and Chin On had brought with them only Lung and Jack, leaving the others behind, but it's so hard to get a handle on exactly how many kids they had. The oldest daughter was married off and stayed in Toisan. Eldest son, Hong, the lusty eater of giant crabs, was left behind to finish his schooling. Now it is unusual for a Chinese family to not take the firstborn son—the little prince of the family. But if that firstborn son is the son of the deceased first wife, as is testified in Yulan's and Chin On's Exclusion files, and just happens to be of a convenient age where the patriarch could sell his slot to either (a) make a profit off, (b) trade a favor for, or (c) use to bring over someone else whom he had more of an immediate need for—like a bodyguard—then that son might be made to stay behind.

Yulan was beginning to have an inkling of understanding that her husband was a big shot in New York, and not just because of the stores that he and his brothers had established. This tong they were involved in was powerful, and now that she was learning that Chin On was high up in the On Leong ranks, she grew a little afraid—if he was the kind of man who needed protection, just like how they'd needed to leave the village for safety from bandits, what would their lives be like in New York?

Much later, the sentiment among the children, by the time they were old enough to realize and make judgments for themselves, was that no one was indispensable for Chin On and his needs—whether it was his firstborn son or, say, another daughter. In truth, although she was rarely mentioned in the family later on, and certainly erased in the official documents, there was a daughter, a youngest one, who was conceived in that gap when Yulan was still nursing Jack and before Chin On set sail again for America.

My grandfather Lung spoke to one of my cousins about this, who was shocked to learn about what they had done.

When I asked her how he reacted to her questioning, she stated, *He just shrugged, like it was no big deal.*

In a thinly veiled reference to his unnamed little sister, Lung said in his oral history, *No one brought over girls to America back then. If you had a daughter, you never admitted it and you sold her.*

How cold and dismissive.

Later, Lung would deny that this form of indentured servitude was anything like being a slave—instead likening it to having another sister who was part of the family—his own grandmother had moy moys who served her and the other aunts, and he never witnessed any real physical beatings that were worse than what he got for misbehaving.

Whether you chose to view this as adoption or slavery, these young girls were extremely vulnerable, and at risk for all manner of harassment, corporal punishment, and sexual assault. They knew better than anyone that they were on their own, disowned by their families, and that if they protested, the abuse might get worse—they could even be sold once again to a different family, where the unknown was somehow even more frightening than the violence that had already become familiar.

I'm not sure how Yulan felt about this—this noi (nu'er) would have been the only true blood daughter that she had. And why did they have to leave her behind, if they were as rich as Yulan was beginning to realize that they were?

Seasickness and advanced pregnancy may not have been the only reason why Yulan refused to get out of bed.

ONE DAY, THE BOYS followed their mother to a higher deck, and down a corridor, to an otherwise innocuous-looking white door. When the door wouldn't budge, Lung wanted to do a flying kung fu kick to open it, but luckily, the knob turned, and suddenly a nurse in white appeared. She waved them into the medical examination room, where they were enveloped by an antiseptic smell like a cloud of parachuting knives.

This examination, which the boys would remember every time they smelled hospital disinfectant, was nothing short of excruciating for Yulan.

She was ordered to disrobe in order to be examined by a white male doctor.

Until now, the only man she had ever appeared naked before as an adult was her husband.

Back home, when a woman "visited the doctor," she sat behind a bamboo screen and indicated the source of her pain or discomfort on a miniature ivory doll. The male doctor never laid eyes on her or touched her the entire time. This had been the common practice of protecting a woman's modesty ("chastity") during both the Ming and the Ching dynasties, but by this time even male patients weren't used to being touched by medical professionals, largely because doctors considered it beneath them.

Here, naked in front of the barbarian doctor who examined her in places she had never examined herself, not even after childbirth, where she had been attended to by midwives and womenfolk, Yulan yearned to wave her hands over the entire ivory mannequin—from her cheeks to her bare bosom to her naked hips and buttocks—which even now was shrinking away on its padded cushion from the Western doctor, in shame.

WHEN THEY ARRIVED AT the port in San Francisco, they waited as the Europeans and first-class passengers were allowed to disembark the ship. *What's going on? Why can't we go too?* they wondered, their belongings in hand and at their feet.

Instead of being allowed onto the wharf like the others, all the second-class and steerage passengers were loaded onto a small ferry, the *Angel Island*, that sailed back into the harbor.

The first thing they saw of the island was a long dock, leading up to a big white house at the base of a green hill. Two stories tall and imposing, it was the widest building that Lung had ever seen, and it resembled a manor with wings on either side, protected out front by four young palm trees. Another house, higher on the hill, was peeking behind. There was a complex of smaller buildings surrounding it, and another large building to the left of a pathway, which they would later learn was the medical facility.

Lung held his mother's and little brother's hands as they walked along the wooden planks, solid under his black slippers. When he wiggled his toes in relief, they moved under the cloth. *Hey, hey! I'm walking on land again.*

Although they did not realize it, even on the ferry ride over, they had been separated in terms of race—whites on the upper deck, Asians in the main hold.

When they came up to the big house, they entered the entrance designated "Asiatics."

Later, they would learn that inside, there were separate staircases, dining halls, and dormitories.

They were ordered into the Asian registration area—by far the largest in the building for any of the races—a loud, echoing hall divided by columns and cages.

They were herded inside the women and children's pen, separated from Chin On, who was herded into the men's area, the gate locked behind them from the outside with the turn of a key. *Why are we being treated this way, like animals?* they wondered.

On the wall hung a sign, "No Smoking!"

On the other side of the fence, a woman was being photographed.

The intermittent flash of the photographer's flashbulb.

They sat on wooden benches, until an official came to check them over and assign them numbers and barracks.

Yulan and the boys were led out of the cage, and followed a matron up the Asiatics' staircase that led to the Chinese women's ward. (Because the children were under twelve years old, they were allowed to stay with their mother.) Looking back through the rows of fenced-off areas, Lung searched for Chin On, but could not make him out in the crowd at the other end of the facility.

The women's second-floor barracks were spartan—three double tiers of metal bunks, one atop another.

Blankets that felt like wolf hair.

The ones who'd arrived long before told them about the suicides in the bathrooms—despairing women who had hung themselves during the wait, so interminable after the long ship journey in steerage—so they took turns walking in and out in pairs whenever possible. They did this even when doing the laundry in the sinks, then shuttling the wrung shirts and pants out to dry on the lines between the barracks bunks. At first this seemed like a marvel—indoor plumbing! no more lugging a bucket from the well—but Yulan would have traded running water for freedom any day.

She cut out drinking tea by the afternoon, and ordered the children not to drink too much at dinnertime, so as not to have to visit the sad, ghost bathroom in the middle of the night.

The food was a slop that Yulan would only have fed to her pigs.

Boiled to death vegetables, rice, and meat that was hard to keep down, meal after meal, day after day. This, after the month of monotonous food they'd had at sea—except that even on board the ship in the forever midnight of steerage they had fresh fruit and vegetables after every port stop, including Hawaii. (While the government had hired Chinese cooks on Angel Island, I later learned that their food allowance was less than that for whites, and far less varied.)

You're so lucky, the others said. *Your husband is a merchant with the right papers. You'll be out of here in no time.*

But when the matrons ordered them into the showers, and ran the hose over their naked bodies, none of them felt very lucky.

Yulan was again inspected, naked and shivering, in the drafty examination room.

They looked at her armpits, the backs of her knees, her groin area, her scalp, the bottoms of her feet, checking for rashes, signs of ringworm.

Did she look like she wanted to bite them? Her mother had always called her *hard-necked* stubborn. I bet she wanted to bite them.

The doctor noted the size of Yulan's pregnant belly and deemed her to be six months pregnant—two months shy of what she really was. He made no address of the poor nutritional quality of the food, which was considered so bad that Chinese detainees later staged protests in the dining hall.

In her file, they wrote: *This is to certify that the above-described person has this day been examined and is found to be* [here, they crossed out *afflicted with* and the inspector wrote over it] *PREGNANT—about 6 months, affecting ability to earn a living.*

That last line, "affecting ability to earn a living," gives me the chills every time I read it.

It was grounds for deportation, and so if they wanted to, immigration officers could have denied our very pregnant Yulan entry. If so, she would have given birth either on a ship back to China or right there on Angel Island if the family had found a San Franciscan lawyer to appeal her case.

The medical examiner whose name is stamped on the document is W. C. Billings, the chief medical examiner for San Francisco. Billings was an ardent eugenicist who hobnobbed with other scientists and philanthropists and presented papers at top-tier eugenics congresses, including at the Museum of Natural History in New York. He believed that immigration was an extremely effective way to weed out *racial impurities.*

"Granting that we cannot breed a superior line from inferior stock one of these immediately important questions . . . is that of immigration. The arriving immigrant of today is the father of tomorrow's citizen, and upon tomorrow's citizen and his descendants depends the future of the country," he wrote in an article published in *Eugenics in Race and State* in 1923.

When I realized that Billings was at the helm of the medical front on

Angel Island, where so many generations of Chinese like my Chin side were subjected to screening, I was sitting in front of my computer in my studio. After reading his published paper, "The Medical Application of the Immigration Law," I immediately burst into tears.

From published accounts and interviews of detainees from the same time period, I gather the following:

In the medical infirmary, they were again herded into separate facilities based on race and gender. Men were left to wait, unclothed, for hours until doctors did their procedures—tapping on chests and spines—and then they were ordered to jump up and down like monkeys.

Everyone, both men and women, was given a washbasin with a number on it.

They were ordered to stand between the rows of hospital beds, and squat down.

At first, few understood what they were being asked to do, despite the doctor making overblown gestures with his hands.

Surely they weren't being asked to do what it seemed like the staff were asking for, so blatantly out here in the open?

Yulan was used to squatting, but in her eighth month of pregnancy, and after a long voyage and life in detention with little fresh fruit or vegetables, and a giant in utero baby blocking her large intestines and bowels, she simply could not defecate on demand.

Chin Shee, the other pregnant mother, who'd also traveled with them on the SS *Siberia*, was bent over the immaculate basin with a look of extreme concentration.

Shouting, in their incomprehensible language, from the nurses who walked the aisles, brows furrowed, and then one of them was shoving a purgative salt in Yulan's face.

She was encouraged to take another, and then another, until her mouth felt like parched earth, and she was desperately waving for a glass of room-temperature water, even though she worried it might make her sick. Boiled water was the only water that my great-grandmother trusted.

Later, Yulan would learn that the doctors were divining whether or not they had any communicable ("Oriental") diseases like hookworm—which, despite being treatable, was also grounds for deportation.

No one knows or remembers how long it took for the family to produce their individual fecal samples, but Yulan was never so relieved to return to the barracks.

Every day, despite Yulan's advanced pregnancy, the matrons woke them up and got them out of bed.

They had meals at set times, seven a.m., twelve p.m., six p.m., daily.

Women could go onto the fenced rooftop, but mostly Yulan stayed indoors and tried to rest.

One day, she was brought downstairs to the registration area, in a cage adjacent to where they had been processed.

She was ordered to sit down on a stool in front of a makeshift wall with a number behind her head.

If new arrivals were in the adjacent pen, they would have been able to watch the number being changed—"1435" to "1436"—as Yulan was being ordered to *face forward, hold still, turn to the side.*

Any newcomer would be watching intently, wondering about their own fate. If there were any faces she recognized, she would have pretended they didn't know each other.

As I stare at her photographs now, I can see that she had taken care with her hair that morning—twisting her bun and securing it with a netting, before tucking a large pin behind her ear to keep everything in place.

Only her eyes, and their shadowy fans of dark circles underneath, betray her emotions.

What I saw the first time and identified as murderous rage has something behind it, just under the surface—deep, abiding, unfathomable pain, and something else, something even deeper: betrayal.

As her body continued to grow the baby, turning in its amniotic fluid, Yulan was questioning if all of this was worth it.

WHEN YULAN AND THE BOYS were finally brought in for official questioning, Chin On was there, having just finished his interrogation.

It was likely the first time they had seen him since their separation.

Unlike her, he seemed remarkably refreshed. (She remembered in that moment that he had gone through questioning several times before, in New York, but never as a detainee, so why was he so annoyingly relaxed?)

Chin On barely acknowledged her, even while the children rushed to him, and were distressed when he was ordered out of the room. Lung and Jack were threatening to cry until the interpreter mentioned that they would see him again.

Mr. P. B. Jones, the chief inspector, whom even members of the staff found intimidating—some went on the record about this long after Angel Island was shut down—was the lead interrogator on both cases.

"Did you ever have any children which are dead?"

"No," she said.

"Did either you or your husband ever adopt any children?"

"Never adopted any."

The stenographer, used to short answers, is already on to the next line when Yulan adds, "What is the use, I have two of my own."

This sticks out, especially today. In my years of reading such files, I have never heard anyone display any kind of personality or attitude in their interrogation. Most folks just endure it like the most painful mental marathon of their lives.

I love her for being four foot ten, pregnant, and lippy—she knows how ridiculous this entire process is, but as a Chinese woman stuck on Angel Island, even a merchant's wife with legitimate papers, there's no getting around it.

Yulan answered questions about their house (*a small hut*) in relation to her in-laws' (*grand, finer brick homes*). What their floor is made of (*bare ground*). Whether or not they have a clock. At first she says *no*, unsure about the question, then answers correctly—the clock is more like a piece of art or furniture, it's been displayed forever, but no longer tells time.

The questions flowed like a river, meandering here and there, sometimes shifting without reason.

"Have any of your husband's brothers' families been in the U.S.?" was quickly followed by "Were your feet formerly unbound?"

Her feet were never bound, but because officials knew that bound feet were a symbol of high status, befitting a merchant's wife, immigration officers searched for these markers. Even now they were scrutinizing her feet the way the Chin women regarded them, and so she said, "Yes."

As in *yes, my feet were bound, but I unbound them before getting married.* There is no explanation given, nor any further questions asked about it.

Each answer was scrutinized to see how it would match up with Chin On's remarks.

They asked questions about the distance from the village drinking well to the house, the distance from her home village of Sai Gwan to his (close—hers was by the Southern Gate, his was by the Northern, but only a bird's-eye view could show them in the same frame). Where the in-laws lived? Who was alive and who was dead? Whom had she met? Which family members had she not met? So much talk about death would have been alarming to Yulan—what a way to start a new life in a new country!—but still she continued, as if it were nothing.

In America, she was learning that it was useful to know how to pretend.

By the sixty-third question, they asked if she wanted to stop and continue the next day, but, even tired and heavily pregnant, Yulan preferred to get it over with, even after the interpreter finished his shift and was replaced by a new one.

When they called Chin On back into the room to verify their identities, the children, who were bored and not subject to questioning because of their ages, rushed toward him. Yulan was too tired to pull them aside.

In the end, Yulan answered seventy-three in-depth questions about their lives in China, even as she could feel the baby turning inside her like an old crank.

She was exhausted at the finish, the circles under her eyes darkening, as they turned the official document in her direction and asked her to sign it.

At first she didn't understand. Yulan could not read or write and had never been asked to sign anything in her life.

They instructed her to make a mark, with their hands making strikes in the air.

At the bottom of the page, she filled in the empty place for her name (Lee Yulan) with an elongated "t" like a sideways cross.

Inspector Jones wrote: *There is a good family resemblance noted throughout, and the testimony was satisfactorily given by each witness.*

If they had known what Jones had written in their file, it would have given them solace, but this was for official purposes only. The family was dismissed, but only Chin On, with his merchant papers, was released that day.

Yulan and the children could only watch him from the second-floor window of the women's ward, jogging down the dock toward the waiting ferry.

Did Yulan imagine that she saw her husband do a little dance as he bounded toward the boat? How could he be so happy and buoyant when they were left behind?

In that moment, while the children called out *Baba!* in vain, Chin On, oblivious and never once looking back, she couldn't have hated her husband more.

LUNG WOULD WRITE LITTLE in his papers about their time on Angel Island, with the exception of the humiliation of being naked and hosed, but younger brother Jack had this recollection:

One day, the brothers were playing near the dock, when a boy around their age, with a heavily pockmarked face, approached them.

Do you want to come with me? My dad works here and I know everything about this place.

Lung and Jack shook their heads.

The boy disappeared. Several moments later, he emerged with something hidden in his cupped hands.

When he opened them, the brothers noticed the dirt encrusting his fingernails and what he was carrying.

Dried scallops.

Take 'em. You want them, don't you?

Jack made no move, waiting for his older brother.

Lung stepped forward. *Those are stolen! I don't like taking other people's property.*

Even at seven years old, Lung wasn't above using the moral high ground when it suited him, especially if the thievery wasn't *his idea.*

The boy ran away, back toward the building. Then, turning back around, he called out something that they didn't understand and threw the scallops in their direction.

They landed several yards away from their feet.

Lung and Jack threw knowing glances at each other and laughed, the sound of their voices pealing out to the edge of the water, where the waves were turning over rocks along the shoreline.

I imagine it was the first time they heard the taunt *ching chong Chinaman*.

If Lung and Jack had asked their mother about it, Yulan would have had no clue what it meant either.

MRS. CHIN, THE NURSING MOTHER they'd traveled with from Hong Kong, was despondent. She had been interrogated the same day as Yulan, but Inspector Jones had harped upon a discrepancy over a painting in their home.

How was I to know what he was talking about? I didn't understand, so I said, "No."

The other women told her to ask the interpreter for more information before answering next time, but they couldn't get her to stop crying.

They called my daughter in to verify, but when I told her what I had told them, they got mad at me, she said, sobbing, her voice reaching a pitch that alarmed them and woke up her baby, so that she had to nurse him back to sleep again. *No talking! they said.*

Aiya, you're getting yourself upset!

Yulan wished there was something she could do for her friend, but even though both of their husbands were successfully landed business-men, here, trapped in the big White House on this Island of Pain, their status conferred no power.

My heart too went out to Mrs. Chin, when I read her file that summer day at the NARA offices in San Bruno, California. There she was, pic-tured with a ten-month-old baby in her arms, and her belly big, another one on the way. She was an older mother like me, over thirty-five and pregnant, but while for myself it was by choice, for Mrs. Chin physical distance and the Exclusion laws determined whether or not she saw her husband—there was a thirteen-year gap between her daughter and younger sons.

The last thing any expectant mother wants to do is give birth in a detention center with a view of Alcatraz.

A few days later, after thirteen days of waiting in detention, the matron and the interpreter suddenly called out Yulan's name.

She was told to pack their things immediately and be ready to catch the next ferry out.

Leaving was emotional, but Yulan was too busy gathering their items and corralling her sons to pay much attention. It seemed rude to be happy in the face of the other mothers' collective misery—everyone wanted it to be their names that were called—so she kept her elation to herself. The whole thing seemed unreal, but once they were past the barracks and the fencing, and heading out toward the open dock, the kids running ahead of her toward the waiting ferry, Yulan finally allowed herself a smile.

They never did find out whether pregnant Mrs. Chin and her son made it through.

WHEN YULAN AND THE CHILDREN arrived in San Francisco, weeks after the first- and second-class passengers from the SS *Siberia* had landed and were allowed to go about their own lives, the wharf was bustling with dockworkers loading and unloading cargo, and other recently landed visitors reuniting with friends and family. Despite how crowded it was, there was no one there to greet them.

Yulan knew to expect this. No one knew when they were going to be released, but even so, in this new country where she knew no one and couldn't speak the language, she had never felt so alone, even back in Chin On's village, in those early days without him.

She had her instructions. They were to go to the family association in a cab, where he would be waiting.

For Yulan, her sense of relief was taken over by the prospect of having to navigate the big city, Dai Fo, without any English, on her own.

Yulan stood there with her big belly and two kids, and her rattan suitcase, and the kids' bundles at her feet, as vehicle after vehicle passed them by, clomping down the busy road. Many without a single occupant.

I can almost hear the children saying, *Why won't they stop for us?* even now, over a century later, or maybe I'm confusing it with her growing anxiety.

Although she tried to keep her feelings to herself, Yulan was livid. *Why hadn't Chin On warned her about the conditions here? Why hadn't he told her how they were going to be treated?*

Then, as yet another cab passed them by, she grew worried.

What if no one stopped for them?

They could take a streetcar, which seemed confusing, or try to walk, which she preferred, but in her late stage of pregnancy, she couldn't carry all their baggage. And then there were those hills. . . .

It seemed impossible. Besides, they didn't even know the way.

Everywhere Yulan looked, they were surrounded by foreigners, with not a single other Chinese person in sight whom she could ask for help.

She was starting to lose heart, when suddenly a hansom cab, with wheels almost as tall as the hindquarters of the horse that drew it, rolled to a halt in front of them.

The driver, a giant Black man, whose vehicle sprang out from under him when he descended from his seat, gave them a big smile. *Welcome to San Francisco!*

In relief, Yulan produced the address from her pocket and gave it to him.

Of course he knew where Chinatown was—it wasn't far.

He piled their bags onto his cab, as the children and an exhausted Yulan grabbed ahold of the bar and clambered aboard. When their driver climbed back on and took the seat behind them, Lung watched in awe as the entire cab groaned under his weight. And then they were off.

When they arrived at a nondescript two-story building in Chinatown, a man popped his head out the door.

He paid the driver, who was already bringing their belongings down to the curb.

Before he left, the driver smiled again and waved. *Good luck.*

Many decades later, the family would remember this man's kindness.

Though they never saw their driver again, the boys always remembered generations later how this Black man was the only one who helped them when they first truly landed as scared, newly released immigrants in California.

INSIDE, THE FOLKS FROM the association informed them that Chin On was out, but they would send word for him to return as soon as possible.

Someone asked if they wanted something to eat.

Yulan shook her head. *No.*

Now that they were safely arrived, she realized she was exhausted.

She didn't want to be any trouble, but if she could just sit down?

Lung tugged on her elbow. *C'mon, Mah, we're hungry.*

Jack looked on with liquid eyes.

Between the packing, the ferry ride, and the wait on the wharf, they hadn't had anything to eat for hours.

Okay, she finally agreed.

It was their first real, home-cooked meal in a month and a half, and it was so delicious that she was surprised to learn that one of the men had done the cooking. *Who else is going to do it?* the cook asked.

They ate slivers of Chinese sausage over steamed rice, stir-fried long beans that grew like sprays of firecrackers—diced and sautéed in sesame oil with minced pork—and the tender hearts of long guy lan choy with hoisin sauce, flavors that reminded them of home.

When their rice bowls were empty, Lung and Jack immediately asked for more.

Afterward, while the boys played in the front room, to distract herself from wondering about where her husband was Yulan went into the kitchen and put on a pot of water over a high flame.

She took a pouch from her pocket and brought out a handful of smooth pebbles collected from their bay overlooking the sea. Her father had gathered them himself, at walking distance from the village where she was born, and had given them to her before they left. They had made the long journey on the SS *Siberia* with them, through the various countries and out over the wide, open Pacific.

She tasted one of the stones with her tongue, before tossing a handful into the now boiling water. They were still salty.

The pebbles sank to the bottom with a clatter, sparking white froth to bubble to the top. Just as suddenly, the temperature of the water lowered, so she had an almost clear view, as if the rocks had settled at the bottom of a lake. Yulan raised the flame to bring them back to a boil, and tried not to ponder where Chin On was, and what he was doing, and with whom, and then the unthinkable arose—a thought that she couldn't quite shake, even as she fretted about the kitchen, wiping her hands on an old cloth.

What if he had changed his mind—what if he wasn't coming back for them after all?

What would she do? She didn't have any U.S. dollars and only a handful of Chinese money that was worthless here. *How long would they be allowed to stay at the association before overstaying their welcome?*

Chin On was supposed to have taken care of everything for them.

"What are you doing, Mah?" Lung asked, coming up behind her. He was tall for his age, and laid his head close to her shoulder.

"Cooking stones from home," she said. "Your grandfather gave this to us, to help with our journey."

Lung stuck his fingers into the pouch and felt the rocks at the bottom.

"What's this?" he asked, finding something else inside her pocket.

"Goong Goong gave this to us too," she said. "Take a look."

Nestled inside a bag, on top of grains of rice, were dried orange peels, from Sun Wui, the neighboring county east of Toisan. The orange peels from this region were so prized for their medicinal value and flavoring for dishes that in the growing season, in the height of summer, folks eagerly pried the deep leathery peel and discarded the fruit by the roadsides, so you could get as much of the tangy pulp that you wanted to eat for free.

Lung inhaled the scent of citrus from the orange peel, and his eyes widened in a smile. Another flavor of home.

Yulan had yearned to make this brew ever since they'd arrived in America, but she had not had access to a kitchen. In detention, she didn't trust the cooks to give her the stones back—she could just see them laughing at her and flinging them out the back door.

Because the food and the water are so different in Gum San, her father had told her, *you need to bring some of the minerals from home to get your stomach acclimated.*

When it was ready, Yulan poured the hot stone water from the pot into three teacups.

She sat in the front room sipping a little, so warm in her hands. It tasted like good, clear mineral-y water, with a slight hint of brine.

The boys, excited about being in a new place again, began tumbling over each other, shouting.

Yulan yelled at them to settle down, but none of the men at the association seemed upset; in fact, they smiled and laughed and played along. For many of the old-timers, it had been some time since they had last seen children.

The Chinese written character for "good" is composed of the symbol for "woman" and "child." In America, this kind of *goodness* was a great big gaping hole in their lives, and so Lung and Jack could really do no wrong.

Instead of scolding them, the old men dug into their pockets and flipped the boys some coins. This delighted the children, who had never seen American money before, and they flung them into the air, racing each other across the room.

Yulan sipped her tea, trying to remain calm, but her thoughts kept coming back to Chin On and where he was, and where they might be if he didn't return.

She could give birth any day now. It was a little early, but stranger things had happened.

Where was her husband?

The sun was lowering in the sky and streaming through the windows, the shadows growing long across northern California, when the door suddenly opened.

The children ran toward the tall figure, shouting, "Baba, Baba!"

Chin On was wearing a tailored suit, with a starched white collar and a hat jauntily tilted to the side. He picked his sons up, one in each arm, not caring about their shoes sullying his clothing, soaking in the attention, the lucky father, the Big Man in America who could navigate the laws so successfully that even his family could come over. Every eye in the room was riveted toward Chin On, as the boys clung to their father like tree monkeys.

Then another man, a tall, much younger one, also dressed in a Western suit, stepped into the room behind him.

"Brother Wong!" the children cried.

It was the butcher's son, the one who had been in the army, whom Lung had always looked up to.

"What are you doing here?" they asked.

"Same as you," he said, standing behind Chin On, his new boss.

Yulan felt such a rush of relief that all the fears and accusations she'd harbored suddenly dissipated like morning dew.

There he was, Chin On, standing there with their boys, the envy of so many men in the room.

Although Chin On did nothing—he didn't hug or kiss her or even touch her, all he did was look her way, assessing her as she slowly rose up from her chair, one hand protectively on her belly, to see if she was all right—she knew. It was the same look he gave her when they first met, on their wedding day, when he removed the cloth over her face, and then later, that night, their first night together, when he gently undid her dress, with the intricately embroidered knot at her throat.

In that one moment, as she stood before her husband, Yulan knew everything.

She didn't need to ask him where he'd been. He'd been gambling, with the Wong man.

And smoking lots and lots of cigars. He was like a plume of cigar smoke, billowing out of the top of his short, spiky hair that stood up as if by static electricity.

And she could smell the alcohol on him as well.

But he had returned to his accommodations, wherever that was, and changed into his best suit, which still smelled like laundry soap and starch, just for them.

"Come on, we're going," he said to them.

Where? Where? the kids wanted to know.

"On a train journey—it's a big, big country," he said. "You'll like it, you'll see."

Yulan drank the last of her tea.

Before they left, she remembered to collect the stones.

PART FOUR

1915–Present

13

Mothers of Mott Street

Ng-Doshim Family Apt. 31 & Chin Family Apt. 23

伍 陳

When Sun Lau was constructed in 1915, a year after Naughton's three-story funeral parlor and horse stable caught fire and burned to the ground, the merchant families of Chinatown, including the Chins and Doshims, wanted in. The new residential building, now six stories high and occupying three lots, dominated the block almost as much as its next-door neighbor, the ornate Catholic Transfiguration Church. From a bird's-eye view, one could take in its dumbbell shape, the classic tenement configuration, but from the street level, Sun Lau, with its winsome bend and good feng shui, presented itself to the community like the overture of a grand opera.

For each of my great-grandfathers, Doshim and Chin On, landing an apartment at Sun Lau was as simple as inquiring about it the next time Laurence Naughton, the landlord's son, who had taken over the family business, came by their stores to collect the rent. The Naughtons seemed to own the half of Mott Street that the church did not.

Move-in day, as I imagine it, was akin to opening day of the city's best department stores, like Macy's or Wanamaker's. Yulan, with Calvin, her toddler, in hand, followed by Jack and Lung, climbed that front marble stair in excitement, past the bound-foot mothers who gripped the wooden handrail in pain, each step a reminder of the crippling cruelties they had survived from childhood, recently outlawed in the new Republic of China but too late for this generation. The Chins rounded the corner to the next landing, where the steps became slate, and then eventually pebbled tangerine-colored terrazzo on each floor.

They were the lucky ones—these merchant families, the first tenants of Sun Lau, who now had amenities that many of them and their peers had never before experienced.

"It was considered a luxury building," Grandma Rose always said, "with a claw-foot bathtub and a toilet in every apartment."

For her mah and the other mothers of 37 Mott Street, this meant no more having to lug a boiling kettle from the stove and give sponge baths to wiggly bodies in the middle of the kitchen.

For the children, it meant no more sharing the same bathwater with your siblings. (In practice, though, many of the families still bathed in the old ways, only now in the privacy of their own bathrooms.)

There was an icebox in the kitchen, and a garbage disposal in the hallway.

Chin On had landed one of the choice front-facing apartments on the fourth floor, along with two others in the back for the store employees. This was a period for the family where everyone was making greenbacks hand over fist. Chin On, eager to strike out on his own, opened his own store on Pell Street, Sun Yuen Hing, which conveniently shared a back office with Ying Chong. Brother Jun, who could never get used to the language, had decided to return home—not to Kwong Hoy, but instead to thriving Hong Kong. It was in the burgeoning Chinese district of Sheung

Wan where he set up their exporting business, the *New* Ying Chong, on Des Voeux Road, named after a former colonial governor and conveniently located near the shipping docks. When Jun proposed buying their own freighters to ship their goods—cutting out the middleman—Hing and Chin On readily agreed.

Already in New York for close to a year, Yulan had given birth almost as soon as they stepped off the train, and she and the others were looking forward to having a more permanent home. So when Hing and his wife moved in, it really was a family affair.

As Yulan and her children climbed the staircase, right behind them entered the Doshim family—Chun, along with her brood of four young children: Oilily, six and about to enter grade school, and old enough to mind her younger brothers; rascally Normon, the oldest son, a little spoiled and rambunctious, with a mind of his own; Johnny, a round-faced toddler with big eyes, who still sometimes demanded to be breast-fed; and baby

Chun, with Normon, Johnny, and Lily, 1913

Edith, held in Chun's arms. Elva brought up the rear, marching everyone up the stairs and carrying the family valuables, even the fine china she and Dek had given the couple as a wedding present, as easily as if the crate were a lunchbox.

Chun, who now wore her hair in a soft bun, was thrilled to have arrived. There were schools for the children only a short jaunt up Mott Street and over on Bayard where they would be with other Chinese kids. The American elementary, the Columbus School, was just up Mott Street and a block over, diagonally across the park. Chinese school was in the other direction, on lower Mott, where they learned to read and write Chinese calligraphy.

Chun especially looked forward to being within walking distance of all the churches and missions that were so active in the community.

I like to think it was here on move-in day that my great-grandmothers happened upon each other—Chun carrying the baby, followed by the others, while Yulan paused at their fourth-floor landing with Calvin, her toddler—the baby born after that long journey at sea and detention on Angel Island—while Lung and Jack raced ahead to their apartment.

Because my great-grandmothers didn't know each other, they wouldn't have called out greetings, but instead slowed down to regard each other.

It's not just that they were of the same age and generation, or that their kids were within a few years of each other, although there was that too.

Chun was still so beautiful even after giving birth to four children that she seemed to embody that Chinese adage about the full moon and the flowers hiding their faces in shame.

But what inspired mothers in the throes of labor in Hong Kong to trust her, now was like a wedge that would harden the faces of the other women in the building long after move-in day.

They were almost eye level—Chun on the staircase, Yulan on her landing.

One dressed like a Westerner in a floor-length dress, the other in a

Chinese loose-fitting linen top and pants. Both wore clothing they had made by their own hands.

One spoke Yingmun with a British-inflected accent and the ease of a Hong Konger, the other spoke only a village dialect.

One could read and write in both Chinese and English, the other could only make two intersecting lines to signify her name.

One was clearly high-class, the other a peasant.

One wore good leather shoes with a slight heel, the other a kind of Mary Jane–like cloth slipper.

Yet, both traveled up the stairs easily, and didn't appear to be in the slightest bit winded or in pain, like the other mothers.

As Yulan paused to watch Chun and the lofan continue to make their way up, she knew right away that this woman was not like them.

BOTH THE DOSHIMS AND THE CHINS had coveted front-facing apartments, where morning light streamed through the windows, offering a panoramic view of the entire neighborhood. On the fifth floor, Great-Grandmother Chun could look up Mott Street and watch Doshim heading to the office. Once there, if he wanted to look out his office window and wave, he could, past the ever-present delivery trucks. Sometimes, she waved back. Up short Pell Street, if she was lucky, she might catch glimpses of Dek Foon heading into his office from Brooklyn, while in the distance, the elevated trains rumbled in and out of the station at Chatham Square.

A floor below, Great-Grandmother Yulan was even closer to the theater of the street. It was as if she could reach out and touch the vegetable hawker, Tony the iceman, or the friendly fruit seller Mr. Chin Song, who was probably the only naturalized Chinese peddler on the block, having arrived to New York even before the Chin brothers. She too could watch her husband—who usually raced out of the apartment to work—crossing the street and heading straight into their store. He never looked back.

Occasionally, if Yulan was sitting by the window, where she liked to do her mending, she caught Chin On and his brother walking south along Mott toward the On Leong headquarters, growing smaller and smaller until they seemed to disappear into a tangle of iron balconies and three-story buildings out of view.

The apartments alone were like the promise of a bright new day, but no one wanted to be on the fourth floor where the Chins lived.

Say, the number four, sounded too much like the word for death.

Naughton, the Irish landlord and undertaker—who cornered the market not only on Italian funerals but Chinese ones as well—knew nothing about these kinds of Chinese customs, and had not made an accommodation to skip up to the number five, the way it was commonly done in cities like Hong Kong. Everyone avoided Naughton and his son at the start of every year—for who wanted to be in the position to wish them a *prosperous* New Year?

Because the Chins had wound up on the "bad luck" floor, they began referring to it as the *third floor*, despite the "4" painted in the corridor outside the stairwell.

It's unknown when Yulan learned that it was *that woman* and her family who had beaten them to the upstairs apartment. She noted with annoyance every time a chair was dragged across the kitchen floor, or a tiny body leapt from the bed like a springboard and tumbled across the wooden floors, ahead of the wail that erupted from the bedroom window and bounced along the air shaft at the back end of the building.

Even in the Chin village, living in the family hut with only the roof above their heads, at least there was no one living above them.

If my great-grandmothers happened to pop their heads outside their windows at the same time, peering out onto the busy street through the fire escape, and by chance caught each other's glances, Yulan's expression would have snapped shut like a lobster cage. She would have immediately gone back inside, slamming the window so that the entire neighborhood heard it, and Chun felt its vibration below her feet.

. . .

CHUN'S MOVE TO MOTT STREET inspired renewed zeal to spread the gospel to the community among Elva and the other lofan wives.

You're in the best building in the neighborhood, they told her one day, after services. *Every merchant family in Chinatown is in your building.*

The idea was simple: focus on the mothers, who would then convince their husbands, and bring the children to Sunday school.

Chun agreed with the strategy, but the other mothers hadn't been exactly welcoming.

You're Chinese, they'll talk to you, the church ladies said. *You'll win them over, you'll see.*

They gave her tiny pamphlets, little folios with pictures of lambs and the cross, even though, as Chun pointed out, most of the wives could not read.

But the ladies looked so excited over the possibility of a new generation of Chinese women and children converts that Chun had no choice but to smile and hope for the best.

She agreed to keep a few in her handbag for whenever she encountered another mother in the building.

ONE AFTERNOON, YULAN WAS holding court in the back staircase with the other wives, where the skylight caught the dust above their heads. She was with the jewelry store mother from the second floor and the carpenter's wife; both had been her neighbors when they lived next door.

Chun came downstairs in her starched white shirt and skirt that reached her ankles—she was the only Chinese mother in the building who wore Western clothing—then waited patiently, until there was a gap in the conversation. "There's a Sunday school for the children, where they can learn English and the gospel," she finally said, perhaps a little too brightly, passing out the pamphlets.

Yulan reluctantly took the paper from her, noting that Chun spoke Cantonese—not Sayyup village dialect like the rest of them.

"I see you're pregnant," Chun said. "I am a midwife. I can help."

"You're from Hong Kong?" Yulan asked in Sayyup.

Chun nodded—Doshim and Dek Foon were Sayyup. She answered in pure Cantonese, "I am."

The other women regarded her coolly.

Cantonese-speaking.

Big-footed.

Hakka.

Yulan frowned, she and the others became silent for a moment before someone changed the subject.

Chun looked down, her eyebrows raised like my grandmother's whenever she saw or heard something she didn't like and couldn't believe, before drawing her skirt around her and heading back upstairs.

"I don't want that Hakka touching me," one of the third-floor wives said, "or my newborn baby."

The other mothers laughed, but Yulan remained silent, watching her neighbor's feet disappear onto the fifth floor.

Later that spring, Yulan gave birth on her own, without anyone's help.

From the back of the apartment, where clotheslines crossed to the back-facing units and the bedrooms abutted each other, Yulan's deep guttural noises seemed to fill the entire space, and wafted upstairs to where Chun could hear her through the open window. Kinny was one of the first children born in the building, the second American in our Chin family to be born in New York.

PRETTY SOON THE hallway corridors were littered with pamphlets.

Chun would find them whenever she left the apartment, and bade Oilily to help her collect them—hating to see tread marks on the cover bearing the cross. Sometimes the moy moys who lived with the families helped them, and Chun always gave them a leaflet, which they slipped into a pocket, and gazed on at night, finding comfort in the pictures and primary colors.

There were so many things that set my grandmother Rose's family apart from the other Chinese families in the building—not only their mixed Cantonese-Hakka marriage.

They spoke English at home, so the children were the first to be thoroughly multilingual, and in school they outpaced the others. Even the Italian and Russian families in the building mainly spoke their native languages at home.

Dek Foon and Doshim did not go by the family name Eng or Ng—the "Number Five" family—but instead used their first names as their surnames.

They did not join the family association like other Chinese because they didn't have to—Dek Foon's civic and Christian networks were large enough to sustain them and better connected to the power structure of politicians and leaders outside of Chinatown. (By the time we moved into Sun Lau, the need for the Chinese Reform Association had mostly dissipated, and the organization that loomed larger in our family life was the church.)

By choosing their given names as surnames, they were declaring themselves self-made men in Gum San. They were re-creating themselves—as a new kind of Chinese, a new kind of American.

Doshim is such an unusual name that to this day, if I meet one, which is admittedly rare, I know that we are related.

Doshim, the New Man, was a busy husband and a father, who traveled for business back and forth to his manufacturing operation in Pennsylvania, meeting new clients. He did not notice how tense and withdrawn Chun had become since their move to Sun Lau. Or perhaps, if he did, he did not address it directly, instead giving her a piece of jewelry, or supporting her favorite church cause.

One day, Elva visited, as she often did from Brooklyn.

Lily and Normon were chasing one another, tripping over their younger brother and all falling into a heap onto the floor. Chun grabbed the two by the arms and gave both a swift rap to the head with a sharp knuckle.

Lily swiftly burst into tears. Normon bit his lip, nostrils flaring, refusing to cry.

Chun flew into a rage—the eldest needed to model good behavior for the youngest children, and here was the toddler Johnny on the floor, bawling.

If Normon was going to be so *hard-necked* obstinate, then both Lily *and* Normon, as the oldest children in the pecking order, needed to be punished.

With a harder rap to the head, they were soon both crying—Normon's face breaking open like a floodgate. Before she knew it, at the sight of them, Chun was herself in tears.

It's unclear if Elva put her hand on Chun's shoulder or cleared her throat and said, *Okay, enough,* but once she'd ushered the children into their bedroom, she returned to find Chun sitting on a chair.

They hate me, Chun said.

They love you—they're just being children.

Not them, Chun said. *The women—in this building.*

Why?

They know that I am different, Chun said, attempting to explain, but knowing it was no use. For Elva, they were all Chinese at 37 Mott, but Chun was distinctly aware of the divisions.

It was embarrassing to talk about such things to her aunt, her only true friend aside from Doshim, and a lofan.

Elva was truly puzzled. "Shouldn't that no longer matter here? You're in a new country! This is America, after all."

Chun's natural inclination to try to please Elva, to pretend that things were fine even when things were so bad that *mo' paa, mo' waa*—you can't crawl, can't scratch—made Elva's misunderstanding feel like an anvil pressing down on her chest.

"Don't give up," Elva finally said, her hand on Chun's small shoulders, so bony like a little bird, now shaking as the tears began to flow. "I know it seems impossible, but there is always a way."

THAT NIGHT, AS ELVA lay in bed next to Dek, who loved to curl up next to her, and always seemed to fall asleep so easily, she would have listened to the sounds of his breathing as she did nearly every night, and contemplated her life. It was a habit she had acquired those years after Doran rejected her, when she lay awake at night in her parents' home, in her childhood bed, and raged against her own body—and why God had made her the way she was.

Aside from the one time Chun brought it up, Elva had never spoken to her niece about why she and Dek had married late in life, or why they never had any children.

I like to think that this was the moment that it fully dawned on my aunt that if she had never been born with an extra appendage, that if she had been equipped with a womb and a pair of silken ovaries, she would have settled down to a life with Doran, raising a family as Chun was doing, and never met Dek.

Without him her life would have been so different—Dek had a zest for improvement and loved debating ideas. He was strict in his Christian mores, and never drank alcohol or smoked—a bit of a drag maybe, but she treasured his conviction. By the time I tracked down Dek's descendants, they confirmed this—Dek listened carefully to his American wife, valuing her thoughts and opinions.

They had worked together on his ironing machine patent, and she helped edit his writing so that it shone with American optimism. They sent it off to a lawyer that she had helped find, who had sent it in for legal copyright.

If Elva had never met and married Dek, that meant there would be no Shim nor Chun in her life, and she would not have become the nana to all these little ones, including the woman who would become my grand-mother.

If she had not been born intersex, Aunt Elva would have led a life completely parallel to my family—rarely exiting the orbit of her first hus-band's world.

Luckily for us, she was, and did.

That night, Aunt Elva prayed for Chun, who was like a daughter to her, and whom she hated to see suffer, and the children she considered her grandkids. She felt lucky to be their matriarch. And with that feeling of gratitude in her heart like a giant balloon that was sailing away across the East River, Elva prayed for all of them: Chun putting all the children to bed after saying their prayers—Oilily, Normon, and Johnny, with the baby asleep in a cradle—and at the kitchen table, Doshim catching up on his newspapers. Even though it had been several years since he had hung up his hat as an editor, and the Chinese Empire Reform Association had long since dissolved, Shim still loved reading his newspapers.

Elva extended her faith and gratitude toward the other inhabitants of the building, wishing they would open their hearts to the little family, and find the message of the gospel so that it spoke directly to each and

Dek Foon and the Doshim children, Elva in
the background, at Bear Mountain, 1916

every one of them, on all the floors, even the ones, or perhaps *especially* those, who were giving her loved ones the most difficulty.

IN APARTMENT 22, CHIN ON was coming home increasingly later and later.

Where's Baba? the children would ask, but Yulan always told them to shut up and eat.

Back when they first left the West Coast, it had all been so different.

The children, with their boundless energy, were so hopeful about the train journey and the prospect of their new lives together. But their father disapproved of their endless chatter and excitement and seemed to grow more and more withdrawn as the journey progressed, until one day he erupted in anger and the entire car went silent.

Lung would later recall that their father could only say "corned beef and cabbage" in English to the server in the dining car. For the duration of the weeklong journey, that's what they ate.

Lung remembered his ancestors' admonition to *never eat cow meat* because of the animal's worthy contribution to saving the Chin ancestor during the era of the last Mongol ruler.

Corned beef. There was no corn—he later learned it was a verb—and the meat was the color of a big cow tongue.

Each bite of beef, an unfamiliar smell and texture, made him nauseous.

But even at seven years old, as sick as the meal made him, he was careful not to show it, for fear of upsetting his father.

Still they hated eating the same meal every day and were eating it only to help their father save face.

It cast a pall over the entire journey.

Once they landed, they hoped it would be better, but as the months rolled on, the newness of being the big merchant family man started to wear off for Chin On.

Whenever he was home, he sat in stony silence for what felt like hours

Chin family, c. 1917

before yelling that the boys were being too loud, or too rough with each other.

Once, Calvin, who was studying the saxophone, hit a particularly wrong note—loudly. Chin On emerged from the bedroom, his hair standing on end from a nap, and everyone in the apartment froze. He grabbed the instrument and opened the back window and tossed it out like a plate, despite Yulan yelling it wasn't theirs, but the property of the *school*.

The boys heard the instrument hit ground level with a crash. They knew right away it was broken beyond repair.

Then there was the issue of other women.

Before he brought Yulan and the children to New York, Chin On was used to living the freewheeling life of a bachelor. He was lean and good-looking, with a full mouth and thick shiny hair like a chow's—on such a coveted canine, it would have been described as a *luxurious coat*; long limbed and lean, he resembled a classical Chinese scholar, but for the pockmark on his left cheek and the fact that his nose had been broken while sparring at his father's kung fu school. Generous while drinking, Chin On was very popular with women, and before long, the seductive lure of Mott Street and Newark's Chinatown beckoned. From Lung's papers we know that there was a well-connected Irish prostitute on lower Mott Street ("You're Chin On's son"); a particularly captivating small-time-operator waitress in West Point, New York; and numerous women in Newark, New Jersey. Sometimes Chin On didn't come home at all.

When Yulan finally complained one day, Chin On erupted, his face a deep crimson red from drinking.

In China, I would be able to have several wives, not just you, he said.

Brother Jun was living the life of a fat man with a wife and a much younger concubine in Hong Kong.

Did she argue that *they were in America now?* That *not even older brother could get away with that in New York?* Either way, Chin On swung so fast, his fist was a blur. When he hit her in the face, the blow was so solid that Yulan stumbled backward, and had to steady herself against their kitchen table, the blood under her skin pooling around her eye.

I can do whatever the hell I want, he told her, the terror registering across her face only making him angrier. *No one can help you here—you don't read, you can't write, and you don't even speak the language.*

She steered clear of him after that, they all did, and when he fell asleep in the living room, she just left him there.

To the outside world, Chin On looked like the big-shot *dai lap je,* or *dai lap mak—the bigwig with the big mole.* In addition to Ying Chong and Sun Yuen Hing, the Chin brothers now owned two restaurants in the Bronx and a pool hall on Mott Street—by all accounts the first Chinese-owned hall in the neighborhood, and perhaps in the whole city—and were looking to expand into Newark's Chinatown. Their freighter ships, including the SS *Monmouth*, ferried goods from Hong Kong to New York, were in constant use, and docked right on the harbor. They bought up investment properties in Hong Kong and Kowloon—good deals that would appreciate in value, especially since they all dreamed of one day returning home. No one suspected, not even Yulan, that Chin On was overextended on his credit, and that opening the second store, which competed with Ying Chong, had caused tension between the brothers.

The crack in the facade occurred when Chin On learned that one of his gambling parlors was experiencing a loss in revenue. *How does a gambling joint lose money, when the odds are stacked in the house's favor?*

It was obvious—someone was stealing, but he couldn't tell who it was. Everyone who worked there, from the manager to the dealers to the "bank," was connected to another On Leong dai lap je.

Chin On couldn't send Big Brother Wong to rough anyone up for fear of upsetting someone higher up.

The next morning, at the crack of dawn, the family woke up to the youngest boy, Kinny, now a three-year-old toddler, wailing at the top of his lungs.

Shut that kid up, Chin On yelled.

But Yulan was too tired to pay any attention.

According to Lung, their father grabbed the cane duster and started beating the boy while he was still in bed.

The others watched from where they had just been sleeping, in shock.

With each hit, Kinny continued to cry, louder and harder. Lung and the others could only watch in terrified silence. Usually, whenever Chin On was upset with one of them, he made the eldest the target for the mistakes of the younger ones, but today he unleashed his anger on the baby.

Yulan, now roused, felt the blood drain from her face—the punch in the eye was recent enough that she still recalled having to ice it and stay inside, avoiding the other mothers in the building.

Did any of them step in, and say, *Come on. He's just a kid*?

Or would that have just made things worse?

Surely my Doshim family upstairs could hear it, so early in the morning and with the resounding acoustics in the building. (Even today, whenever the window's open and anyone takes a phone call in the tiny courtyard downstairs, or a neighbor plays the radio too loud, you can hear it all the way to the fourth floor.)

By the time he stopped, the child was covered in red marks, which later darkened into bruises.

Yulan realized that she had never hated someone so much in her life. The next time that Jesus woman from upstairs looked at her with big empathetic eyes as they passed each other on the stairwell, Yulan wanted to stick her compassion in her rear with a sewing needle.

WHILE THE MOTHERS OF MOTT STREET may have shunned Great-Grandmother Chun, the Chin and Doshim children had become fast friends.

One day, Chun found herself cooking dinner not just for her own kids, but for Lung and Jack as well.

She drummed up a feast of traditional Hakka fare. Delicate braised tofu (dow fu) stuffed with a shrimp, pork, and chives mixture. Country-style stir-fried noodles. A stir-fry over rice.

For the Chin brothers, it was just as good as their mother's food, but slightly different.

Even the apartment was identical to their own, with the same number of kids, but more orderly.

The Doshim mom was so nice and pretty and the food so scrumptious, they didn't mind the blessing over the meal that the father gave in English, a kind of gratitude chronicle for their *daily bread*, even though there was no actual bread on the table. The father translated the text into Toisan for their benefit.

They shrugged off Chun's queries over when they were going to Sunday school.

When they returned home and told their mother about what they'd eaten, Yulan frowned.

Not to be outdone, Yulan told her sons to invite the Doshim children downstairs for dinner.

The next week, when Lily and Normon arrived at apartment 22, Yulan noted how well-behaved they were. Not beating each other up at the table or wiggling around uncontrollably—it was rumored they knew how to eat with a fork and a knife.

She asked them questions, which they seemed to readily understand, although they answered in Cantonese.

Our baba is Sayyup, they said. *Our mother is from Hong Kong. At home we speak English.*

English! She was bewildered. *What was going* on *upstairs?*

Yulan served ham yue fan—the fish that she had salted herself and air-dried on a rack in the bathroom.

A variety of chay (tsay), or homemade dim sum.

Each small, individual morsel (*a little spot from the heart*) was made by her own capable hands.

I got a bicycle for my birthday, Normon told the Chin brothers, watching their eyes grow large over their bowls.

He doesn't know how to ride, Lily said.

Once I learn, Normon said, *you can all have a go.*

Who wouldn't love being neighbors with the Doshims? While their own father wouldn't be caught dead trying to learn how to ride a bike at his age, quiet, bespectacled Mr. Doshim was often seen wheeling around the neighborhood in a three-piece suit like an English dandy.

All you have to do is watch out for the shee-shee, Doshim had instructed his son. Horse manure lay in piles on every road in the city, and especially seemed to accumulate on their busy corner.

Perhaps Normon was doing just that as he pedaled along cobblestoned Mott Street, doing a wheelie outside of Doshim's office.

It was five thirty p.m. on a Friday, and school had let out hours before.

The delivery express driver had just made his last delivery of the week, and out before them stretched the promise of the weekend.

Normon likely never saw the express truck backing up; this was, after all, the early days of motor vehicles—long before warning bells or crossing guards or traffic lights, and vehicles often drove upon the city sidewalks, even beyond narrow Pell Street.

If Chun had been looking out the window from the fifth floor, she might have seen the truck hitting the bicycle, Normon thrown into the air like a doll, and then the nauseating crush of both bike and then child under the back wheel.

But luckily, Chun did not actually witness it.

Any of the mothers of Mott Street, if they were looking out of their front-facing apartments, would have been able to see the crowd that was forming. News of Normon's death reached the building and front stairwell even before his body did. Later, they carried him into the landlord's basement funeral parlor. Mr. Naughton took one look at the boy and indicated they place him on the porcelain enamel prep table.

The coroner would list the following cause of death:

Internal injuries.

Fractured skull.

Run over by express truck.

As a nurse in Hong Kong with a stint at the children's hospital, Great-Grandmother was no stranger to copious blood flow and broken limbs. Her first instinct upon seeing her son lying there, unmoving, would have been to make bandages, but even she knew that absolutely nothing could be done. Still, I imagine her trying to rip the bottom of her cotton dress into strips that could patch the boy together.

But they say, even with her training, Chun nearly collapsed when she saw the extent of his injuries.

. . .

Out on Mott Street, for months after, Normon's death had a ripple effect throughout the community.

The death of a firstborn son not only rips a hole in the family fabric, it also creates a giant fissure in a community where children are rare because of immigration restrictions. Such children, who either miraculously made it through the border with their families like Lily or were actually *born here* like Normon, were luminous creatures as marvelous as golden phoenixes representing wealth and prosperity, abundance and fecundity. This, in a culture where a common wish for newlyweds was *May you beget many children.*

Children are not supposed to die before their parents, as all Chinese know.

According to Chinese custom, there was no funeral service, no public grieving, no parents in attendance when Normon's casket was lowered into the gravesite.

Only Elva attended his burial, with Uncle Dek by her side. Normon had been a surrogate grandson for them both, and Elva could not bear for him to be buried like an orphan.

If for the next few weeks, Chun refused to get out of bed, wondering why she had ever allowed Doshim to buy their child that bicycle, who could really blame her?

If she snapped at her husband, or was short with her other children, or if she wasted hours recounting the times she had been angry at Normon or exasperated by his hard-necked stubbornness, who are we to judge?

And so what if she indulged in the slippery practice of *What if*?

As in: What if she hadn't let him go riding that day? Or insisted that he stay at home—at home for the rest of his life? If she did that, would he still be alive today?

So what if she spent her time in the darkness of their bedroom, and could not bear to enter the children's room at night, where Normon's bed lay starchly made and empty and Oilily cried herself to sleep and Johnny, only three years old, kept asking *Where's Normon? Where's Normon? (Go-go, I want Go-go!)* So what if she found solace in the baby, who still clung to her, and allowed her to forget for a while, as she got caught up in her feeding and sleep cycles? But Chun found it so hard to eat, and now her milk was drying up and it was time to move the littlest one to the kids' room, but she still wanted her close, the small body, like a hot loaf of comfort.

What if she whiled away her time dreaming of all the what-ifs, including ripping her clothing into ten thousand bandages, wrapping Normon back together again *whole*, a little mummy boy with blinking eyes, and then flying with him through the air all the way back to Hong Kong?

Perhaps, if they had never left, he would be safe.

He would know her family, her poa poa and his own grandparents.

What if they had never come here?

Was it worth it? she wondered. Perhaps the answer was no. *Perhaps they never should have left at all.*

THE KNOCK ON THE DOOR was just a series of small taps from a tiny, insistent hand.

When Chun dragged herself from the sofa to the door, she found her downstairs neighbor in a housedress and slippers, carrying a brown clay casserole dish.

Yulan wordlessly placed the dish on the kitchen table. She meant to dash—what was there to say? *Sorry about your son? Sorry we treated you like cow dung all year?*—but she couldn't help peering around.

The upstairs apartment's layout mirrored their own home, of course, but aside from that it was completely different.

Nurse Chun, favorite niece of Elva's, kept the living area spotless.

You don't have to return the clay pot, Yulan said, indicating the dish. *My husband imports them from Hong Kong.*

The next week, Yulan brought some of the small delectable chay that she knew the Doshim children loved.

She wasn't the only one. Soon the other mothers of Thirty-Seven, down the hallway and on each of the floors, including the jewelry store mother and the wife of the wood-carver, brought food to Chun too—food for the whole family. There were tonic soups—chicken cooked in wine with red jujubes floating on top, and pork trotters in black vinegar—the same braises and stews given to birthing mothers to support their kidneys, those gateways to life, and to keep their strength up. They knew she was still breast-feeding her youngest daughter.

Chun took to keeping a bowl of candy by the door, instructing Oilily to offer it to each visitor before leaving.

Although they were a Christian family, they were still Chinese. Although Chun was a native Hakka Hong Konger, she was still born and raised in Guangdong Province.

Each gesture of kindness by the women of 37 Mott Street was reciprocated with a confection wrapped in colorful paper that they ate on the way back to their own apartments.

May you go in sweetness.

THAT SUNDAY, WHEN CHUN was finally able to get the kids ready, with Doshim's tender help, she put on her favorite white linen dress and they gathered the children and headed down the staircase and out the front door.

It was her first time outdoors since Normon's death, and I imagine the fresh summer air felt good against her face. Chun would not have wanted to even look at that part of the street where her son had been run over, but luckily, the walk to church was a straight shot from the building down the middle fork of the intersection of Mott and Pell, and then right to the house of worship that sat at the same angle that echoed their building.

When they entered the humble mission that resembled any other three-story brick building on the block—passersby would know it was a church only by the cross hung in the window—Chun would have been surprised to see the Chin brothers there, accompanied by their mother.

Yulan nodded at her approach.

I thought I should see what this was all about, she said, answering an unasked question.

It's not hard to imagine that this was the first time in a long while that my great-grandmother Chun truly smiled.

EVERY TIME I WALK past 44 Mott Street, I too think of Normon Doshim.

These days the street is consumed by a giant build-out that the community uses like a mini patio overlooking the neighborhood. There's even a barbecue grill permanently parked outside by the manager of the take-out snacks place—the same building where Great-Grandfather Doshim had his business. During the first year of the pandemic, they gave out free food to the community and essential workers.

Even today, as I walk past on my way to Mei Lai Wah to get a roast pork–filled pineapple bun, or head to my favorite open-air display fish-monger on Mulberry Street, I sense the shadowy outline of his presence. It's like a car crash on a highway that results in a slowdown as rubber-necking drivers slowly edge past, only this family trauma originated over a hundred years ago, when there were still horse-drawn carriages and boys wore short pants, even in the winter.

Chun and Doshim had no real control over it, like any of us.

As parents, we cultivate an illusion of safety for our children so that they may grow and be innocent and fearless.

Even now, every time I pass it, I see Normon, the five-year-old showing off his new bicycle, finally feeling like he was getting a handle on things.

I think of myself at five, in Chinatown, tossing mini poppers on the ground, each to ignite in a tiny spark of gunpowder and end in a waft of smoke and black smudge on the sidewalk.

My daughter follows in my footsteps, every Chinese New Year's, popping long tubes that end in confetti streaming through the air, completely unaware.

LATER THAT FALL, both of my great-grandmothers swelled with orange heat, like the fruiting of giant persimmons. When the calendar year flipped like a wall chart, they entered 1917 heavily pregnant.

Nineteen seventeen was important on more than one count: the U.S. entered the First World War, and Congress passed massive immigration legislation. Chinese Exclusion, now in its fourth decade, provided the foundation for the Immigration Act of 1917, and its creation of a "Barred Asiatic Zone." Like an exponentially expanded version of the Chinese Exclusion Act, this zone barred anyone from the mountains and plains of Afghanistan to northern Mongolia to the Indonesian islands from immigrating. Full stop.

Downstairs, Great-Grandmother Yulan and Chin On had yet another son, Ngo.

His birth—the birth of yet another boy—was celebrated with a red egg party where all the Chin relatives and close friends throughout the building gathered.

Upstairs, Great-Grandmother Chun gave birth to a baby girl.

Although Chun and Doshim had been hoping for another boy, they did their best to hide their disappointment.

Elva, who was present, as she was for all the Doshim children's births in America, called it *God's will*.

I want to linger here, as Elva peered over the baby who would eventually become my grandmother. There are no photos of her from this time period, so I have no clear picture of what she looked like.

Did baby Grandma look like my own daughter, who resembled my adult grandmother even in grainy in utero shots with a ski-jump nose in profile so striking that even my uncles remarked upon the likeness? When I gave birth to her, the sixth-generation New Yorker in our family, she emerged with a rose-red mouth, the most delicate fingernails, and a nose that resembled a lingchi—the mushroom of longevity that appears as a scepter carried by mythic deities in Chinese paintings, porcelain statues, and wood carvings. Is this what my grandmother looked like as a baby?

What we do know is that Elva, in charge of the American names, picked out Rose, perhaps after the baby's own rosy lips.

In honor of Aunt Elva May, my great-grandparents gave Rose her Chinese name Mai. Pronounced like the month, "Mai" functioned well in English as well as Chinese, where it means Beautiful and is the same character for America.

The Beautiful Country.

And because every girl of her generation was given the character "Oi," like the oldest daughter, Oilily, baby Grandma's full name became Mai Oi. Beautiful Love.

Beautiful Love's parents did not know it at the time, but they had welcomed into their family the infant who would become the smartest girl in Chinatown.

THAT SUMMER, THE MOTHERS of Mott Street bonded with their new babies on their backs. When Yulan couldn't bring the children to church on Sundays, Chun picked up the Chin boys on the fourth-floor landing and brought the whole gang over.

Sometimes, the Chin brothers brought Johnny Doshim down with them to Boy Scouts.

Even with their front-facing apartments, the mothers had several windows that faced the back, where lines of laundry crisscrossed to the apartments where the Chinese bachelors and the Russian and Italian families lived. As anyone who has lived in a communal situation knows, *it's just rude* to leave your clean, dry laundry hanging too long on a shared line, and one can imagine the minor squabbles and hurt feelings involved over so-and-so's *lack of consideration*. It was at Thirty-Seven that Yulan picked up a few Italian words, like scusi, bene, and basta!

The U.S., still in the grips of a powerful eugenics movement, saw many politicians, philanthropists, and civic leaders vested in the belief that the betterment of society depended upon a "pure" stock. As European immigration was at an all-time high, the federal government also enacted a literacy test in a chess move to stem the flow of the poorest and least educated immigrants, namely eastern and southern Europeans. Everyone from Italian grandfathers to the Lithuanian milkman to the shtetl tailor was excluded, but most especially women.

It's hard to know if my family was aware that the nation's restrictive immigration policies that had started with us were now targeting their closest neighbors. Certainly Dek Foon, who was still working part-time as an immigration translator, would have been aware of it, as was Doshim, whose business partners were also immigrants. I can see from the census that about 25 percent of the building was European—mostly Italian families, who could now, like my own family, consider themselves lucky to have gotten through.

Nineteen seventeen was also the year New York finally granted women the right to vote, ratifying the bill two years later.

But this right would not be given to the women in my family.

When American women were finally granted suffrage by the federal government, Aunt Elva was excited about the prospect of voting in the upcoming presidential election. But a brutal new reality confronted her.

Only a few years after she and Dek were married, with little fanfare, and minimal coverage in the press, Congress passed a law affecting women's citizenship.

The 1907 Expatriation Act, which targeted dual citizenship, stripped native-born women who had married foreigners of their U.S. citizenship—claiming it now reflected that of their husbands. A woman who married an English, Dutch, or German man became English, Dutch, or German.

The law was retroactive.

Suddenly Elva, in the eyes of the law, became *Chinese*. White women who married outside the race, like Elva, were seen as traitors.

Even wealthy heiresses who married European nobility—think Cora Crawley, Lady Grantham, in *Downton Abbey*—were viewed as deserters for another reason. Not only were they leaving the American gene pool, they were also spreading their resources and money outside of national borders.

Aunt Elva and the other wives of Dek Foon's band of brothers had no idea on that early spring day, March 2, 1907, when Congress signed the Expatriation Act, that they had all become Chinese.

Since most women were not aware of this act, there's a pretty good chance that our Elva had no idea that she had lost her citizenship until she registered to vote. I can only imagine her expression and indignation when she opened her mail that day and found a letter denying her registration application on the grounds that she was not a U.S. citizen.

How does it feel to suddenly learn that you are no longer a citizen of the country in which you were born?

Then, when she learned *why*, and that, unlike women who had married European foreigners—or any other foreigners, for that matter—husbands who might later become naturalized American citizens, because Chinese were prevented from becoming citizens she too might not ever be eligible to regain her citizenship or to vote . . . Elva's rage is red-hot and alive to me more than a hundred years later.

How could this happen?

How was she no longer "American" but "Chinese"?

What did that even *mean*?

I imagine that her mind looped as mine would have if I had found out that my country had deserted me based on my marital decisions and gender, ex post facto.

As AUNT ELVA CONTENDED with the loss of her citizenship, that technically she was no longer "an American," Great-Grandfather Doshim was busy trying to prove that *he was*.

By this time, Doshim had expanded out of laundry supplies to include banking, and set up his office upstairs on the second floor of 44 Mott Street. His business, Lun Tai, was now well established in the neighborhood as a "foreign money exchange," with the Bank of Canton, headquartered in San Francisco, as his chief affiliation. (The Bank of Canton was the first Chinese-owned bank in colonial Hong Kong, and started by overseas Cantonese.) Chinatown then, as now, was largely a cash economy, and banks often refused to give loans to Chinese. With international banking between the U.S. and China practically nonexistent, many Chinese could find help only within the community itself—going to bankers like Dek Foon and Doshim.

I was researching Doshim online via Ancestry, when I stumbled upon his draft registration card.

On September 12, 1918, forty-year-old Doshim left the office early and headed toward the draft registration board on Baxter Street—the shop signage transforming from Chinese and English to Italian. Once there, he voluntarily enlisted to serve the country.

He was middle-aged and myopic, and never a likely draft pick. Unlike the other side of my family, Doshim had never even thrown a punch. The man jokingly referred to as Bowtie Jesus really did believe in *turn the other cheek*.

He didn't have to register for the draft. His age and position as head of household, with so many young ones under ten years old, exempted him from service.

At first, I couldn't figure it out. Why risk your life by signing up for the armed services to represent a country that prevented you from becoming a citizen, no matter how hard you tried? Why register in the first place?

I looked at his date of registration. Doshim had registered for the draft on the very first day that registration opened for his age group—*Doshim had marched over to the registration offices on the very first day he was eligible.* And after sifting through more records, I learned that he did it again for World War II.

There was only one possible answer.

Great-Grandfather, and the other Chinese like him who enlisted in the draft that year, may have been past their prime as soldiers, but they still wanted to prove to the U.S. government that they were *patriotic Americans.*

That explained the exuberantly large signature on the World War I draft card, with a "D" the size of a platter and a long "m" for the finish that dangled like a panther's tail from a treetop.

I am here, that signature said. *You cannot deny my efforts.*

14

The Flu of 1918

Ng-Doshim Family Apt. 31 & Chin Family Apt. 23

伍 陳

In the fall of 1918, New York City succumbed to one of the worst epidemics it had ever seen.

They called it the Spanish Flu, the Flu, and the Three-Day Fever. Residents who were fine one day could not get out of bed the next.

Hospital patients gasped for breath as their lungs filled with "frothy," "bloody" fluid.

It overran the city, hospitals were full to capacity with sick patients, and children were forced to triple up in beds.

Great-Grandmother Chun, no stranger to a pandemic, flew into action.

Every window in apartment 31 was flung open, creating a cross-draft from the street to the back of their apartment.

Nurse Chun enlisted the help of Doshim and the children to open the hallway windows on every floor, including the back and the front stair-wells, so that even the corridors had circulating air. She even solicited the landlord to keep the rooftop doors open as well.

When the other mothers asked what she was doing, Chun used words like *ventilation* and *air circulation* (calling it air *chi*, likening it to a kind of feng shui) and instructed them to open the windows in their apartments.

She instructed them to wash their hands several times a day, and have their children do so too.

Chun was used to quizzical or blank expressions on patients' faces in Hong Kong from her days tending laboring mothers and their family members on Western hygiene. She didn't think that her neighbors were backwards or look down on them when they asked about drafts and staying warm. Like them, she grew up in a village where there was no running water—where you had to get your water from a well—and knew that basic hygiene had to be taught, like she had been taught by the nursing matron in Hong Kong.

She instructed the other wives to wear layers, even around the house, and to keep the "cold" off their organs and necks with sweaters and scarves.

Chun was grateful to live in a new building with running water in every unit, and for her training. Although it's likely she never heard of Jacob Riis's efforts to modernize New York City tenement living, she and every resident of Sun Lau benefited from them: every room in every apartment, even the bathroom, had a window that faced either the street or a courtyard. (I'm hoping too that she was equally unaware of how awfully racist Riis was about Chinese residents of the Five Points.)

When the Board of Health nurses came to Chinatown, Chun was there to help distribute the fresh linens and supplies to all the Chinese families in the building (they turned down the soups, preferring their own). She translated questions and answers as best as she could.

The pandemic spread globally, infecting a third of the world's population, and nearly three-quarters of a million Americans would die, including tens of thousands of New Yorkers. Although it's unknown how many residents of the building were saved by Chun's efforts, certainly in part thanks to her, no one in the Doshim or the Chin household that year died from contracting it.

Then, later that very same year, the city found itself in the grips of yet another disease—one that attacked the very young and the very old, including our vertical village at 37 Mott Street. They called it the "plague among children," the "throat distemper," "the kiss of death," and later, diphtheria. Many considered it a death sentence.

One morning, all the members of the Chin family suddenly woke up with sore throats and swollen glands. Although nearly everyone recovered in a matter of days, Ngo, the youngest, had symptoms that only worsened, and his tears became more copious.

When he opened his mouth, Yulan noticed a strange growth blooming at the back of his throat. Soon he was making noises like he was being strangled. After consulting with Chun upstairs, she quarantined the child from his siblings, sleeping on a cot in the living room, away from his brothers, who were grateful to be free of the noise.

Then, one morning, they simply couldn't hear him anymore.

Although a treatment had recently been developed, it wouldn't be rolled out to the general public for a few more years, too late for the youngest Chin son on Mott Street, whose body was brought to the undertaker downstairs.

This time it was Great-Grandmother Chun's turn to make food— good, solid Hakka soul food—knocking gently on her neighbor's door.

CHIN ON PRIDED HIMSELF on being a stoic and a pragmatist. No one had ever seen him cry, not even for the death of a toddler son.

Why waste tears on the inevitable? We all die sometime.

By this time, the Chin brothers had bought up more property in Newark's Chinatown—purchasing a multistory warehouse in the heart of the community that contained:

1. a ground-level gambling parlor
2. a second-floor tea parlor
3. an opium den in the basement
4. a top-level brothel

Details about this multiuse establishment are scarce, but Chin On was delighted by the cash that came streaming in. It was noted that just like in the early days of Tammany Hall, the local Newark police were only too happy to take bribes to look the other way.

The Chin brothers imported high-end silk items, porcelain, various teas, and fresh caladium bulbs that could be forced to bloom for Chinese New Year. Their freight ships transported their cargo from Brother Jun's business, New Ying Chong, in Hong Kong, for not only their own stores and restaurants but top department stores like Macy's and Wanamaker's as well—their network spreading up and down the Eastern Seaboard and to the Midwest. ("It was a big, big business. A big, big business," my great-aunt later recalled.) According to Lung and Jack, whenever they arrived at stores to meet with buyers, their father never had to wait.

Mr. Chin is here, the receptionist would announce, and they were always ushered right in.

At first, the opium exporting started with their own consumption, back when it was still legal, but as the laws changed—the Smoking Opium Exclusion Act was the first law criminalizing a drug in the U.S.—and their own habits and demand for it grew, they began smuggling it into the country, eventually bringing in huge quantities of it nestled inside giant soy sauce containers.

Chin On was bringing home serious money. Giant twenty- and fifty-pound paper sacks full of money, which he carried up the front stairwell and into the apartment. On those nights, he was beaming when he flung the door open—whenever Baba came home with a giant sack, everyone knew it was going to be a good time. Sometimes he even tossed the money high up into the air, so that they were showered with lucky, fluttering greenbacks.

One night, as the children crowded around, and Yulan watched from the sidelines, Chin On dumped the contents of the sack onto the kitchen table.

Suddenly they were surrounded by piles of banknotes, singles, and five-spots the color of iceberg lettuce. *Gimme gimme gimme!* they cried, despite Yulan's admonitions: *Don't grab.*

Chin On allowed his sons to help count the bills. There was so much money it overflowed the table and took the entire family's help to collect it, but they listened to Baba's directions—all the money facing in one direction like soldiers—while their mother calmly nudged the contents closer to the center of the table, catching whatever fell to the floor.

Yulan and the children were also busy with their own branch of the family business.

When Prohibition went into full effect, Yulan, who had already been making the rice wine version of bathtub gin in a bucket in their claw-foot tub, ramped up production in apartment 23. She wasn't the only one—several mothers, except of course Chun, the church lady upstairs, also began brewing it in their bathrooms. It was so easy—this Temperance thing was making her Mott Street hooch a real commodity—that it seemed stupid not to continue making more, so she had Chin On get her a few more lidded containers and tripled the quantity. This way, she single-handedly provided rice wine for their establishments throughout New York City and New Jersey.

Even the children were put to work. Calvin, one of the younger sons, recalled delivering brown parcel-paper-wrapped packages to stores and underground gambling parlors in his knapsack when he was still in grade school. Often, the proprietors tipped him and gave him a treat. Only later did he learn that he had been transporting packages of opium for his father.

No ONE KNEW WHEN IT STARTED EXACTLY, but sometime around the 1910s and 1920s, Uncle Dek began actively helping new arrivals get their foot in the door.

Perhaps it started with a villager that he knew, or that villager's cousin or good friend. Perhaps after that, the word began to spread that there was an interpreter on the inside who could help uncle or auntie through the system.

I learned this after finally tracking down Dek Foon's descendants in Hong Kong and Virginia, and while many of the details are fuzzy, this is what we know for certain:

By the 1920s, our fellow villagers from Shun On, fleeing a famine, traveled by boat to Hong Kong. Once there, they lodged in a building that Dek had purchased for Chow and his family, until their ship came in, before it was time to enter the long hold of steerage, as Dek himself had done so many decades before.

They took passage through New York or Boston, depending on the period, hoping they would land Uncle Dek as their interpreter. They could consider themselves lucky if they did. During the grueling inter-rogations, Dek Foon would stall to give them more time. He coached them when they answered incorrectly or simply didn't know.

Just open your mouth and say something, he would prompt them, after which he gave the immigration officer and stenographer the correct answer.

Exactly how many times this happened no one could confirm, but my sense is this occurred for years.

I couldn't help but think back to how Dek Foon and his band of Christian brothers fought so hard for our rights, and how, after Chinese

Exclusion was made permanent, their dreams of it ever changing within their lifetimes were dashed.

Instead, this man whom I had always seen as boringly *squeaky clean* continued to do his best by helping from inside the system—even though he put himself at risk of deportation.

In addition to the many villagers who got through with his aid, I learned about others he had helped from his Exclusion file in Boston. There was the Chinese American Gertrude Chew, who married her Chinese college classmate and subsequently lost her citizenship like Aunt Elva. Once she returned to the U.S., after divorcing her husband, she got stuck in Seattle detention for months. A Wellesley graduate with a U.S. passport, Chew was shocked at how they were treated. It was Uncle Dek who greased the wheels, enabling her and her child to eventually be freed.

I later learned that Uncle Dek acted as an informant as well. In his file, not only were there notes by Wiley that he had provided material evidence against Chinese trying to enter the country, but there was a memo written by Dek, tipping officials off to some who had been smuggled into Boston's Chinatown. There were even two letters sent in by irate Chinese calling him "cunning and wicked," a "turtle," and a "stub-tailed dragon." (Some of the names and return addresses turned out to be fake.)

I was initially dismayed about Dek's whistleblowing against other Chinese. Was he really a traitor or *on the take* as those anonymous accusers claimed? Knowing him through the family stories and the written record, I didn't believe that Uncle Dek was actually extorting money, although the evidence showed that he reported others for trying to enter illegally—illegal solely for being Chinese. But while it's hard for me to stomach the idea of him turning in his fellow countrymen, like all of us, suspicious until proved otherwise, Uncle Dek would have felt the pressure to prove his loyalty to his American colleagues and bosses.

It must have been a heavy burden trying to decide whom to help and whom to call out, or simply stand aside, and watch them enter, unaided, the web of suspicion that wrapped around us all.

Luckily, after an investigation, his colleagues at immigration dismissed the charges.

WHEN OLD TOM LEE passed away a few years earlier in 1918, a grand funeral procession made its way through the neighborhood. Chinatown locals and passersby stood five rows deep along Mott Street to watch the hearse—a glassy carriage with lit lamps, drawn by six horses, each animal flanked in netting and tassels that nearly brushed the ground—followed by a full Italian brass band, a Naughton specialty, playing "Nearer My God to Thee," until they made it to On Leong headquarters. It was the end of an era. Although there's an omission in all the English-language books about the succession of power, according to my grandfather's papers and oral history, and essays written by Uncle Jack and Uncle Calvin, Chin On and his brother were only too happy to take the reins.

Lung enjoyed bragging that whenever his father gambled, "he never lost." That's because Big Mr. Wong—Dai Lo Wong—stood behind him, his big arms crossed, glowering at the other gamblers. As Chin On's losses piled up, he simply ran up his credit, and the proprietors looked the other way.

But whenever someone borrowed money from the Chin brothers, and couldn't or wouldn't pay back their debts, Chin On sent Dai Lo Wong to pay a visit.

"Do you want me to use the gun or the hatchet?" Mr. Wong once asked.

After a careful pause, Chin On replied, "The gun makes too much noise."

Although Big Mr. Wong had a reputation among the Chin children as being a gentle and watchful enforcer, the butcher's son was never hesitant to turn an enemy of the family into human pork.

But those were the early days, when the Chin brothers needed to uphold a certain reputation.

After Tom Lee passed, Hing and Chin On led the charge in scouting out a new On Leong headquarters. The feeling was that On Leong had outgrown its dilapidated three-story home on lower Mott Street across from the Port Arthur, and after the death of Lee, it was time for a change. To usher in a new era in the organization, they purchased the building at 41 Mott Street, just two doors up from Sun Lau, and hired an architect to design it as a brand-new Chinese-style building.

Three years later, in October 1921, the new On Leong headquarters, with its open balcony terraces and red-tiled pagoda-shaped rooftop, was ready to be christened—its opening timed for the national On Leong convention. The building had a restaurant on the first two floors, residences, and a teakwood-paneled reception hall for On Leong members on the top floor. Just like our building, 41 Mott would be colloquially referred to by some in the neighborhood as the "New Building," Sun Lau.

On Mott Street, thousands of On Leongs, who traveled in from across the country—upwards of six thousand delegates from chapters in twenty cities across the East and Midwest—stood shoulder to shoulder with curious onlookers. To signal the shift in power, Hing, now president of On Leong, carried the ceremonial porcelain urn, representing the organization, in both hands. Great-Grandfather Chin On, the treasurer, carried the bright yellow On Leong flag with the red, white, and blue circle at the center like a bull's-eye. Together, they descended the steps of the old three-story building followed by the other leaders of On Leong and gathered on Mott Street. Just like today, the top brass wore suits and ties, but also fedoras. Lung and Jack, now adolescent teenagers, noted that their father looked up Mott Street with his jaw set, eyes watchful and serious the entire time.

Although there was a lull in fighting, Chin On and his brother knew that war between On Leong and Hip Sing could break out at any moment. All along the parade route, their enforcers and lieutenants, including Dai Wong, stood armed and ready.

Yulan and the mothers of 37 Mott Street watched from their windows above.

Even if Chin On was not carrying anything, Yulan would have been able to pick out her husband from his shoes and the angle of his fedora as he approached the elbow of Mott Street.

By the time he and his brother arrived at the building and turned to face the crowd, Yulan would have been holding her breath, watching from her window, while down below, a pair of lion dancers paraded before drummers and the building entrance, festooned with tall plants and red celebratory paper. Did the Chin brothers stand guard in front with the other leaders of On Leong, to receive the lions' blessings, as is done today, or did they go up and watch from the balcony, where it was safer? Either way, because of tensions with Hip Sing they may have forgone the firecrackers.

It was only after Yulan witnessed her husband and brother-in-law disappear into the building, the other On Leongs following behind, a sea of hats, that she shut the window and could breathe freely again.

But within a few short years, the peace deal between On Leong and Hip Sing would be scrapped.

English-language news gives cursory accounts of an On Leong by the name of Chin Jack Lem being expelled from Cleveland in January 1924, along with several of his followers, and, upon landing in Chicago, switching sides to Hip Sing—the ultimate betrayal. (Chin Jack Lem had been involved in an earlier tong war in New York in 1909, and most certainly my Chin family knew him from those days.) Around the same time period, according to family stories, a feud arose in Chicago (my grandfather's writing is infused with passive voice whenever our family members like his father may be potentially involved). Uncle Hing sent in his hatchet man "to settle the issue." When a Chin was murdered, Hing was blamed.

Coincidence? Probably not.

Either way, a Hip Sing placed a hit on his head, which was announced by the pounding of a declaration on the public notice board around the corner from the Chin brothers' stores. That Uncle Hing was a "wanted man" was nothing new, but because of the ferocity of the infighting both within On Leong and between the two tongs, this would be the greatest threat Uncle Hing had ever encountered up to that point.

He and his family were forced to move out of 37 Mott Street and flee for their lives.

By November 1924, the negotiations were so fraught that the head of the Chinese Consolidated Benevolent Association, the Reverend Lee To, the good pastor who had given Uncle Hing a landing place when he first arrived in New York, and who was the Doshim family's pastor as well, had a heart attack upstairs in the dining hall of the Port Arthur restaurant. This, while attempting to broker the kind of peace accord that Dek Foon and friends had celebrated there nearly two decades before.

Soon, Chins were being targeted throughout the neighborhood, up and down Mott Street.

Mr. Chin Hing—a restaurant worker from Brooklyn, and also not our relation—walked into a restaurant on Doyers Street near the Chinese Theatre. When gunshots rang out, Hing hid in a nearby booth. The police arrived sometime later, only to discover him dead, his body riddled with bullets.

A dentist, Dr. Wah S. Chan—Chin and Chan are the same names, despite the vowel difference—was found stabbed to death at his clinic on Mott Street.

On December 14, Mr. Chin Song, the amiable neighborhood fruit peddler, closed up his stand on Pell and Mott, and headed home early, just across the street. He was juggling a bag of sweet mandarins and his keys as he opened the front door to his apartment in the rear of the building next door to ours, when some men caught up to him and shot him in the head. He was discovered lying in his own threshold, with $240 in his pocket, surrounded by oranges. According to the press, the killers slipped away from police-lined Mott Street, tossing the gun behind them, because the inner courtyard muffled the noise; but our families' apartments had rooms facing that area, and the Chin and Doshim mothers must have heard the gunshots from their kitchen windows as they were preparing dinner.

Much of what happened next is sketchy at best.

For his own safety, my great-grandparents plucked Lung, now a teen-ager at Stuyvesant High School, out of public school and shipped him off to Mount Hermon in Massachusetts—the same prep school that Doshim had attended at the turn of the century.

Shortly after, when Jack, while running an errand for his father on Pell Street, witnessed a man get shot in the head, and returned home in shock and covered in blood, they sent him to Mount Hermon as well.

Was Chin On surprised when a hit notice for him appeared on the public notice board around the corner from our building? I don't think so.

Although my Chin family swears that Great-Grandfather Chin On had nothing to do with the murder in Chicago, being Hing's brother and business partner, he was soon implicated for it.

With the eldest boys safely tucked away out of state, Chin On and Yulan decided it was best to leave town.

Big Brother Wong traveled with Yulan and the youngest Chin sons as they took the cross-country train along the northern route. In his Exclusion file, Jocko, whom I was surprised to find a file for since he was born here and a citizen, is pictured as a wide-eyed four-year-old sporting a bowl cut and a sailor suit.

But who was to protect Chin On?

Right before they sent him off to prep school, sixteen-year-old Lung had grown into something of a playboy bruiser. Lanky and handsome, he loved smoking and gambling and had trained as a boxer. He regularly cut school to hang out at the pool halls in the neighborhood, including the one owned by his father, until Chin On got wind of it and chased him out.

On the weekends, when Lung wasn't boxing or practicing his kung fu, he and his brothers took the train up to the northern tip of Manhattan, a kind of wild New York, where they went fishing and brought home fluke and flounder. Big Brother Wong taught them how to shoot and throw knives, and soon Lung was the best shot of his brothers.

It was already feared that Lung was succumbing to too many of the temptations of Bowery life—*a tiger father does not sire little puppy dogs,* as they say in our dialect. Even Yulan could see that Lung was taking after her husband.

Although he was nearly denied entry because he admitted to smoking, Lung arrived at boarding school that year, bringing with him a case-load of cigars, Cubans, rolled by the hand of local Chinese cigar-rollers. A budding entrepreneur, he sold these individually to his new prep school friends at a profit. He also brought several bottles of his mother's home brew.

After class, he started a social club, his own version of "study hall," where he tipped the liquor into tiny glasses and taught the boys on his floor how to play Chinese poker. As the house, Lung naturally took his cut, and had soon amassed a tidy sum that meant he didn't have to completely rely on the nominal amount of spending money his father provided him—for all his bags full of money, Chin On was still a notorious cheapskate.

When the hit was placed on his father's head, Lung was yanked out of prep school and ordered to protect him.

Chin On and Lung traveled out of the area by train, retracing their steps across the country, only now Lung was the one carrying the gun.

He just hoped he wouldn't have to fire it.

BACK IN CHINATOWN, as the Tong Wars escalated, local police were soon joined by federal agencies.

Soon the entire Chinese community was cordoned off and placed under scrutiny like a living specimen under a lens. Starting on September 11,

1925, the police, working alongside the federal secret service, conducted a series of midnight raids that sometimes lasted until the sun rose—smashing windows and busting down the doors of gambling parlors, businesses, and even family association buildings on every block from the center of Chinatown to Allen Street in the Lower East Side. They harassed any Chinese they encountered, demanding to see their registration IDs. If the person questioned didn't have it, he was arrested, shoved into a police wagon, and brought before a judge.

A new law had been proposed the year before—the most restrictive immigration law the country had ever seen. Under the Immigration Act of 1924, all nationals from Asian countries were banned from immigrating, with the sole exception of the Philippines—and with a brand-new quota system set up for other countries. The quota, based on the 1890 census, allowed higher immigration from English-speaking countries and western Europe, while limiting everyone else. It easily passed with a two-thirds majority in the Senate and House, during the presidential election year of Calvin Coolidge.

Police raided the Chinese Theatre on Doyers Street, site of our fundraiser for the Jews of Kishinev, and the nearby Thalia Theatre on the Bowery during full-blown, standing-room-only performances. Officials emptied the theaters, dragging out every Chinese attendee onto the street in order to check their paperwork.

The New York Times reported that the actors and band continued their performances to absolutely no audience.

That was the custom of the Chinese, according to one police detective. *These artists were under contract to give the performance . . . and living up to the Chinese tradition of good faith, they continued to the end, audience or no audience.*

This may have been true, but here's another more salient reason: continuing to perform provided the performers a measure of insulation from scrutiny.

By performing, they proved they were *artists, not laborers.*

But as time wore on, and the tong war violence continued, the U.S. district attorney doubled down on the raids, conflating the war between On Leong and Hip Sing with illegal immigrant activity. They raided restaurants, workers' dorms, pool halls, and tong headquarters. They pulled laundrymen from behind their ironing boards, took proprietors from their restaurants, and harassed students learning English at the local Baptist church right in the middle of night class.

They returned to the theaters, and this time brought in both the audience *and* the performers.

At midnight on September 14, a peace deal was brokered between On Leong and Hip Sing, but the district attorney announced that the searches would continue.

"If the Hip Sings and the On Leongs are going to get along without killing, well and good," he said, quoted in *The New York Times*. "But the Immigration Law is the Immigration Law. . . . Chinese unlawfully in this country are subject to deportation, whether there is or is not a tong war. . . . Those found unlawfully here will be deported."

When the officers began raiding homes, they came around to every residence in Chinatown, banging on doors, including on Mott Street.

Downstairs, the Chin family had long since made it safely back to our villages in Kwong Hoy.

Eldest son Hong, in charge of Ying Chong while Chin On was away—someone had to hold down the fort—was just about to close up shop when law enforcement burst through the door. While he was legitimately a *son of a merchant*, because his father had given his identity away so many years before, Hong had to show officials the papers that Chin On had purchased for him.

On the fifth floor, the Doshim family could hear the police and secret service storming the buildings up and down the block. Doshim was now a rich and well-connected merchant, with a laundry supply business that extended from Canada, up and down the Eastern Seaboard, and out to

Havana, Cuba, where there was a significant Chinese population in need of Paragon washers and Dek Foon's ironing machines, plus his banking business and ticketing agency for the Great Northern Railway.

But even Doshim's connections couldn't prevent the raids that were unfolding all around them.

At Sun Lau, agents entered through the front doors and rushed the vestibule.

They banged on each apartment, one by one, and the sounds of their fists against doors and their footsteps echoed through the building. Thankfully, the children had been put to sleep early, and Chun shut the window, before going back to her prayers.

Great-Grandmother Chun, several months pregnant again, was deeply afraid.

The family had grown to include another daughter after my grandmother Rose—five children now in total. Although Rose and most of her siblings were American born—birthed at home in Brooklyn or on Mott

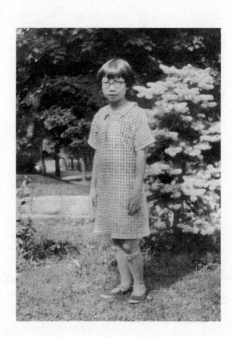

Rose, age nine, 1926

Street—you'll remember that Chun and Oilily had no papers. They were undocumented.

It's unknown whether or not Lily, now a willowy sixteen-year-old with a flapper haircut, had any understanding about her status. No other nationality had to have papers with them at all times, and as a child, Lily had largely been cushioned from immigration pressures. I'm sure Chun and Doshim kept this information from her as long as possible.

When the authorities approached the fifth floor, the children were asleep, tucked into their room, far from the entrance. At Doshim's warning, the adults remained quiet. Earlier that day, because he couldn't have moved the family without flagging officials, Doshim had put out an urgent call to Dek Foon at the immigration service.

I'll see what I can do, Dek had said.

Our uncle made several calls from the office, but because the raids involved several different agencies, including the feds, his sources were powerless to stop them, although they did give him information. Dek left work immediately and, upon arriving home, began packing a bag, when Aunt Elva inquired about what was going on.

That evening, sitting very still in his chair, Doshim felt like the nervous Shim of yesteryear, despite the streaks of gray that now appeared increasingly at his temples. He had been the one who convinced Chun to leave her home and family behind for the wonders of the West and New York. Although he could have easily fixed it for her by purchasing papers, Chun had never wanted to live a lie and under an identity that wasn't her own.

They sat quietly in the living room, listening to the sounds of banging and shouting still audible through the closed doors and windows. As Doshim sat waiting for the knock on their door, he couldn't help wondering if they had done the right thing after all.

When officials banged on their door, it was loud and insistent, and the door rattled in its frame. *Police, open up!*

From outside, the door looked like any of the others. They banged again, this time threatening to break it down.

When the latch finally unlocked and the door creaked open, the police may have been quite surprised to see a tall, middle-aged white woman—her considerable girth filling the doorframe.

Elva May Foon, dressed conservatively in a dressing gown that practically touched the floor, granny-style, glowered at the agents from behind little round glasses with all the displeasure of a Sunday school teacher.

It must have struck something like fear in the heart of each man standing there.

Instead of rushing in, like they did when they raided other households, they paused.

"What is the meaning of all this?" she asked, never taking her hand away from the doorframe.

Elva, who had volunteered to come when Dek informed her about the raids, wasn't about to let them take her family away.

For the officers standing at the threshold, Elva resembled their angry, disapproving mother, aunt, or teacher. Who could blame them if they had an almost visceral, knee-jerk reaction—a current of fear coursing through their torsos up to their faces now reddening with shame, caught within Elva's stern gaze?

"Sorry, ma'am, we're looking for Chinese," they said. "You know, evading the law."

"Does it look like I'm a Chinese?" she asked, leaning in, with a slight tilt of her head.

"Sorry, ma'am, didn't mean to disturb you."

"You should be ashamed of yourselves, disturbing good people in the middle of the night!" she said.

Did they apologize again? Or did they thank her, trying to get away from Elva's hard stare as quickly as possible?

When she slammed the door shut—hard—the sound reverberated down the hallway like a slap in the face. It was only when they heard the sounds of the footsteps retreating that the Doshim family, Aunt Elva included, felt like they could finally relax.

Nearly one hundred years later, I read about these raids in newspaper articles from the safety of my studio. After several moments where I can feel the blood draining from my face, I try to shake off the feeling, and continue reading.

In the end, the midnight raids continued for days, rounding up more than 1,200 Chinese. Some of them were arrested more than once because the police didn't trust them when they said they had earlier been brought up in front of a judge and dismissed.

Even allowing for the double arrests, this number is estimated to be one-third to one-half of all the Chinese residents of Chinatown.

Two hundred and six Chinese, mainly seamen laid off in New York at the end of World War I who couldn't afford the return fare home, were processed for deportation.

I FEEL A HEAVINESS IN THE CHEST, like it's hard to take a deep breath. Over the course of the next hour before lunch and then again in the midafternoon, I take several breaks away from my desk and the articles and books that are breaking my heart.

Get water.

Make tea.

Prepare a snack.

My aversion to reading these articles is real, and my body wants to put as much distance between them and myself as possible.

I want to protect Chun and Oilily as much as possible. I want to place myself as Elva did like a barrier between my family's fears and the knocking on the door.

The family would have been split apart, like so many Chinese families during this period. Chun would have given birth to their next baby in Hong Kong.

In the family portrait taken the following year from Grandma Rose's album, Dek and Elva are sitting in the center, surrounded by the Doshims, the patriarch and matriarch of us all.

Chun has given birth to the new littlest Doshim daughter—Dorothy, a big-eyed toddler in a white dress and black leather lace-up shoes, sitting on her mother's lap.

Chun, who has always looked tired to me in this picture, appears guarded, eyeing the camera suspiciously. She is thirty-eight years old in this photo, but she looks a full decade older. I had always assumed that this mother of six was simply worn out from running after so many young children, but now after reading so many of these news articles, I sense that much of this is fear of the authorities, and what might happen to them if she was found out.

I can't shake the feeling that she was gazing out at us back in 1926, as if the photographic evidence might do her some harm.

NEARLY A CENTURY HAS PASSED, and my family no longer has to endure such treatment, but I think about the undocumented men and women of this generation from so many countries who are living in fear today. I teach in the most conservative borough in New York City, and whenever the discussion of immigration comes up, I've heard students say, *It's not fair if these people skip the line. My family had to wait, these people should wait like everyone else.*

It's the law.

My heart rate grows rapid whenever I hear this, and so I always have to pause a moment. My *these people should wait their turn* students are espousing an idea that immigration is a level playing field, when for so long we know that hasn't been true.

I can always feel a certain unease within myself—at its worst it feels

Chun, 1927

*Chun and daughters, flanked
by Elva and Dek, 1926*

like blazing annihilation, where everything is being torn apart from under my feet—and I'm sure this is similar for many of the immigrant and first-generation students in the room. For me the question is, Why are exclusionary practices still so persistent to this day? Why is the fear of the Other so potent in the cultural imagination, when in truth, we live in such an interconnected world?

15

Paper Families

Wong Family, Ng-Doshim Family Apt. 31 & Chin Family Apts. 22 and 23

黄 伍 陳

When Great-Great-Grandfather Yuan Son arrived home after nearly three decades in Gum San, he did not resettle in Hong Kong as Dek Foon's son, Chow, and the eldest Chin brother, Jun, both did—Chinese who had developed a taste for big-city conveniences. Instead, the former railroad worker turned Boise merchant returned home to his village near the center of Toisan, where he was lauded as a rich, prosperous man.

The homecoming feast lasted for days and included all the Wongs in the village—practically the entire town—and each of the neighboring villages within walking distance. Platter upon platter arrived, a never-ending party of braised and stir-fried delights, including fresh-caught seafood; local eel and salted fish casserole atop mounds of rice, the bottom crackling in the clay pot; legendary portions of roast pork; sautéed cauliflower and lap cheong sliced by the hands of the aunties, the cauliflower a local variety with spaced florets resembling white sea coral.

It was food Yuan Son had not eaten in decades. Country-style yet subtle—not too ham or ho ham, disdainfully salty, or sai gwai gum ham, deathly ghostly salty. No, it was sheer perfection, and at the first morsel his eyes watered from the pleasure and the pain of what he had been missing—this village by the stream, surrounded by fields of banana groves and hairy root vegetables, this land tilled by the strength of Toisan people, and the lone water buffalo that created the grooves for the year-round planting that this lush and humid climate afforded.

Perhaps his eyes welled up for what could have been, but which never was.

Now middle-aged, Yuan Son, whose name meant "distant and new," or a New Distance, settled down, married, and grew potbellied. His wife, whose name has been lost to history, blessed him with children, including two sons.

These two sons were given the kind of education and advantages that a Gold Mountain man like Yuan Son could afford. The eldest, Woon Mun, who was more adventurous than his brother, was restless at school. He yearned to cross the ocean like their father and try out his hand at the Beautiful Country.

Sow Lei, the younger son, excelled at school, taking the imperial exams in the final years of the Ching dynasty, and like my Chin great-grandfather, he too landed a placement as a teacher. Sow Lei eventually had several children of his own, including a rambunctious son so beautiful his sisters dressed him up like a doll, my grandfather Kai Fei, later known as Gene.

The Wong (黃) family traced their lineage all the way back to

Huangdi, the legendary Yellow Emperor, a mythic ruler credited with creating the lunar calendar, and laying down the basic tenets of Taoism and the foundations of Chinese medicine. Genealogically speaking, tracing your ancestry back to Huangdi, whether he was a historical figure or a myth, was rather the equivalent of being a *Mayflower* descendant or discovering you were descended from Cleopatra or Julius Caesar, except the Yellow Emperor predates them all (2697–2597 BCE).

Aside from Huangdi, our next most esteemed ancestor was Wong Yue, a scholar who, during the earliest years of the Song dynasty in 965 CE, had placed at the top of the imperial exams, earning his name, Highest Mountain Peak. Wong Yue eventually became a governor, and later, a minister of the military bureau of a regional northern city.

A rich and prosperous man, Wong Yue had three wives, who each bore him seven sons. (*What about the daughters?* I always wonder, but the stories never include the daughters.) Because of the continuous threat of warfare and military coups in the region, Wong Yue ordered all but his three firstborn sons to relocate, spreading out farther south to seek their own fortunes.

It is from one of these *non*-firstborn sons that Yuan Son was descended.

Although it felt good to be back in his village, looking at the familiar mountains, so gentle compared to the soaring Sierra Nevada, and married life, retirement, and a gaggle of grandchildren suited him, Yuan Son couldn't help but think back on his time in America with some wistfulness.

What had they done to his store? he wondered. What of his friends? How was it possible the white people he knew could have turned on him so quickly?

He never told his family about the heartbreak of getting pushed out until way later, saving it up for the next generation, his grandson, my grandfather Gene.

He remembered the train journey back to the West Coast, some two and a half decades earlier, his seurng sum, his sinking, downward heart, threatening to descend into his spleen.

But he also recalled the way the locomotive ran on the railroad that he and the others had built, and how the landscape opened up all around him.

All along the track, where there was once only plains and prairie, sage and desert brush, herds of buffalo, mule deer, pronghorn, and big-horned sheep, small towns and settlements had cropped up along the edges of the stops like wildflowers after a spring rain.

Here and there, a train station, a white church steeple cutting into the wide blue sky, mountains in the distance, families waving, so that he too began waving, as they pulled out of every town.

It would happen again and again, as they crossed into states and territory on track that he and his countrymen had laid so many decades before, the familiar terrain and his teenage memories of it now made anew, as if gilded by a paintbrush.

When the train left the desert, a red dustbowl at his back, and began its slow climb toward the great Sierra Nevada, with its snow- and conifer-covered mountains, Yuan Son saw the mountain range he had not seen since he was a teenager.

The Sierra Nevada appeared as vast, impervious, and impenetrable as it did when he first laid eyes on it, except he knew the fuller story.

He held his breath when, with a sudden whoosh, they were swallowed by the first tunnel.

Inside the winding artery of the mountain, he wondered, *Who had he been when he was last here and helped blast and dig through this tunnel?*

Who was he now?

When the train emerged, his pupils contracted to the size of small black dots, blinded by a white, snowy landscape, a pastoral disturbed only by the sound of their locomotive.

He was the same, but he was different.

Yuan Son thought of his friends and countrymen whose remains lay buried under the snow and a carpet of pine needles, forced to forever wander about as ghosts in this barbarian land. Ghosts that if the gwai lo had their way would be separated from their ghostly brethren, still drawing up laws to separate and exclude them, chasing them from their eternal slumber with torches and guns.

He looked over the vast landscape, covered in a blanket of snow, so silent and seemingly untouched that it was almost as if he had never left.

WHEN HIS OLDEST SON begged him to send him to Gold Mountain, Yuan Son was hesitant.

What if what happened to him, happened to his son? The laws against them had only worsened and become permanent by the time Yuan Son had landed back in Toisan. How could he protect his son against the outbursts of an angry mob? (*Stay alive,* I can hear him saying, *just stay alive.*)

But the firstborn son had his heart set on the Beautiful Country.

By this time, it was several years after the earthquake that had created a giant rupture in the wall of Exclusion through which my family now hoped to enter.

Intrepid Chinese, escaping the years of chaos and warlordism that had broken out in this early Republic period, could now claim that they or their fathers were born in California. And as a "son of a citizen," each could now gain a foothold in the scaffolding of Exclusion.

They called themselves "paper sons."

Entire networks were created from mounds of "paper."

Paper fathers. Paper uncles. Paper relatives.

And later, paper wives and paper daughters.

The first time I heard the term "paper name" while staring at that envelope at my grandparents' house addressed to "Sun Ming Wong," and later "paper son," I thought of daisy chains of paper children. I could not

Gene Wong, 1939

understand what it had to do with anyone in my family, or the people we knew.

It was only later that I learned about how American laws had reduced us to paper people—flat, two-dimensional sheets of biographical fiction, date-stamped and cross-examined and scrutinized for errors and inconsistencies, then made into duplicate and triplicate before being slipped into folders in drawers, only to be drawn out when another paper person sought refuge in America.

Finally, Yuan Son relented.

Although his son's paternity would list another Gold Mountain man's name, Yuan Son and I both knew that in reality the railroad builder's firstborn was a son of America.

And later, my grandfather, who left after him, one of its grandsons.

MY FAMILY REMEMBERS WHEN Chin Gee Hee, the Seattle-based merchant whose wife, Lenoi Louie, had lost their baby during the anti-Chinese attacks decades before, returned to our region in the early twentieth century, and hatched a plan to build a railroad. The Sun Ning Railroad, financed by overseas Chinese money and Chin Gee Hee's deep pockets, extended from the northern part of Toisan, before spreading out to our southern villages. Old Yuan Son, now white-haired and walking with a wooden cane, helped advise the construction team.

By the time my grandfather Kai Fei was born in 1920, the railroad extended through Toisan City and out to the neighboring villages. When Sow Lei became a leading official in the town, Kai Fei was entering elementary school; his father had risen up from school principal to town magistrate—he even had an office at Sun Ning railway. I imagine this was when Yuan Son started opening up to his grandson, my grandfather, about his days on the railroad.

Central Pacific.

Southern Pacific.

Union Pacific.

There he was, learning his first words in English, and one of the first stories he would tell me was about Yuan Son, over fifty years later and half a world away.

Grandpa, a notoriously incorrigible student ("I was so bad, I used to kick my books at my tutor and chase him out of the house"), noted the names of the country's railroad companies in English better than any history lesson at school. His pride in the accomplishments of his grandfather shone in his eyes whenever he recounted them.

When he was growing up, his uncle returned home intermittently from America to see his wife and children, and had taken on the American name of George. Uncle George lived in New York City and was working as a waiter in a Cantonese restaurant in midtown Manhattan. (*So many lights, you can't even see the stars at night. In Manhattan, the buildings take the place of stars!*)

Before he left, Uncle George had told the immigration authorities that he had four sons. In truth, he had two, but the extra slots were in case anyone else in the family needed them, or in the event that he needed to make extra money. Why not profit, as the Americans did, off the system in place that caused so many of their countrymen so much misery?

Come join me in America when you get older, Uncle George said, when Kai Fei was a crafty twelve-year-old who preferred playing games and riddles over school. This was just before Uncle George sailed back out again.

It was 1926 when Chin On finally returned back to New York, after several years in Hong Kong—years spent gambling, drinking, and most of all, smoking opium. In the family portrait taken just a few years after his return, the Chin patriarch sits on a leather couch looking thinner, his face harder, his jaw tight, while Yulan sits beside him, face rounder, her mouth set into a slight frown. There is clearly ill will between the pair, with Yulan not liking his being back home one bit.

Hong sits with his and Annabelle's growing family—two young sons and a daughter, Shirley, the oldest—on one end of the couch, while Lung sits on the opposite end of the row, in an armchair, flanked by his younger brothers Jack and Calvin; the littlest sons are crowded around their father. Each of the Chin boys has inherited Chin On's long, thin hands with the piano-length fingers (and for the first time, I see where I get mine from as well).

Although successful, it wasn't easy for them, even in Chinatown.

When the children were first starting out at elementary school, they were picked on by the Irish and Italian kids, who'd yell, *Go back to where you came from!* It was common knowledge that if you walked home by Mulberry Street, which was its own Italian neighborhood, you were going to get the crap beaten out of you.

Even the adults had to contend with such abuses.

Once, older brother Hong, a married man with a growing brood of children, was working downstairs in the basement of Sun Yuen Hing on Pell Street. A drunken man appeared at the top of the open hatch doors, and vomited straight down the stairs.

Hong rushed up to the street level. "What are you doing?" he said, more a statement than a question.

"I'm a white man," the lofan yelled. Hong could smell the alcohol off his breath. "I can do anything I want in Chinatown!"

When the stranger rushed toward him, arms flailing, Hong knew better than to meet him head-on. Instead, Uncle Hong stepped to one side—thrusting his fist out as the man lunged forward. It was a perfectly executed lesson in kung fu mechanics.

A moment later, according to Jack, the man was "spitting teeth like kernel corn from his bloody whisky-stinking mouth."

When the on-duty police officer, whom the kids all called Frank the Cop, took one look at the situation he told the drunk, *Beat it.*

CHIN ON FIGURED THAT HE AND YULAN would stay in New York until his retirement, after which they could return in style to Kwong Hoy, or relocate to Hong Kong. Until then, he soon discovered that there were still business opportunities open to someone who wasn't afraid of a little risk.

While the city was enjoying a burgeoning jazz movement, and women cut their hair into bobs, tossed their corsets, and raised their hemlines, Chin On, the consummate gambler, invested in a giant luxury nightclub-restaurant on Broadway, the Palais d'Or. Formerly a French restaurant sporting the "largest restaurant dance floor in New York City," the Palais was the venue for the big band era—serving high-end Chinese food with a hefty dose of glamour—with resident bandleader Benny A. Rolfe and his Palais d'Or orchestra performing live radio broadcasts over upwards of forty stations, reaching millions of listeners. With renditions of "Let's Do It (Let's Fall in Love)" and the swoony "Lover, Come Back to Me,"

*Lung, Hong,
and Jack, 1929*

they were the leading band on the radio, and their performances helped fill the nine-hundred-capacity restaurant with droves of diners and big band music lovers. Chin On loved the glamour, the party atmosphere, the revenue, and the attention from women that came along with being a big-shot owner.

Ever since returning home from prep school, Lung was on course to becoming the biggest good-for-nothing in Chinatown. Aside from his job as headwaiter at the Palais d'Or, for which he wore his best suit and pomaded his hair, Lung preferred to spend his free time cartooning, shooting pool, and writing love poetry to white girls who patronized the restaurant.

Now that Chin On was back, perhaps the one thing that he and Yulan could agree upon was that twenty-two-year-old Lung should straighten himself out and get married—perhaps to some nice jook sing, an American-born Chinese. But once they started asking around, they discovered that nearly everyone in Chinatown considered Lung a "bad boy," a sui jai, who *didn't like to work too much* or have a boss lording over him. No self-respecting Chinatown girl wanted to have anything to do with him, including my Doshim family, who, while they may have had a certain fondness for the Chin boy, still did not want Lily or any of the others to be near such a one as he. Even one of the witnesses for Lung's Exclusion Act file observed of the brothers working at Ying Chong, "Jack, I have seen in the store waiting on customers, but the other boy, I have never seen him doing anything."

The family would have to do it the old-fashioned way—in China, through a matchmaker. It was decided that Jack would also get married, and younger brother Calvin would go to boarding school at Lingnam University in Canton to get a good Chinese education; Yulan and other female family members would be in charge of coordinating with the matchmaker. And so they purchased tickets from Doshim, who booked their passage back home to Kwong Hoy.

According to Lung, when folks in California learned that he and Jack were going home to get married, the Chinese Californians, who called them "the rich Chins," took a picture of him and proclaimed, "The Prince of Merchants is going back to the Orient!"

They stayed in Kwong Hoy, in Yulan's village—the Lee village within sight of the ocean—while the matchmaker worked overtime trying to find candidates to their liking.

IN LATE OCTOBER 1929, the Roaring Twenties skidded to a halt, as the stock market crashed. Walking distance from Mott Street, bankers jumped from office windows to their deaths.

My grandmother Rose was twelve, and excelling academically, a bright spot.

Luckily, Doshim was not overextended, and he had a diversified portfolio long before that was a commonly used investment strategy. When desperate clients came to his office demanding their money, Great-Grandfather calmed them down, mainly because he was able to give them what they needed without going belly-up himself. Dek Foon, who, after handing over the reins of his banking business to Doshim, had moved with Elva to Boston for his work as an interpreter there, still maintained a significant bankroll as a backup. In addition to the bank, Doshim also worked for the Great Northern Railway Company—its only Chinese employee in the New York office. His own second-floor office on Mott Street, Lun Tai, was the main railroad ticket agency in the neighborhood.

So even while makeshift tent and cardboard cities cropped up all throughout the city, and folks slept in the parks and green fields in every borough—there was even a Hooverville in Central Park—Grandma Rose Mai and her siblings were largely shielded from the woes that other American families experienced.

As the Depression rolled on, Rose was a shoo-in for top honors as she approached graduating from PS 23. But it was decided that only boys could be valedictorian, so she would have to settle for salutatorian.

Nearby Stuyvesant, which the Chin brothers attended, was boys only, so Grandma chose to go to Wadleigh, a prestigious high school on the Upper West Side, plus Chinese school. Unlike the other jook sing kids, Rose and her younger sisters—the Doshims never did have another son aside from Johnny—were a dedicated group who studied not only the Bible but also Chinese language, writing, and culture.

Tiny like her mother, but bespectacled like Doshim, little Rose did not see herself as beautiful like her eldest sister, Lily, who had grown into a tall, willowy version of their mother. Rose considered herself more like her father—introspective, decisive, and practical.

When a Cantonese opera troupe arrived in town, offering to teach the Chinese students the ways of Chinese opera, Rose and her younger sister Alice leapt at the chance.

Rose, 1930s

The first notes of the wooden clapper captured my grandmother's teenage heart.

When she sang, others noticed. They could not believe she was a jook sing, an American-born Chinese.

Onstage, Rose Mai transformed from bookish know-it-all to exemplar of Chinese arts and culture.

She did not balk at the restrictive movements dictated for women. For as far back as I can remember, my grandmother extolled the virtues of a lady never using her hands while speaking, so perhaps it wasn't such a leap for her to conform to the small steps and lotus hands.

She sang the female lead for all their productions, but by far her favorite role was as the White Snake.

The story of the White Snake is a never-ending Chinese tale about a female Snake who falls in love with a Scholar, and who at great personal risk transforms herself into a woman in order to be with him. A folktale one thousand years old in the telling, the twists and turns in the narrative are like the trunk and roots of an ancient banyan tree. Did she dream of a love as grand as that of the White Snake and her scholar? Did she believe that the greatest testament to love was the ability to endure numerous trials and tribulations at all costs—that love conquered all? In a photograph from the period, Rose is center stage, kneeling in a white embroidered silk costume before a microphone. At sixteen, she has finally allowed her hair to grow out, and it tumbles past her shoulders. She is lovely and luminous. Even in the dark grainy black-and-white of the theater with the lights down, she has that glowing complexion the color of milk that she would retain throughout her lifetime, as a grandmother and even great-grandmother.

Chinese Opera cast, Rose, middle row,
second from left, 1933

A nonagenarian former resident who went to school with my grand-mother and her younger sisters and sat in the audience told me recently that Grandma Rose and Alice were a marvel to behold onstage, showing the entire male-dominated Chinatown what American-born girls could really do.

In September 1930, just months after Lung and Jack picked out their brides and got married, Dek and Elva, newly retired from immigration service work, decided to relocate to Hong Kong, sailing halfway around the world. Their money they knew would go further in the British colony, and for Uncle Dek, it was a wish fulfilled to live the remainder of his life closer to Chow and his family. To make Elva happy in their new city, Dek purchased a large, two-story house with multiple bedrooms at 37 Cumberland Road in the leafy residential area of Kowloon Tong—a neighborhood filled with single-family homes and villas that was popular among Portuguese and British businessmen and expats. The Foon family home, a palace by Hong Kong standards, with both a front and back yard, was near a triangular park where Elva liked to stroll early in the mornings before the heat had her ducking back indoors.

This was not their first trip to Hong Kong—Dek had brought Elva to the harbor city, which Cantonese refer to as Fragrant Harbor, in 1923—and, like that first time, everything in the beginning was a wonderful novelty: the magnificent views of the harbor and the mountains, the semi-tropical climate, the freshest seafood, even the intense smells. She felt, though, that she could have done without the squat toilets.

But in the intervening years, some things had not changed. Chow, though now a family man, continued to live his life as an incorrigible trust fund baby. After his stint in the United States, he had returned to Asia, and for the past decade had liberally invested, thanks to his father's bankroll, in business ventures that never panned out. Luckily his wife, whom they called Dai Mah, or Big Mother, a tiny but fierce bespectacled woman from Toisan with intelligent eyes and rather long ears, proved to be a stabilizing force who largely kept him in line. But even Dai Mah's influence had its limits.

A few years before Dek and Elva moved to Hong Kong, Chow had secretly taken up with a young woman in Shanghai.

When Dai Mah discovered him living with this very beautiful girl, flush with the glow of pregnancy, she didn't have the heart to turn them away, especially when she saw the woman's big belly poking out from her loose-fitting top. Soon, the woman, whom they later referred to as Sai Mah, or Little Mother, became Chow's second wife.

For Dek and Elva, especially, this was a difficult situation. They were a Christian family that did not curse, drink, gamble, or cheat, and this polygamous situation was antithetical to their values. They would have liked to take Chow to task and berate him for his actions. But by the time they arrived in Hong Kong, with all their heavy American furniture and wardrobes and Bohemian tea sets in tow, they found a family building with Dai Mah and her son occupying one floor, and the younger Sai Mah on another, nursing the baby, a lovely little boy.

Chow was a grown man, living in a culture where it was common for wealthy men to have multiple wives. Although he and Elva did not approve, Dek, ever consumed with guilt over not being there in his son's formative years, found his hands tied.

AFTER JUST A FEW MONTHS, life in Hong Kong started to lose its color for Aunt Elva.

The Chinese population of the colony had increased drastically since the time they had last visited, and she saw things that perhaps she had not noticed before. The poor and the dying lying on the streets, and the bodies of the dead left to decompose, abandoned by families too destitute to give them a proper burial. The prostitution of girl children. The ways that Europeans sometimes hit their rickshaw drivers with sticks or umbrellas, or made their payment by casting coins to the ground.

Then there was the language. She couldn't make heads or tails of Cantonese, despite knowing some words of politeness, like good morning and thank you, of which there were two ways that she kept confusing. One would not have thought that she had been married to Dek Foon for nearly thirty years. Perhaps Uncle Dek blamed himself for this—as their marriage progressed, his English improved, but Elva's Chinese remained basically nonexistent. Even when Shim and Chun lived with them back when the young couple were just starting out, everyone spoke English at home in deference to Elva—that and no one could decide whether to teach her Cantonese or Toisanese.

Sometimes, when Dek and Elva were out and about in the hustle and bustle of Hong Kong and needed transport, the rickshaw drivers took one look at her considerable American girth and balked. Some even claimed they were off duty, before scuttling away with their big-wheeled, handheld carriages.

But it wasn't the rainy season and its torrential downpours, the dai fung big wind typhoons, drenching her dress and threatening to snatch her umbrella from her hands, or the heat and humidity that finally got to our dear Elva so much as the colonial society into which she found herself dropped like an interloper at a tea party. While many foreigners enjoyed their country clubs and life along the "Riviera of the Orient" high atop Victoria Peak, no Chinese or Eurasians were permitted to reside in the district or join their clubs (the Peak "looks down on everything and everybody," wrote one anonymous writer for the English-language press). Dek and Elva were excluded from the white social clubs—the Hong Kong Club, the Cricket Club, the Jockey Club, and even the Ladies Recreation Club.

Although there had been a few prominent Chinese merchants who married white women, like the founder of the midwifery training hospital where Chun had been educated, within the British social caste system these kinds of intermarriages were anathema.

That Elva was an American only made the colonial ladies look down upon her even more.

Put simply, much like Chun in the early days at 37 Mott Street, Elva had no friends.

Although the particulars have long been forgotten, over the course of a full year in Hong Kong, the snubs and the lack of invitations to society dinners and charity balls—no St. George's or St. Andrew's balls for them—all began to add up and take their toll. It wasn't the first time for Elva—our family remembers how when Uncle Dek was working for the Boston Immigration Station that "Elva was nearly run out of town for marrying a Chinese." But the combination of social isolation from the English-speaking expat community, coupled with having to adjust to a new culture, would have given the slights even more weight. In the U.S., she could hold her ground and deem them all *racist snobs*, but here in Hong Kong, where she was caught between the locals and elite foreigners, and struggled with even the basics of communicating to their servant, Elva began to feel as lonely as when she had retreated to her parents' home after Doran left.

Finally, one day, when their moy moy presented her with ham yue, the salted fish that Dek loved with minced pork and fashioned into a patty over steamed rice, the sharp odor of which filled the kitchen and clung to the curtains like the pungency of fried kippers, Elva had had enough.

She opened the window wide and flung the entire casserole out—watching it sail across their backyard and over the fencing.

I imagine that the arc of Elva's throw was magnificent, and the servant girl, mute with fear, stood there with widened eyes.

Don't ever make that again! Elva said, wiping her hands on a towel and throwing it into the sink.

. . .

WHEN UNCLE DEK RETURNED home later that day, he found Elva at the small triangular Essex Crescent park, only a block and a half away from their house. She was sitting under the shade of a giant Chinese banyan tree amid its twisted roots, her favorite place to rest. The sun was starting to set, just behind the mountains, and his long shadow joined hers.

I'm sick of it, she said. *There's nothing for me here.*

Dek's soft heart sank straight into his spleen.

He couldn't help but feel guilty. All his dreams of being reunited with Chow and the grandchildren, of living out the rest of their days in a semi-familiar landscape, climate, and culture, had brought them here, as a couple, to this very moment.

Dek had underestimated how difficult the adjustment would be for Elva, perhaps convincing himself that their family, money, and the strength of their marriage could alleviate the stresses of moving to a foreign country in their fifties and sixties. She had trusted him wholeheartedly, and moved halfway around the world to make him happy. How could he ever have been this wrong?

From a photograph I have from that period, Dek and Elva are standing in their back garden. Because of the extreme heat, Elva has shed her usual modest clothing and is sporting a long housedress, her arms bared to the shoulders. While Dek Foon appears trim and tan, in a crisp white shirt, and happily in his element, Elva stands by a towering hibiscus bush. Although it is in full flower, and she proudly shows off a prominent bloom to the camera, everything about her expression proclaims her unhappiness, from the mournful eyes to the deep lines around her downturned mouth.

Even in retirement, with his hair more salt than pepper, but still as thick as a horse brush, Uncle Dek stood there in the park in his button-down and formal slacks, unable to meet his wife's eyes. Despite the warmth of the afternoon sun, his hands felt numb.

It's my fault, he finally said. *You've risked everything for me—your family, your friends, your country.*

If you'd never married me, you'd be accepted by these people, he said. *Back home, you'd be able to vote—*

Please, she said finally, putting her hand out. Did the aerial roots of the banyan tree hanging overhead stir in the breeze? Could she almost feel them trying to suck the moisture right out of the air?

If it weren't for you, I would still be living with my family, Elva said. *You accepted me when no one else would.*

I love you for that, and for everything that you are.

But I'm not happy here, she said, looking into his warm brown eyes that were appearing golden and syrupy in the light. *I want to go home.*

LATER THAT YEAR, the couple sold the big house on Cumberland Road. With the money they received, Dai Mah, the ever-practical wife, was able to purchase the adjacent building next door. In this way, the family with the two wives could flourish in these two apartment buildings, in one of the fastest-growing areas in Kowloon, renting out one to various tenants, while continuing to house future villagers who needed safe passage to America.

Even Chow couldn't mess up a financial arrangement this good, they thought.

No one could predict what would happen when, within a few years, Japan would invade China, the Japanese army pushing farther and farther south until it reached Hong Kong, and everything in our family's lives would inalterably change.

But this was still 1932. Just a year and a half after the Chins had left with their new wives, Dek Foon and Elva waved goodbye to their kin and set sail back home to New York, traveling in a first-class cabin on the SS *President Lincoln.*

Doshim and Chun, and my grandmother and her siblings, were elated about Dek and Elva's return, as I was, reading about it from his Exclusion file, so many decades later.

They were finally returning home.

I was so happy for them that for a moment I forgot myself, flipping through a digital copy of the file on my computer in my studio on Mott Street. I had just finished reading Uncle Dek's return permit form with his mixed block and cursive handwriting and all of the stamps of approval from the American Consulate General of Hong Kong in English and Chinese, when I was confronted with the following memorandum:

> NG DEK FOON, Chinese, a former interpreter at our Boston office, and his wife, ELVA M. FOON, are reported to be returning to this port on the SS PRESIDENT LINCOLN due January 2, 1932. Each should be in possession of an immigration return permit . . .
>
> If these aliens are admissible on primary examination, you will please have executed the enclosed forms in duplicate and returned to this office.

Elva Foon, 1931

I shook my head at "these aliens." *What did my family have to do to prove that they belonged?*

Then, in neat cursive handwriting, a note from the Boarding Division Inspector in Charge:

"Arrived 1/3/32.
Aliens admitted on primary inspection.
Forms and reentry permits herewith."

16

A Homecoming

Chin, Ng-Doshim & Wong
Families Apts. 22 and 23

陳伍黄

There's a 16mm black-and-white film from this era with footage taken on the rooftop of 37 Mott Street. Hong's wife, Anna, and their daughter, Shirley, are waiting by the stairwell when Lung appears in a white button-down and dark slacks—tall, handsome, somehow with an even greater swagger than before.

Right behind him, Mak Lin, his new wife, appears, sporting a severe bob, and because this is the fashion, she's got a bobby pin tucked into the side to encourage a wave. I pay special attention to this woman who is my grandmother, whom I have only ever seen in pictures at my father's house. It is 1930 and she is newly arrived in New York—this is her first time on the roof, and she is squinting from the bright light. From this portrayal, I can see why my father thinks I resemble her; she is outside her comfort zone, and her face looks a little hard as mine does when I'm on the defensive. She's also two months pregnant, and barely showing under her loose-fitting top.

Like her mother-in-law, Mak Lin was a Kwong Hoy girl who spent her childhood growing up by the sea. She was from a respectable family—her brother was studying to be a doctor, and would later set up his own hospital in their town. The farthest she had been out of the village was Toisan City, but now she found herself in this New York enclave of Toisan folks, and a society more patriarchal than the one she left behind. There was also Lung to contend with, who, since their marriage, had become even more like his father than anyone in the family liked to admit.

The morning after their wedding in Kwong Hoy, Lung had told Mak Lin to bring him his pants. When she did, he asked her to step into them.

Mak Lin was swimming in his trousers. She tried to keep them around her waist, folding the excess with her hands, but when Lung ordered her to let go, they slumped into a pile around her ankles.

"Now you know—I wear the pants in this family," he said, while she looked down, humiliated.

In Hong Kong, whenever she sidled up to him in the early days of their marriage, excited about something new she had seen, he made her walk several paces behind him.

And before leaving, he had made her cut her hair into a flapper-style bob like the white women of the Palais d'Or—which all the modern Chinese girls were doing. Perhaps she would not have understood the irony of this independent women's hairdo being imposed upon her as the hairdresser used the cutting shears and her long locks fell to the floor, but she would have known that her husband was doing everything in his power to show her who was boss.

It didn't need to be that way. He had every advantage. Mak Lin was living in a new country, in a new city, where she knew no one and couldn't speak the language. He held all the cards, just like his father before him. Her in-laws dominated the building, so much so it was practically a Chin village.

In a series of Jenga-like moves within 37 Mott Street, Lung and Mak Lin moved into a front-facing two-bedroom apartment diagonally across the hallway from Yulan and Chin On. Hong and Annabelle and their growing family moved to another floor, and eventually out of the building altogether, so that Jack and his wife could live in their old apartment. If the brothers and their wives each looked out of one side of their apartments, they could wave to each other from across the air shaft.

For my grandmother Mak Lin, it would be a very long pregnancy. Tiny and diminutive in stature that she was, her belly grew and then continued expanding like a giant gourd, to the admiring eyes of the other family members, well beyond the nine months of a normal term. When she entered her tenth month, Yulan and the other mothers of the building brought over boiling broths of black chicken steeped in rice wine home brew with red jujubes floating on top, and pork trotters simmering in pungent black vinegar.

Sometimes, I wonder if Chun came downstairs to help the new Chin wife give birth. As the resident midwife in the building, it's certainly possible that my maternal great-grandmother might have been there to help Lung's wife bring their firstborn into the world, especially since it was by all accounts a terrible labor—*Such a big baby! So slow in coming out!*

But even if she was there to finally witness the top of my father's bald head emerging into the world (the "crowning"), Chun could not have known that this innocent, hefty, ten-pound baby boy with the big lungs and wailing cries that echoed throughout the building and out the open window to Mott Street below, who was born during the Spring Festival—on a day that Chinese consider the darkest of the year, when folks light red illuminants—and whose Chinese name would be Bright Lantern, would later grow up to be the crown prince of Chinatown.

She could not know, as none of them could back then, even as the family threw his red egg party, to which all the Chins in the building and those in the neighborhood were invited a month later, that this baby with the curled-up fists and watchful eyes would grow up to be smart and handsome, whether it was because Chin On was rubbing the top of his recently shaven head with a dyed red egg before the entire congregation of New York City Chins, or because of their connections, or some combination of the two. That same day, Lung played the Chinese lottery and won $1,000—the boy was lucky! My father's birth would inspire poetry and line drawings—and even, later, as he lay swaddled on Lung's lap, a pivotal moment in the introductory chapter of a bestselling book on 1930s New York's Chinese by Carl Glick (*Shake Hands with the Dragon*). This treasured, fat baby boy would grow up to become one of the community's first lawyers and run to be its first-ever elected politician and, eventually, the initiator and cause of so much collective heartbreak for so many generations of women in our family.

LATER THAT SUMMER, across the hall in apartment 23, Chin On was sitting at the kitchen table with his head in his hands.

It was the third year of the Great Depression, and unlike the Doshim family upstairs, it was not looking good for the Chin family.

In the theater world, Broadway was a shadow of its former glory, with productions closing and its brightest stars moving to Hollywood. Patronage at the cavernous Palais d'Or slowed to a trickle. Even the exuberant B. A. Rolfe and his orchestra with their mighty radio presence had left for deeper pockets at NBC.

When the captain of the SS *Monmouth* wired that it was stuck in Japan, needing money for fuel to make it back home across the Pacific, Chin On became desperate.

He attempted to call in his debts, even sending out Big Mr. Wong to hunt folks down, but many stores were shuttered. At the few open ones, they could promise to pay him back only if their businesses survived.

He arranged for folks to buy his cargo in Japan, but as people knew a bargain when they saw one, he was forced to sell at a loss.

The captain and his crew abandoned ship. Soon, he lost the other freighters as well.

In order to cut his losses, Chin On gave up the warehouse in Newark, the Bronx restaurants, and the pool hall on Mott Street. But even the remaining establishments had problems. Without a steady flow of goods coming in, the shelves at Sun Yuen Hing and Ying Chong displayed holes where merchandise once lay—and because there were no customers, a layer of dust coated what few items remained.

Everyone was in the same position, and now folks were suing Chin On for money that he owed. They were five months behind on the rent for all their residences, plus the rent for the stores. It was a doubly bad situation, as the Naughtons were their landlords for all their rentals.

Chin On was sitting at the kitchen table with his head in his hands, when Yulan and the boys approached with an idea. *Why don't we turn the store into something else?*

He looked at them as if they were speaking gibberish.

What if we turned it into a coffee shop or a small restaurant, not anything cheen-cheen like Palais d'Or— Lung said.

Something small, more home-style, Hong interrupted.

Hong and Lung wanted to sell coffee for five cents a cup ($1.05 in today's dollars, still the going rate for coffee in Chinatown today). No one else was selling coffee in the neighborhood—they would corner the market!

I could make small savory pastries to go with the coffee, Yulan offered.

Crazy people, Chin On said. *We have no money!*

Maybe you *don't,* Yulan said. (In the film version of this scene, I see her saying this with a slight smile.)

When Yulan revealed what she had—wads of long green bills stacked neatly into hundred-dollar bundles—Chin On looked so astonished, everyone laughed.

How do you have so much money? he asked, incredulous.

I stole it from you! she said.

For years, whenever Chin On came home with one of his bags full of money, making the children count it out bill by bill in tall stacks on the kitchen table, Yulan had siphoned off a little. At first, it started with a dollar at a time, but when she realized that she could slip several into her apron pocket without anyone noticing, she was emboldened.

In the beginning, even she had to admit that it may have been partially out of spite—he wanted to stay out all night gambling, or being ham-sip (salty and wet) with all those chickens around town? It was going to cost him. But when it became clear that his carousing and spending money on other women and all those gambling losses he was incurring—Chin On was such a narcissist that he felt like *he could never lose*—was never going to stop, Yulan realized she was doing it for more than just pay-back.

Stealing from him became a necessity—she was no longer the little wife back in their village hut, scraping by on what little he gave her, wondering when her husband was coming home.

Chin On was always going to be out drinking and chasing women, and the only thing she could do was look out for her family and herself, and make sure her husband didn't leave them destitute.

And now that this arrogant man was sitting in her kitchen, a deflated balloon, she could finally reveal what she had been doing all these years.

As everyone laughed, Yulan knew that she was going to enjoy this moment and the memory of the look of dawning surprise on her husband's face for a very long time.

IT WAS A CRAZY IDEA—pivot to a new venture during the Great Depression—but after buying a few Silex coffee makers and installing a two-burner stove, the Chin family converted Sun Yuen Hing into China-town's first coffee shop, the Sugar Bowl.

They started with Chinese pastries and coffee—the kind of chay that Yulan was known for throughout the building.

Then they moved into the "something-over-rice" dishes—beef and broccoli over rice, spare ribs in black bean sauce over rice, etc.—according to Lung, they were the first to create this kind of Chinese food phenomenon, now a staple of the Chinese restaurant lunch trade. A big favorite was hamburger dan fan—hamburger with a fried egg and savory soy sauce gravy on top over rice—like an early version of a Hawaiian loco moco.

Hong, with his muscular arms and robust palate, proved himself to be something of a baker, specializing in pies. Apple pies. Blueberry pies. All with a flaky, homemade crust. He could even whip up a killer lemon meringue.

The coffee shop caught on, and eventually locals started ordering Sugar Bowl coffee with the same frequency of nai cha (milk tea). Yulan's home brew was always available, but this "special coffee" was kept in a separate Silex container in the back, hidden from the authorities. It was sold at a higher price, naturally.

By 1935, PETITE ROSE DOSHIM was graduating from Wadleigh, again at the top of her class. In her autograph book, classmates wrote "Success to a girl with plenty of ambition," and "To the Chinese nightingale! Who so beautifully interprets the music of China."

When an acceptance letter to Hunter College for this exceptional girl arrived at 37 Mott Street, it was met with excitement, as well as a bit of consternation.

Hunter College was arguably the best women's college in New York, rivaling Columbia University's Barnard. Extremely competitive, Hunter was a public college that was welcoming to first-generation daughters of New York City, many of whom would otherwise be turned away by the restrictive quotas against those who were considered "socially undesirable" imposed by other elite women's schools. Called the "Jewish Girls' Radcliffe," Hunter was a way into a teaching profession for many of its graduates.

While it was Rose's heart's desire to attend, Doshim and Chun, as progressive as they were, hesitated.

Who would marry her?

Chun, having gone to nursing school, was more sympathetic to their middle child, but Doshim, who had graduated from City College after Mount Hermon, and was one of the few Chinese of his generation with a college degree, was adamantly against it. Even now, in the 1930s, a generation later, only the most exceptional men attended university.

If Rose became a college graduate, her pool of eligible bachelors would shrink. Doshim knew that most men, Chinese or otherwise, wouldn't want to marry a girl who was better educated than themselves. Allowing their daughter to attend college would be tantamount to throwing in the towel and calling her a spinster at eighteen.

I'm not sure when exactly they told her, but I know that on Rose's part, there were uncharacteristic tears and a lot of door slamming. She had worked so hard for so long, doing everything right—getting the best grades in American and Chinese schools, earning the female lead in all the local Cantonese operas—that it's not hard to feel her total and utter frustration. She knew that most Chinese families would balk at allowing their daughters to go to college, but they weren't like most other Chinese families in Chinatown.

How could the most progressive Christian parents in Chinatown refuse to allow their daughter to attend college? It seemed so contrary to their values. Both the Reverend Lee To, their friend and former pastor of the Morning Star mission, and Kang Youwei, the head of the Chinese Empire Reform Association, had allowed *their* daughters to attend Barnard and Columbia. Mabel Lee, Lee To's daughter, a supporter of women's suffrage, became the first Chinese woman to get her PhD in economics at Columbia.

When Uncle Dek told Aunt Elva about Rose's acceptance letter to Hunter over dinner that night, she was overjoyed. The couple were back in Brooklyn, living in a house in a spacious, residential neighborhood.

The first girl in the family to go to college! Not even on her Lisk side did any of Elva's relatives attend university.

She's so bright and talented, Elva said. *Surely, she has to be allowed to go.*

Dek was not so convinced; he too thought it would mar Rose's prospects.

Although Oilily and Normon had lived with them when the family was just starting out, Rose had been a favorite of Uncle Dek's from the time she was able to string together sentences. She was bright and funny and observant, with a deadpan delivery that always made him crack up. When she performed Cantonese opera, Uncle Dek and Elva made sure to see every single performance, taking the family out afterward for dinner and treats.

He knew that Doshim and Chun both wanted the best for Rose, but no one could quite agree upon what that would be.

The next time Elva was at church, she talked to the others about it, and learned about the Ging Hawk club. Ging Hawk, which meant Striving for Knowledge, was a social network and support group for Chinatown's smartest girls, the first to attend American universities—it was founded by the Young Women's Christian Association, giving it the right imprimatur.

Luckily for Grandma Rose, the next time Dek and Elva visited them at the apartment, her aunt weighed in.

Surely, she should go, Elva said, in her matter-of-fact way. *She's so smart and talented and it could challenge her in a good way.*

We worry she won't be able to find a husband, Chun said. *Even boys that have college degrees do not want to compete with a wife with a college diploma.*

Do not hold her back, Elva said. *Times are changing. Do you know about this Ging Hawk club?*

Chun and Doshim were aware of it, started only a few years before.

Rose, 1938

It's growing, Elva said. *And it would be a good group for her.*

My great-grandparents sat there blinking, unconvinced, while Rose tried to hide her excitement.

She will find someone, Elva said, regarding her husband, who was playing with the youngest, Ruby, another P.S. baby, who had been born while she and Dek were away in Hong Kong.

Dek, looking a little worn out, tried to push off the shortness of breath with a quick smile.

Rose will find someone who will love and support her, Elva said, with a quiet confidence. *No matter what.*

That summer, despite her parents' reservations, Rose was allowed to enroll at Hunter College.

AT APARTMENT 23, I wish I could say that Chin On's carousing had slowed down once he hit his golden years and his hair became tinged with gray. But in time, as the Sugar Bowl picked up steam, and he was able to return to On Leong, this time as president, with a little bit of time and money back in his pockets, Chin On had returned to his old ways.

Only now, Yulan was older and wiser too, and with the kids now out on their own, she discovered that she had options. Instead of fighting with him—*You dead dog, you stinking penis, you want me to vomit to death?*—she just stopped everything, no cooking, no cleaning, no nothing, and walked away.

Sometimes, on days when he drove her particularly ti sin, muttering *Kai ai* under her breath, Yulan disappeared over to Lung and Mak Lin's apartment across the hall to make the pastries for the Sugar Bowl.

Occasionally, she stayed the night, not bothering to return home.

As Rose was studying her French, Latin, and statistics up at Hunter College, trying her best to get all As—it was hard to land at the top when you were among so many other girls who also strived for excellence—half a world away, Japan invaded China. It was the beginnings of the Second Sino-Japanese War.

While Japan had already taken over Manchuria a few years before, renaming the puppet state Manchukuo, this was different. This was full-on war.

It began first with the attack on the capital city, Nanking (Nanjing), followed by the bombing of Shanghai. If the losses continued, the Chinese government would be forced to retreat farther inland. . . .

Dek Foon was especially worried about Chow and his family, and the villagers back at home. Doshim had arranged a large donation to help the Nationalists purchase planes for their defense. But with the advancing invasion, the lines of communication were breaking down, and it was getting harder and harder to wire anything through, even to Hong Kong. (At the same time, the Chin family was also monitoring the situation, concerned about the investment properties they had in the colony.)

In Kowloon, Chow proposed a move to Singapore, but Dai Mah, knowing that there'd be other ever-younger, more beautiful women to contend with, told him that while *he* could go, she and the rest of the family were bou ci mei baak (keeping their complexions, by staying in the shade). Besides, who else would help the villagers on this leg of their journey to America?

This was when Uncle Dek, who'd received the diagnosis of a ballooning bulge in his aorta only a few years before, suddenly started complaining about shortness of breath and pain in his chest.

At home in Brooklyn, on the advice of his doctor, they moved Uncle Dek from the upstairs bedroom down to the first floor. Elva kept him company during the day, playing the radio or reading scripture aloud in the living room, and at night, watching as he slept on the day bed, the bones on his face becoming more and more visible with every passing

Ng Doshim family portrait, 1937

day. He was cold, so they piled on the blankets up to his nose, until he began to complain that he could barely move.

The Doshims visited when they could. Doshim's everything business was as commercially successful as ever (*You need a train ticket?* Go to Doshim. *You need to send or borrow money?* Call Doshim. *What about laundry supplies, washers, notaries, or immigration papers?* Doshim's your man!), and now Johnny was working in the office with his father, learning the ropes. So many of the now-adult children were getting married and starting families of their own. Oilily had married a former employee of Doshim's, a journalist and consultant to General Chiang Kai-shek, who was out of town more often than he was home; the couple had a toddler daughter, and another on the way.

That spring, Hitler annexed Austria—Europe was inching toward war. Closer to home, as the city trees unfurled new leaves and the Brooklyn magnolias budded, Aunt Elva came downstairs and found Uncle Dek on the living room floor, unmoving.

China lost control of Shanghai to Japanese forces, and soon after, their capital, Nanking. In the news, a photograph circulated of a crying baby, badly burned at the Shanghai train station, on fire after a Japanese air attack, its mother presumably dead, just out of the frame ("Bloody Saturday"). It was just the beginning. Word spread across the country of the atrocities against civilians in occupied Nanking, the medical "experiments" done by Japanese doctors on living patients, the ways in which the Japanese army practiced their military drills by tossed crying babies into the air and jostling one another to stick them with bayonets.

Is it any wonder that this man with the soft heart, who called Brooklyn home, had finally reached his limit? Everything was shutting down, the flow of oxygen moving to a trickle, as he lay there on the living room floor, the carpet making an impression under his cheek, until Elva dropped to her knees, covering his body with her own.

Our countrymen were desperate for aid from Western allies, which was slow to materialize, so Chinatowns across the nation went into overdrive.

Businessmen like Doshim donated large sums of money to the Nationalist government.

Grandma's opera troupe and the Ging Hawks fundraised for the war relief.

A giant Chinese flag—red, with the white sun on a blue background—was unfurled and carried in a somber parade procession down Mott Street. The mothers of the neighborhood, including Chun and Yulan, threw open their windows and tossed coins from fire escapes and balconies, out to the slowly moving flag below.

Back in Brooklyn, the medical examiner stated that the cause of Dek Foon's death was myocarditis—a severe swelling of the heart.

I first read Uncle Dek's obituary in his Chinese Exclusion Act file in Boston's National Archives office so many decades later. I opened the folder and there it was, a small clipping from *The Boston Sunday Globe*, published just a few days after his death. A colleague must have cut and pasted it onto an eight-by-eleven-inch piece of paper and placed it at the beginning of his file, where the endnote became the beginning.

The obituary notice was so small, only two inches by half an inch, and it broke my heart to read it. "DEK FOON—On Friday, April 1st, 1938, at his residence on East 15th Street, Brooklyn, NY, in his 78th year, beloved husband of Elva Lisk. Funeral services Sunday, April 3, at 8pm, thence to Kimlau's Mortuary, 28 Mulberry St. New York City to lie in state until Tuesday, April 5. Interment in Woodlawn Cemetery." Kimlau's mortuary was right around the corner from 37 Mott Street on Mulberry—also known as Death Street, Say Gai, in our dialect. Even then it was garnering a reputation throughout the community as the unlucky street of funerals and wakes.

The official cause of death—severe swelling of the heart—and the underlying complications of the bulging aortic nerve, seemed so tragic yet so fitting for this gentle man who had done so much for our family and community during his lifetime, battling for our civil rights and *inclusion* with his big expansive heart.

WHEN WORD OF THE JAPANESE ATTACKS and pillaging spread to our villages in Toisan, Guangdong Province, my great-grandfather Wong asked his brother about purchasing one of his "paper" slots for sixteen-year-old Kai Fei.

They booked him passage from Toisan to Hong Kong, and then a ticket to America, where Kai Fei would transform into Sun Ming Wong.

When I asked him about coming to America, my grandfather recalled the following:

Sailing day was filled with bright blue skies, the fish were leaping out of the water.

He was sixteen years old and looking forward to this brand-new adventure.

The ship, the *Empress of Japan*, was, despite the name, a large, white Canadian Pacific cruise liner—the fastest on the route. Although he did not know it then, American baseball legend Babe Ruth and his family had sailed to the Orient on the *Empress* only a few years before.

Kai Fei knew it wasn't going to be easy. His grandfather Yuan Son had warned him about the fickle nature of the lofan and how it was best to always have a bag packed with his papers and important items *in case he had to run.*

But good-looking, spoiled Kai Fei was born with such a happy-go-lucky attitude and a gambler's optimism that he *just knew* everything was going to work out.

His mother had given him three American $1 bills—the equivalent of $59 today—and his passage across the Pacific had been paid for. He even had sponsorship for a job waiting for him in New York City (the fact that young Grandpa had never had a job in his life didn't seem to deter him).

He just needed to remember to study for his interrogation, and not gamble away everything on the journey over.

In the beginning, he memorized his new identity by writing the following out in neat script in a little black notebook.

I
Am
Sun
Ming
Wong.
SunMingWong. SunMingWong. SunMingWong.

It was like transforming into a brand-new man: the name was revolutionary in spirit—New People—suggestive of a brand-new democracy. Even the convention of one's first name preceding the family name was thrilling. He was lucky, the others told him—his family had bought papers from a family member, whereas the others, desperate to escape before the Japanese invaded Guangdong Province, had no choice but to hastily memorize information about families they had never met and villages they had never visited.

He began calling himself Sun Ming for practice, but it never caught on with the others. Never a good student, Kai Fei started to slip, reviewing the answers only once or twice (he had fallen asleep the second time), even though he knew that if he failed, he would be deported on the spot and sent back home. (Did he think the devastation would be less great in Toisan than in Shanghai? Perhaps, for why would the Japanese want to invade our small rural villages?)

The day their ship docked in Shanghai, he and his friends climbed to the deck, excited to see it for the first time, but the city lay in ruins. Back home, they had heard of the atrocities, but something about seeing the bombed-out buildings and the red and white Japanese flags flying from the top of occupied edifices, and smelling the smoke that filled the air, even from the relative safety of the harbor, filled Kai Fei with anger and fear.

The *Empress* would land in the coastal cities of Kobe and Yokohama, Japan, but because of the war, none of the Chinese were allowed to get off.

Grandpa was only too glad when the *Empress* set out across the Pacific.

BECAUSE THE *EMPRESS OF JAPAN* was the fastest cruise liner on the route, it took only about a week for them to arrive in Vancouver, British Columbia. Grandpa never told me that he and the other Chinese bound for the U.S. switched to the *Princess Marguerite*, which ran up and down Puget Sound, to finish the journey to Seattle, Washington—I would have to look through his Chinese Exclusion Act file to find that information. The *Marguerite*, a stunning ocean liner with a black and white hull, would only a few years later get requisitioned by the British Navy during World War II, and be sunk by a German U-boat in the Mediterranean.

But back then, according to the ship manifest, Grandfather was traveling with other boys from neighboring Hokshan and Hoiping counties, who also claimed that they were U.S. nationals, and were in the same predicament as he was—*sons of American citizens* fleeing the war.

Grandpa and the other Chinese landed in Seattle's detention center in late November 1938, just a few days after Thanksgiving, in that period when things throughout the country start to slow down. Because no one knew how long it was going to take, the wait must have felt interminable. When the authorities finally called him in for questioning, it was the last week of January, the following year.

He had been in detention for two months.

When I asked him what it was like back then, at his home in Flushing so many decades later, Grandpa just glossed it over. "It wasn't bad, there were lots of boys there—we played games," he said.

Because there was no school, and there was lots of gambling, he claimed that he didn't mind it.

Now, after hunting down his files and traveling out to Seattle, decades after he first told me these stories, I can see how difficult it really was. Their outdoor area was fenced off with barbed wire like a prison yard. The food was by all accounts inedible. From his interrogation file it's clear that he had not been studying. He tripped over questions about how far his village was from the center of town, and couldn't even properly name his village. He was able to identify Uncle George, whom he called Baba, but he was unsure about the others, including his paper grandparents.

The interrogations had grown longer and more intense as the giant web of Exclusion grew wider. Now in its sixth decade, questions covered not only the domestic sphere of whether or not there was a clock or an ancestor tablet hanging on the wall, or how far the well was from the house, but the proximity of other towns to the village and how one caught a bus to the center of Toisan City.

It took yet another month before Uncle George's and the paper grandparents' testimonies in New York were completed and sent back to Seattle. Until then, Grandpa whiled the weeks away gambling and playing card games. Reading through the pages upon pages of testimony, and knowing how they were dragging out the whole process, drives me bonkers even now, some eighty years later.

I left the National Archives building after several hours of sifting through his file, weighed down and saddened by it all. In total, he had been detained in rooms with caged screens and bars over the windows for nearly the entire winter. Even though I had read the Exclusion files on so many of my family members, my heart broke all over again for my teenage grandfather—my real father figure, the consummate storyteller who cooked for me nearly every weekend of my childhood. But as I looked past the conifers and the chain-link fence, I realized that I was one of the lucky ones.

LATER THAT AFTERNOON, I arrived at the former Seattle Detention Center, where Grandpa had been held as a teenage boy.

Now a sprawling arts complex filled with artists' studios, I was reading a sign commemorating the site, when I met a painter who had been in the building since the early days of its conversion. She was kind enough to show me around.

We visited the outdoor recreation area where Grandpa walked and played ball. It was nothing but a concrete patio, which must have felt like a prison when the bars were still in place.

In her studio filled with encaustic art, the painter recounted the following story:

"Sometimes, when I was in my first studio, late at night, I would hear what sounded like marbles rolling around the floor," she said.

When she first inquired with her upstairs neighbor about it, he claimed that he hadn't heard anything because he hadn't been at the studio. Then, he began hearing the noises too.

They later found out that those studios had been just under the boys' dormitory, where so many Chinese boys, including Grandpa, were held during the Chinese Exclusion era.

I was still thinking about the ghostly noises as we walked downstairs to the basement. This was the loading area where Chinese immigrants like Grandpa were separated from the others and ordered to line up single file.

As I stood there, in the dark corridor, I suddenly remembered a conversation I'd had with my grandfather many years before.

It was Thanksgiving and my family was watching the Dallas Cowboys on television. We were in my grandparents' sunken living room in Queens, and I was interviewing Grandpa with the tape recorder going. ("What's she doing?" my uncle asks, before everyone erupts in disbelief at a play.) When I asked Grandpa what Seattle looked like from the ship when he arrived, I was imagining scenes from films and television shows, where immigrants arrive in New York Harbor and see the Statue of Liberty, pointing and hugging each other in delight.

Grandpa sucked his teeth at the notion and waved his hand dismissively. "I didn't see anything!"

Standing in the basement of the former detention center, where immigrants were made to enter after having disembarked their ships, I too couldn't see anything for several moments.

But as my eyes adjusted to the dark, there, against a long wall, two sets of painted handprints appeared, hovering like disembodied appendages.

I placed my hands within the closest prints. Once, a lifetime ago, my sixteen-year-old grandfather placed his here too—as did countless other men and boys after him—submitting to getting frisked.

I stood there, thinking about my own questions from the past that I had asked, *What did Seattle look like when you arrived?*

I could taste my old innocence dissolving in my mouth as I swallowed, hands growing numb against the wall.

WHEN THE IMMIGRATION OFFICERS finally released him, it was late February 1939, and the weather was just starting to warm up.

Grandpa headed straight to Chinatown. It was so close, he walked.

Things had changed in Seattle since the anti-Chinese riots when Lenoi Louie lost her baby so many decades before. After a fire wiped out so much of the city in 1889, Chinatown moved from its home on stilts above the tidal flats, first to south of Pioneer Square, and then—after a city works project forced it to move again—farther inland until it occupied several blocks along South King Street.

By the time Grandfather arrived, the population of Chinatown had been greatly reduced because of the Exclusion laws, but he found a vibrant Japantown (Nihonmachi) and Manilatown thriving on its outskirts.

Filipinos, mainly working as farm laborers, were allowed to freely migrate during this period, until the country gained independence from the U.S., after which its citizens were barred from entering, like other Asians.

Three years later, President Roosevelt would declare the entire western part of the country a military zone, and the Japanese American community would be forced into internment camps. Some Japanese would even be extradited from other nations. Only Asians were interned en masse.

When Grandfather finally arrived at the family association, to prove his lineage he recited a tenth-century poem that he had learned when he was a child. Even before he was of an age to go to school, Grandpa could recite this poem, written by our Wong ancestor, by heart.

Although I like to think it begins in the second person, *You are a handsome stallion*, its opening line is:

The handsome stallion boards the journey to afar . . .

I think of the foreign realm as my own,

And then, my favorite: *You are in foreign lands as you are home.*

As Grandpa recited the verses, the association men called over another young Wong man, who rubbed his ears and joined in with the last few lines:

Do not say that fortunes are determined by chance,

The seven sons of my three wives do themselves fortify.

This man was not from Kai Fei's village but, like him, was one of the many descendants of the seven sons of Wong Yue who had traveled throughout the southern provinces, only to meet up here in the Beautiful Country. Because of this connection, they called each other *cousin*.

Grandpa had gambled away most of his money while on the journey over and in the long hold of detention—only one of the three American dollar bills remained in his possession, which he called *his lucky dollar* and didn't want to spend. In order to have enough money to get to New York, where his paper father and sponsorship were waiting for him, he took a job working in a gambling parlor working side by side with his new cousin.

But young Grandpa soon realized that gambling dens are bad places for gamblers like himself—he was spending his off hours playing Chinese poker and mahjong and eating there as well, and running up quite a debt, which his cousin warned him was bad practice if he ever wanted to get out of town.

To pay back the money he owed, Kai Fei found himself another job working in a laundry.

But this kind of manual labor was not to his liking—cleaning the never-ending piles of other people's dirty socks and underwear that came in every day was for him akin to torture. Luckily, the abuses of unlaundered clothing, which offended both his olfactory senses as well as his sense of dignity, were such that when confronted by this new sense of poverty, he pushed through it.

It took several months, but finally he was able to pay back his debts and purchased a ticket to New York City, where his paper father, Uncle George, was waiting for him.

IN THE LATE SUMMER OF 1938, Yulan was not feeling well in apartment 23 and found herself unable to get the food to the table.

The family had all recently returned from Bradley Beach, and it was thought that Mah was just feeling tired.

When Lung came back from the Sugar Bowl, it was already too late.

Yulan had lain down in the front-facing room, her favorite spot in the apartment, where she could see everything in the neighborhood, and did not get back up.

She was sixty-two years old. If she was looking outside in those last moments, Yulan could have seen the new restaurant that had overtaken the Chinese Delmonico, closed some years before, the flock of city pigeons swooping across the neighborhood, the elevated train still rumbling in the distance, the trolley slipping beneath it like a little brother, coming and going on its own schedule, and Lung exiting the door of

The Chin family at Bradley Beach, 1930s

their establishment. Nestled among the vertical hanging signs, our SUGAR BOWL was one of the few written entirely in English, the letters laid out to evoke the shape of a bowl, outside the restaurant that had grown into a mainstay of the community and which would continue to support the family for generations.

The adults gathered around her bed, shutting the curtains, and whispered *growth*, which in our dialect could have meant *tumor* or *cancer*, before shuttling the children out of the room.

Yulan was buried shortly thereafter.

I would like to say that someone had nestled the stones from Kwong Hoy in her grave, but in truth, these had been given away years before to help other new arrivals, and the orange peels long consumed. Unlike the early Chinese pioneers whose remains were shipped back home, Yulan, who never forgot her roots, brought a bit of that seaside spirit to the Chin family plot just north of the city.

After the funeral, at 37 Mott Street, Chin On, who had barely spoken a word to any of his children in the days between their mother's death and her burial, broke down and cried. It was the only time that Lung could recall seeing his ironclad, suit-and-tie father, now even more stoic in middle age, *in tears*, and he and the others looked away in embarrassment.

As the years passed, and even after the youngest sons left home, alone in apartment 23, Chin On refused to sit in the room that he called *hers*. Although it was by far the nicest in the apartment—the room where Mott Street opened before them like a kind of theater every time they drew the curtains, and receded once they closed them, where the music of the street had kept her company as she worked, making and mending their clothing, ironing, or just closing her eyes in those small, precious pockets of time when she could rest—even the sunlight streaming in through the window every morning never failed to remind him of her.

And because few of us can think of those closest to us who have passed without reflecting in large part upon who they were to *us*, and who *we* were in relation to them, that light also reminded Chin On of his worst moments—his thundering rage, stubbornness, arrogance—and how he had treated her all those years.

ALMOST EIGHT DECADES LATER, after interviewing Yulan and Chin On's youngest son, and my father's cousins, now spread out all across the country, I found a photograph in one of the family albums of that summer the family spent out at Bradley Beach, New Jersey. There was my father, a lanky seven-year-old, sitting atop Uncle Hong's shoulders, his younger cousins on the steps between Uncle's knees.

My father is pensive, like he's aware that at any time someone might be watching him, yet he has his arms spread out, as if the world will someday be his.

In the background sits Yulan, beaming at the camera, relaxed, having kicked off one slipper, her big toe pointing out—those big feet that caused her so much ridicule when she was growing up, but which enabled her to navigate the world. She has spent an entire summer at the shore, free of Chin On, free of city life, walking to the ocean to feel sand beneath the pads of her feet, and the tides moving in or out against her calves as she waded in. The fishmonger's daughter, who grew up shucking piles upon piles of oysters and mussels, being at the shore, even if it was half a world away from where she grew up, and able to watch the next generation scampering around, so many grandsons and granddaughters, looks truly happy.

What is it they say, about all bodies of water being connected?

In these years of living in America, she has grown fat and round, with sturdy workman-like hands, her hair thinning. In that way that some middle-aged women have, she has a kind of carefree attitude about her appearance that shows she could care less about how she appears to her husband, or any man for that matter. For the past few years, she and Chin On have avoided each other as much as possible, and a full summer away from him has put life back into her.

This is the only time in all my years of piecing together her life that I have ever seen Yulan relaxed, smiling, and I find it impossible to keep my eyes off her.

IN THE FALL OF 1940, Rose Doshim was working as a ticket seller at a movie theater on the Bowery—one of those large, former performance halls now converted into a movie theater after all the live talent had left for Hollywood.

It was seen as a bit of a disappointment for Chinatown's smartest girl.

While at Hunter College, Rose had dreams of becoming a school-teacher.

She was plucky, patient with children, and, being a bit of a know-it-all, only too happy to instruct.

As a Chinese opera singer, she had taught the younger girls how to project their voices across the stage so that audiences could hear them, even without a microphone.

At home, she often tutored her younger siblings in areas where they were struggling, like geometry and algebra, and loved the orderly nature of mathematics. She loved it so much that she decided she wanted to become a math teacher.

Hunter had a reputation for turning out stellar teachers in this era when women had few choices of profession, mainly nursing and teaching. But the physical examination conducted by the city's Board of Education was exceedingly rigorous by the time Rose graduated. When the doctor heard the swooshing noise that her heart made through his stethoscope, Rose was immediately disqualified, even though her heart murmur was benign ("innocent").

All those years of study, gone to waste, they said.

She took a job as a secretary, but the moment she let it slip to one of her coworkers that she was a Hunter graduate, the information made the rounds of the other secretaries, who conspired to get her fired. Within a week, Rose was given a pink slip and told to pack her things. She learned to hide the fact of her degree after that experience.

Grandma told me this story when I was a child, and back then, I took it as gospel.

But I now know how difficult it was for Asian Americans of her generation to land jobs outside of the community—the discrimination was the reason why so many American-born Chinese (ABCs) continued to work in their parents' restaurants or laundries, or sought employment in China—so it's likely that she was being conspired against not just for her education, but for being Asian.

Eventually, Rose found a job as a bookkeeper.

By this time, only Rose and the youngest daughters were living at the Doshim abode. According to the census, the family had moved out of 37 Mott Street five years before—waving goodbye to Yulan and the Chin boys, before packing up for Bayard Street, across from the elementary school and Columbus Park.

Although the northern reaches of Bayard were only two and a half blocks away from the old homestead, it was like a different neighborhood. Here, they were among the first- and second-generation Italians, Germans, and Greeks, and unlike at Sun Lau, the Doshims were the only Chinese Americans in the building. But while they missed their neighbors—the mothers of Number 37 had finally embraced Chun, although some still referred to her as the *Hakka woman* or the *Jesus amah*—and in this new building, they were "the Chinese," it was considered well worth it, as the landlord had allowed Doshim to rent two adjoining apartments, and connect them by knocking down a wall. Now the family had room to breathe, plus a parkside view.

During the week, Rose worked her day job balancing the books for a custom jewelry company in the garment district, where she earned more than most of the fathers in their building. She brought home mother-of-pearl bracelets and dangly screw-back earrings and small, jet-black purses no larger than her palm, inset with rhinestones—handheld bags so marvelous and tiny there was barely enough room for a lipstick and mirror.

In this era of fur-collared coats, where American women paraded around in fox stoles like a kind of bestiary, Rose and her sisters adorned themselves in veiled hats, white leather gloves, and the mother-of-pearl jewelry she brought home.

At school, Rose had a reputation of being one of those subtly quiet girls who could unleash the kind of one-line zingers that had her peers rolling with laughter. She and her sisters had grown from skinny, bespectacled Chinatown girls to slim-figured banker's daughters in oxfords and peep-toe shoes, sporting finger curls and victory rolls to frame their faces. The Doshim daughters may have been wearing glasses since grade school, and well knew the Dorothy Parker adage about men seldom making passes, but no one could deny how well their half-up, half-down dos emphasized their cheekbones.

The Ging Hawks, that Chinatown network for college girls, opened a whole new social scene for them. There were Thanksgiving turkey trots and nautical-themed dances ("Yacht Dance on the SS Ging Hawk"), Jack O'Lantern socials and Mad Hatter's Marathons—where they met boys from across the Northeast who traveled in to attend their events, and in the process also raised money for the war effort in China. By 1938, Ging Hawks had raised $288—close to $5,700 in today's dollars.

Although not listed in the Ging Hawk program guide for their play *Gift of the Gods*, as "Prettiest" or "Best Dressed," or the Ging Hawk girl the "Boys Liked Best," like her other friends, or even "Champion Fancy Ice-skater," like her sister Edith, Rose, who played the role of "musician," attracted plenty of suitors with whom she went on double and triple and quadruple dates. There were large group outings to Coney Island—where she developed a taste for frozen custard and saltwater taffy and rode the Comet, laughing, with a scarf tied around her hair—and ferry rides up the Hudson to Bear Mountain. ("A young gentleman from Philadelphia always looks forward to seeing Rose when he's in town. . . ." the anonymous editors of the program guide wrote, breathlessly, under the gossip column "Meow!!" "In spring a young man's fancy . . .")

From the few photographs of this era, she favored a side part and liked twisting her hair so that a section swept over her forehead like a roll, highlighting her eyes and carefully tweezed brows.

There was the aspiring architect, who was bound for university in China. He asked her to wait for him until he completed his studies, but when he returned to New York before the outbreak of the war, he said that she was "too American" for him, and preferred to marry a *real* Chinese girl instead.

There was the nice-looking young man whose name has been lost to history, who used to help her with all her opera performances. Folks noticed how he appeared smitten at the end of every show. But each time they went out, Rose noticed that he had eyes for a certain waiter at a restaurant he liked to frequent, and although that wasn't a deal breaker for many Chinese families (as long as couples had children, especially sons, no one cared about sexual preference), Rose knew he wasn't for her either.

There was the gentleman from Philadelphia, whom her family knew through their Chinese civil rights and manufacturing connections, but whom Rose found *incredibly dull*.

None of these boys interested her for very long.

Because she was bored and had nothing else to do and wanted to get out of the house, and because she liked earning her own money, Rose strapped on her walking heels and took on a semiregular, part-time weekend job as a ticket seller at one of those dilapidated, low-frills places on the Bowery that had seen better days. She spent the duration of her shift reading a paperback or crocheting a cashmere hat, while perched cross-legged on a stool, in a glass ticket booth that was completely covered in paper.

Although she couldn't actually see the patrons, more often than not she heard their footsteps approaching, even over the rumbling El that made the windows of her booth rattle, or the dinging of the trolley rolling past, before a shadow appeared. She would receive a request for one or two tickets, then a dump of money being shoved through the slot. She was always quick with the change.

One day, she felt someone's approach, and then a tall, thin shadow with a rich voice asked in halting English for *one ticket, please.*

She told him the amount, and then, when there was a hesitation, she said it in Cantonese.

The money magically appeared, and she was about to place the ticket in the dish, when she saw a pair of eyes looking up at her through the slot.

The eyes appeared young, around her age, but there was a depth to them that reminded her of Aladdin in the "Arabian Nights." That they belonged to that resonant voice that had made the hair at the nape of her neck rise up like shoots sprouting at the first touch of spring, was even more thrilling.

The young man had been intrigued enough by the sound of her voice—a voice that I remember in childhood as being warm and tonal whether she was speaking English or Chinese—to crouch down with some effort in order to catch a glimpse of *her*.

Thank you! he said with gusto, and she caught a flash of a smile before he straightened—according to his shadow, he must have been tall, much taller than she—and disappeared into the theater.

Rose Mai had a rush of feeling, rather like when she used to perform on the stage, that she was actually being seen.

Doshim and Chun were not pleased when Rose Mai introduced them to Kai Fei, or Gene Wong, this young immigrant who was working as a waiter in a Chinese restaurant. Unlike Rose's friends, who practically swooned when they saw him and then looked at her with big eyes (*such a catch!*), her parents were not swayed by good looks.

By the time Rose had graduated from Hunter, young, ABC, jook sing, Ging Hawk girls like her had risen to become the crème de la crème of Chinatown.

Ging Hawk girls had bright futures.

They married well.

They married Ivy League boys from the Northeast—other ABCs like them, whose accents reflected their education.

They were supposed to marry like Edith, the fancy, champion ice-skater who'd met an MIT graduate who saved her from drowning after she fell off a boat at a Ging Hawk event. *Who knew electrical engineers could be heroic?* Her husband came from an exceptional family with humble laundry roots—Uncle Hammie's brother was the first Chinese American to pass the bar in Massachusetts.

Ging Hawk girls were not supposed to marry working-class immigrants who enjoyed drinking and gambling and whose only aspirations were at best to become bartenders or restaurant owners—restaurant suppliers, that was different, but not owning actual restaurants themselves, that industry was seen as too risky and dependent upon customers with excess incomes, which were few and far between since the onset of the Depression.

Plus, if Rose married him, her own U.S. citizenship could be imperiled like Aunt Elva's. They knew that Kai Fei, who liked to be called Gene, was a paper son, whose citizenship was established as the "son of a citizen."

They didn't begrudge Gene his status—most of Chinatown was composed of paper sons, some of whom, it was rumored, had obtained their paperwork through Doshim.

Of course it wasn't the young man's fault that the immigration laws were the way they were, but they didn't like their daughter taking an unnecessary risk. If officials started doing raids in Chinatown again and he was found out to be here under a false alias, then he could be deported, and where would that put Rose? They couldn't understand why she would even consider risking her own citizenship and status and her entire future for a man with such low prospects.

For his part, Gene understood Rose's parents' view.

Back home in our villages, he would have been considered an extremely good marriage prospect, because of his father's land and money. But in New York, he was little more than a nobody.

When Gene first arrived in the city, he had reached out to his paper father, only to find that the restaurant where Uncle George worked had shuttered and that his uncle was out of town, seeking other work in Boston.

He spent the next couple of nights at the Wong association, where he found a job in a local Chinatown restaurant washing dishes and sweeping the floors. He slept in the back, each night looking up at the flypaper, yellowed with age and unrolled like a tongue, having caught numerous flies over the months before, hanging from the ceiling above him, wondering when things were going to get better.

He began saving up a little money, and had dreams of one day becoming a waiter where the tips were better than dishwashing and busing tables. He even began taking English classes at the Church of All Nations on Canal Street, the busy thoroughfare that bisected the neighborhood, from Chinatown to Little Italy; it was the same church my Doshim and Chin families now attended. For the first time, the formerly rich, lazy boy became a student who actually applied himself. If he wanted to make more money, that meant interacting with lofan clients, and so he did his best to memorize hospitality vernacular.

Did he read question-and-answer books written in dual English and Chinese, with sections that pertained to "Duties of a Waiter"? ("What will you drink? Tea or coffee?" "Do you want some more meat?" "No, thanks, I have had plenty. Here is your change, Waiter.")

It was at night class at church that he learned how to say *one ticket, please* and improved his vocabulary—the fifty states and their capitals, with some scripture slipped in—building upon the railroad names that Yuan Son had taught him.

One ticket, please, he said, when he approached the movie theater that day—the first time that he finally could splurge on a film—a Sunday, his only day off from work. He was surprised to hear the young lady's voice answer him in both English and perfect Cantonese.

It felt so long since he had seen a *real Chinese girl*—over a year and a half—and that's when he crouched down to see what she looked like. Seeing Rose sitting there in three-quarter profile, reaching for the tickets, her mouth in full bloom, the barely there round glasses, her black hair carefully twisted in a half-up, half-down hairdo with victory rolls, and a complexion so clear it was like the surface of a lake, was for Gene like looking at *the beloved* through a telescope. He would never forget that thrilling moment when she looked back at him, her eyes open wide behind her spectacles, unblinking.

Gene returned to the movie theater again and again, finally mustering the courage to inquire about her name, and when she got off work, and if he could walk her home. Gene and Rose strolled together up Pell toward Mott Street, then north, past Doshim's office, hooking past the school where she was once top student. At the mouth of the park, across from her building, they lingered until the sun went down, and the neighborhood transformed into twilight, and the gaslight streetlamps hissed and flickered before firing up, and she had to beg off, knowing her parents would wonder where she had gone.

BUT GRANDMA WAS NOT to be deterred, and that spring, after several months of courtship, where she turned away the gentleman from Philadelphia, Gene put an engagement ring on her tiny, size 4 finger.

As the weather started to warm up, and the snow and sleet increasingly turned to rain, there was a course of excitement throughout the city that winter was receding, but in Chinatown, Great-Grandmother Chun, the kind, honest Hong Kong beauty whom strangers fell in love with and babies cooed at upon first sight, was beginning to smile less and less.

In the photos we have from the summer before, even though she sits at the beach with her hair styled in rolls and a bun, as was the fashion of the times for *mature* women, on a blanket with her daughters and a new grandchild, Chun sits with her body facing away from the others—an island unto her own.

She stares at the camera with suspicion, brows furrowed, one eye hooded, even though it is a family member taking the shot.

Chun passed away the following March, at home with her daughters. The story that filtered down through the generations of our family was

Chun with daughters and grandchild, 1940s

that Great-Grandmother had given birth to too many children—eight over the course of twenty years—her last having been born when she was forty-two. Certainly being pregnant for so many years is taxing on a woman's body—and as Grandmother Rose noted, during a time when there was no prenatal care. But I can't help thinking that this alone is not the full answer.

In addition to the heartbreak of losing her son, Great-Grandmother lived most of her life in this country undocumented. Unlike Yulan, who had papers listing her own name, Chun didn't have such protections, and she could never quite shake the fear that had continued to eat away at her, long after they weathered the last raids on Chinatown.

Although Aunt Elva had thrown off the authorities, what about the next time, or the time after that?

After the seurng sum of Chun's passing, Doshim seemed to disappear into his work—staying at the office later and later, sitting at his desk and often falling asleep there. Johnny would find him, with his glasses off, near a photograph of Chun, taken during happier times, her hair parted in soft finger waves, her lips slightly parted, looking out at him from the frame.

As the daffodils and daylilies began pushing out of the earth, blooming all across the five boroughs, Rose and Gene dressed up in their finest
attire—he in a dark suit with a silk handkerchief in his lapel, and Rose in
a white silk cheongsam with embroidered flowers festooning the front.
The Doshim sisters came and took photographs; one of them gave Rose
a corsage of three white orchids and pinned it on her lapel. Someone
wrote "Rose Doshim Loves Gene Wong" in white chalk on the pavement at their feet.

They beam at the camera—pleased-as-punch smiles that illuminate
the entire frame.

It is April 23, 1941.

In another eight months, Japan would attack Pearl Harbor, and the
U.S. would declare war on Japan, pulling us into World War II.

Even with its arsenal of bombs, the country could not hope to defeat
Japan on its own. For this, we would need China as an ally in the Pacific.
Within two years, China's First Lady, Madame Chiang Kai-shek, who was
educated in the U.S., would make a persuasive speech on Capitol Hill, as
would Pulitzer Prize–winning novelist Pearl S. Buck, arguing for the repeal of the Chinese Exclusion Act; with the endorsement of the president,
Congress would pass the repeal by voice vote.

And then finally, on December 17, 1943, Franklin Delano Roosevelt
would sign Chinese Exclusion's repeal, sixty-one years after it was enacted.

In that moment, everything for us would change.

China would receive military aid from the United States.

For the thousands of Chinese living in America, our roadblocks toward citizenship—first placed so many years before by senators from out
west—were now removed. My family members and others like us could
finally become naturalized and access the right to vote.

As he did at the start of World War I, Doshim had registered for the
draft on the first day that he was eligible in 1942. Although too old to

serve, Great-Grandfather Doshim, at age sixty-four, born four years before Exclusion was signed into law, made clear his most patriotic intentions.

I can almost feel Great-Grandfather Doshim's and Grandfather Lung's elation as they applied to naturalize just a few years later, fulfilling a long-held dream of becoming American citizens.

But some things didn't change.

The immigration quota was so stingy it could be argued it barely counted—only 105 Chinese were legally allowed to immigrate per year.

The paper family network would continue to proliferate, out of necessity.

The War Brides Act of 1945 would provide a workaround for those who joined the military—family members who enlisted in the war would be able to bring over their brides from China.

And out west, the internment of 120,000 Japanese Americans was about to enter its third year.

WHILE FAMILY MEMBERS WAITED for their naturalization papers, Gene and Rose welcomed their first two children—a son as rambunctious as Gene, the other, a little mama's boy. Then Rose gave birth to a daughter.

She was one of Doshim's many grandchildren, and by some accounts the prettiest baby in New York—she was so pretty, strangers even offered to hold her on crowded subway trains and buses, as Rose, like any mother of three in the city, struggled with shuttling the kids across town on mass transportation.

They named her Laura, after the 1944 film about a woman so beguiling that men fell in love with her portrait alone ("Few women have been so beautiful, so exotic, so dangerous to know"). Decades later, when the immigration laws shifted, and our quotas finally became more equal to that of other nationalities, a new generation of young Chinese Americans would come of age. Little Laura would grow up to become the most beautiful woman in New York's Chinatown—even crowned Miss China-town, where she waved from floats in elbow-length gloves and sat with politicians in open-air cavalcades—before she started dating Stanley and, eventually, became my mother.

17

37 Mott Street

Even now, so many generations later, these stories still cast a spell over me.

One hundred and fifty years after Yuan Son and his countrymen helped complete the nation's first transcontinental railroad, I have traveled out to Promontory Summit in Utah to celebrate his accomplishments. I have sat at the foot of the Chinese Arch, a natural rock formation marking the site where he and the others camped, surrounded by sagebrush and chaparral, breathing in the desert air as he did, gathered together with other Chinese Americans to honor Yuan Son and his legacy, and the legacy of all the Chinese contributions to the railroad.

On May 10, 2019, I am standing at the railroad grade where the last spike was hammered in by the hands of Chinese workers, along with hundreds of other descendants of railroad builders. We are a massive crowd, like a multigenerational flash mob in colorful Chinese attire in front of two mighty locomotives, under the wide, open skies. Ten thousand attendees have joined the festivities to witness and honor this moment. My genealogist friend Amy Chin is with me—sometimes folks confuse us because our names are so similar, but we just laugh it off and call each other *sister*—along with others who can trace their lineages back here to *their* first American ancestors.

We turn our faces toward our friend, photographer Corky Lee, who stands on a ladder, and dozens of other photographers and news agencies, beaming like the sun, representing our ancestors' contributions in unifying the country—we are claiming that recognition in ways that were so long denied to so many of them in this American history.

My family and I have camped out at Angel Island, and toured the old detention center with the late historian Judy Yung, whose family had also been interrogated there. The barracks that Yulan and my grandfather Lung and uncle Jack had been confined to have long since burned down, but the men's dormitory, where Chin On stayed, remains. It was on these very walls where so many Chinese wrote, then carved, poetry—the wood bearing witness to their testimonies of suffering, anguish, anger, one shaving at a time.

Closer to home, I have traveled out to the end of Long Island to trace my finger across Dek Foon's gold medal of honor, feeling his etched name under my fingertips, and to see this object of pride with my own eyes. It appeared in a lot at a Florida auction house some years before, where a collector of Jewish antiquities purchased it, falling in love with its story. It hearkened back to a time when Chinese and Jewish folks came together, and spoke of the promise of immigrant America lending each other a hand. It would be easy to dismiss such a thing as being the stuff of myth and legend, but this brilliant medal with a patina darkening with age, festooned with a yellow Chinese flag and an American eagle, with diamonds encrusting his initials, "D" and "F," is a testament to those ideals.

ONE EXCEPTIONALLY SUNNY SPRING morning in 2019, I traveled with my family to Woodlawn Cemetery in the Bronx, so that our daughter could see where, in one of the oldest corners of the cemetery, Doshim and Chun were buried in a family plot listed only as FOON.

Unlike other Chinese headstones that list birthplace (Toisan), and real name in Chinese characters, and often the paper name in English, Dek Foon's stone is plain, American in its simplicity.

The space next to Uncle Dek was empty, except for a foundation stone for another headstone. Suddenly, I remembered why.

When I was a child, my grandmother told me this story.

After Dek passed, Elva became distraught, living alone in that big house in Brooklyn. When he was still alive, the house had been robbed one night while the couple attended the theater in Manhattan. Now alone, Elva grew more and more worried it might happened again.

In the last family portrait I have of that generation, everyone is still alive. Dek and Elva sit on the side, Uncle Dek growing more gaunt and ghostlike, the tips of his fingers running cold, his body suffering from poor circulation. Elva sits beside him, looking small and faraway, even a bit flyaway—such a contrast to the robustness she exudes in prior family photos.

As the story goes, when Elva refused to give Uncle Johnny all of her and Dek Foon's money, Johnny, who had grown from sweet little brother to money-grubbing pixiu, had her committed to a mental institution in Brooklyn. When she passed, five years later, the cause of death was "terminal bronchial pneumonia," but the contributory cause was *senility*, or "senile paranoid psychosis." (The feeling that people are trying to steal from you is common in folks with dementia, but given what we know about how Uncle Johnny treated my grandmother and their other siblings, the story could very well be true.)

Grandmother Rose recalled that Elva's coffin was supposed to be buried near Uncle Dek, right where I was standing. But Elva's family had taken her away and buried her in their family plot in Brooklyn instead. Apparently, even as happy as they were that Elva had finally found someone who loved her, they still didn't want her buried next to a

Chinese. (They used a more derogatory term back then to refer to Uncle Dek.)

Ever since I read Nathanial Hawthorne's *The Scarlet Letter* as a teenager, I have been haunted by the last chapter: although the two main characters were buried side by side, Hawthorne writes, the dust on their grave sites never met.

How is that even possible? Adolescent Me practically screamed back then. *Damn you, Hawthorne, after all they shared and their dust can't even meet in death?*

In that moment, staring at Uncle Dek's headstone and the empty foundation stone next to it, I knew what I had to do.

Even though it was eighty-one years after Uncle Dek Foon had passed, I dug up a bit of earth from his grave with my fingers and a spoon that came with our takeout. The earth was dark and loamy and I made sure to pick up some field garlic (a hardy plant in the onion family) along with it, before tucking the whole heaping spoonful into a plastic bag I had fished out of my knapsack. Even though you're not supposed to take anything from cemeteries, this felt important enough to bend the rules a little.

Life takes over as it does when you're a parent of a small child and juggling work commitments, and it was only after the seasons turned from summer to fall that I headed out to Brooklyn's Evergreens Cemetery on a bitterly cold November day. It was so blustery that my hair whipped around my face, and the wind nearly slammed the door of my car shut as I was taking out my belongings.

I couldn't believe that her family had separated the couple twenty miles and several boroughs away from each other.

Finding Elva's grave wasn't easy—they had buried her with her mother and brother, with no tombstone of her own, and so she's in a marked version of an unmarked grave. *Why didn't they at least give Elva her own tombstone?* I muttered to myself.

Although I overshot it and had to retrace my steps, I finally found her family headstone on a slight hill near a tall oak tree.

"Hello, Aunt," I said, dropping to my knees.

Because there was no way to know exactly where they placed Elva that day, nearly three-quarters of a century ago, I would have to take my best guess.

The dirt was dry over the grave as I dug in with my spoon, like the earth was parched, and I wished that I had brought some water. It slid from my spoon into the bag like silt—a mass of soil and small stones.

Then I brought out Dek's dirt—somehow it was still rich and loamy after being tucked away in my refrigerator's vegetable bin, although the field garlic had long since disintegrated (I had a lot of explaining to do to my family in those months)—and poured it into the small depression I had just made, no larger than my palm.

I wanted to light some candles and burn some Chinese funeral papers for Elva, but as a Methodist, I knew she wouldn't really take too kindly to what she and Dek would have considered Chinese superstitions.

So I just sealed the baggie and stood up, waving goodbye to the grave-site even though there was no one there to see me.

Suddenly, as I was heading back toward my car, I could hear Elva's voice inside my head. *Take me to him, right now.*

I was surprised. Uncle Dek had never been so demanding all those months in our vegetable bin.

But there it was again.

Take me to him—right now!

Three days later, on a much sunnier, calmer, practically balmy day, I was back in the Bronx, making my way once again through the gates of Woodlawn Cemetery. I'd had some time to look up a little of the history of the place—Woodlawn was where the rich and famous New Yorkers of the era were buried, including Irving Berlin, who waited tables on a restaurant on Pell Street not too far from Uncle Dek's office, musician Miles Davis, and even the founders of stores like Macy's and Woolworth's.

I rounded the bend and headed down the road, within sight of the storefronts along Jerome Avenue. As I approached the Foon marker, my heart quickened, as if the excitement were not mine alone.

When I got to Uncle Dek's headstone, I felt Doshim's and Chun's rising interest, like flowers following the afternoon sun. In the distance, groundskeepers drove lawnmowers across the hill, crisscrossing and weaving among the headstones; someone was using a leaf blower. These noises drifted over to where I was crouching down before the unmarked headstone placed next to Dek's grave.

I had been away from this site way too long, and the place where I had earlier dug up Dek's dirt had smoothed and recovered with growing grass in the ensuing seasons, as if my minor theft had never happened.

Should I put Elva's dirt over his grave? I wondered. Or should I put her next to Uncle Dek—side by side—where her body should have gone back in 1945, if she had gotten her wish?

Nineteen forty-five.

JUST A FEW SHORT YEARS BEFORE 1945, Aunt Elva would have been able to reapply for her citizenship and become an American citizen again. In truth, she would have been able to do this after Dek died in 1938, but it's not clear that she would have known that, nor perhaps would she have wanted to. Perhaps out of loyalty to him, she would have abstained. Perhaps when Doshim and Lung were putting through their naturalization applications, Elva might have considering doing so too—but by that time, she was not of sound mind and body. By 1940, she was already institutionalized. (Neither Elva, nor Great-Grandmother Yulan, would ever gain the right to vote).

When I think back on Elva being committed, and the diagnosis on her death certificate—senile paranoid psychosis—I can't help but wonder how much of her decline was contributed by forces beyond her control.

How would any of us feel if the government stripped us of our citizenship for nothing more than marrying someone who accepted us for ourselves, but who couldn't naturalize because our laws forbade it, and then that same government continued to turn the screws by rendering us an entirely different *nationality*?

When I first learned about Aunt Elva being intersex, I was so worried about revealing her secret, and all the questions it raised about their relationship and sexual orientation. There was still so much that I didn't know, nor would I ever know for certain because there was no one alive to ask.

But what became clearer and clearer to me as I tracked down older family members for stories, tracing Dek's and Elva's footsteps from Brooklyn to seaside Winthrop, Massachusetts, to Kowloon Tong, Hong Kong, was not just the fact of her physicality, but that with Dek and our family, Elva was able to be herself. That acceptance alone is radical, both then and now.

We live in an era when intersex bodies are routinely altered surgically after birth, in hospitals, where doctors and parents make permanent decisions about a newborn's gender. Sometimes they guess right, but other times, the child grows up and those early medical interventions prove to be very wrong.

This acceptance of Elva, exactly as she was, by both the family that raised her *and* Uncle Dek, was radical, progressive love.

May we all experience that kind of acceptance and love.

I sifted half of Elva's dirt on the spot above Dek's grave, among the clover and the golden ginkgo leaves, their fan-shape stitched needles fluttering in the breeze.

Then I scattered the rest onto the place where she should have been buried—right next to her husband.

It was pleasant at Woodlawn, and I had to thank Dek and Elva for having the foresight to get a family plot here. After I collected my things, I stood up and headed back toward the road again.

As I was leaving, I could hear Uncle Dek saying, *Oh, my love, my love, my love.*

I could hear him as if he were speaking right behind me, quietly but connected, even over the sounds of the lawnmowers and leaf blowers. This was significant not only for its clarity but also for the word itself. One rarely hears Chinese people using the L-word—generally, they use the other more modest *like*. This struck me as notable and profound. So, I left them under the ginkgo and the pin oak trees, as one does when one exits a great party, leaving the friends behind who haven't seen each other in ages, allowing them to reconnect in that heartfelt way, unobstructed, gazing and talking and touching, as if no one else mattered in the world.

THE FIRST TIME I went back to our village in Toisan, I was a newly minted college graduate, still trying to figure out what I wanted to do with my life. I had only a cursory understanding that my grandfather had left this area as a rather spoiled sixteen-year-old who had a sudden wake-up call when Japan invaded China, and from that point onward as a fresh new immigrant in America in 1938, lacking the benefit of close family to protect him, needed to think fast on his feet.

It was January 1994. Hong Kong had not yet been handed back to China, and China wouldn't become the "New China" for another few years or so. I was traveling with two activist friends who were like brothers to me, and my uncle from the Bronx, who coincidentally was in nearby Guangzhou visiting at the same time.

What was I doing here? I wondered, looking out the car window at the countryside, as we drove with our guide at length through a winding road up a mountain, on our way to the cemetery site. What was it that a jook sing, a Chinese American, like me, could possibly hope to do?

When we parked, there was nothing to indicate that we were at a cemetery, from a Western perspective—none of the manicured lawns of fancy cemeteries or even the rows upon rows of headstones that made up so much of the borough I was born in. We were on a small mountain with views of the countryside all around us, and it felt like we were very far from the center of town.

We followed our guide through knee-high brambles, past small conifers and dead grass. It was a mild January in semitropical Toisan, and I was dressed in jeans and a T-shirt topped with my grandfather's plaid shirt. There is a Chinese belief that the best place to bury your ancestors is on a hill with a view, and this one had all those elements—a walkable mountain, a view of the valley.

When we stopped, in the middle of nowhere—surrounded by spring ferns, young pine trees and old grass the color of hay. I watched, puzzled, until the guide and my uncle pulled away the grass and twigs and suddenly revealed a dried-mud mound embedded into the hill with a tombstone in it.

It was my great-great-grandfather Yuan Son's gravesite.

I had never seen a gravesite so unkempt and unassuming. I had traveled all this way from America to find myself standing in front of a mound of mud on a hilltop, marked only by a sand-colored headstone with his name on it, Yuan Son Wong. (*Where was my great-great-grandmother buried?* I wondered. But no one seemed to know for sure.)

I pulled out from my messenger bag red tapered candles on sticks, incense with red handles, gold- and silver-on-orange squares of funeral paper, a suite of apples and oranges.

Although no one else in my Lutheran family paid respects at the grave the Chinese way, I wanted to pay homage to our Chinese heritage. I might not have known what I was doing, but I had a gut sense that I wanted to do the most Chinese-y thing possible.

We began clearing the plot of the remaining dead weeds. Soon only a few twigs and baby ferns remained. We set a trio of apples and oranges before my great-great-grandfather Yuan Son's headstone; my uncle brought out his lighter, and we lit the candles and then the incense. We held the incense between our palms and bowed three times while the incense turned into ash and little ringlets of smoke hovered beneath our chins.

Then we placed the incense together into the ground right before the headstone.

We did the same for my great-grandfather Sow Lei.

I took out a small accordion of firecrackers—I had never lit firecrackers in my life, but it seemed to be the right thing to do.

The sound of *pop-pop-pop* rang across the valley, and I pressed my ears closed to protect them. Even the acrid scent of gunpowder felt right, the faint line of black powder marking the earth.

My grandfather would have wanted to be where I was standing on that hill in front of his father's grave. He was sorry that he never had a chance to say goodbye. I had only a vague notion, as the fog crept across the valley so that it looked like we were about to be enveloped in a cloud, that what I was doing was the right thing.

After I returned home, I had the photographs developed.

In one, I am standing with my uncle in front our family burial mound, framed by young conifers and a small carpet of ferns. I am slightly smiling, my hands behind my back, gazing into the lens, my grandfather's flannel plaid shirt my only layer over a V-neck T-shirt.

I am young, present, and happy to finally be there.

In another, we're pouring rice wine into tiny red cups—a drink for the dead, who enjoy libations—the temperature has warmed up and I've peeled off Grandpa's shirt, which is now casually tied around my waist.

I sent these to my grandparents, then went back to my daily life of freelancing, and trying to grapple with which direction I wanted my life to go.

I received a phone call from my grandmother.

"Grandpa is very proud of you," she said from their apartment in Flushing. It was their way of thanking me.

I didn't know it at the time, but my journey to China sparked a deep desire within my grandfather Gene to return home.

Due to the wars and the reigning Communist government, he had never gone back, but now he was retired and in his early seventies.

I want to see my village, and the place where my father died, he said. *I want to see the mountains again and eat the food of my people.*

They made plans to travel that fall, but first he had to get his passport.

My grandmother helped him with the paperwork that summer, filling in all the information about Uncle George and the rest of the paper family, and including a copy of his Chinese Exclusion Act certificate of identification. They had all long ago passed on, these people I had never heard of before this, but who were so important to our family.

By late August, my grandparents received the following letter from the Department of State's National Passport Center:

> *Dear Mr. Wong,*
>
> *Your application for a passport was not accompanied by the necessary proof of United States citizenship. . . . Please submit your father's U.S. citizenship papers if you were not naturalized.*

Grandpa's Chinese Exclusion Act certificate of identity listed him as being a citizen on the basis of being *the son of a citizen*. He had never been naturalized in any other way, and neither had Uncle George. Fifty-seven years after Grandpa Gene had been released from detention with his official paperwork—over half a century after the official end of Chinese Exclusion—today's bureaucrats were unable to recognize or handle this original paperwork from an earlier era, despite the fact that it was our government that had engineered this red tape in the first place.

Was Grandpa going to have to go through the entire rigmarole again— something he had been dreading the entire sixty-plus years he was living here, trying to get by under the radar?

Was he really going to risk deportation, just to be able to see his hometown again?

He knew that he should have done it earlier, back when passports were not mandatory for travel into the U.S. But back then, he had been too afraid of being found out, and preferred not to rock the boat.

So now here he was, in his twilight years, attempting to return home, one last time.

Grandpa Gene, the paper son otherwise known as Sun Ming Wong, gathered his materials and walked them over to the large post office in downtown Flushing, now the city's thriving third Chinatown. He hesitated before pushing the large envelope into the slot, hoping that it would be enough.

WHAT HAPPENS WHEN a young country closes its doors against a nationality, and then a "race," and an *entire continent* to which your family once belonged?

That kind of disenfranchisement leads to all sorts of negative occurrences—not the least of which is a perpetual "otherness," a cloud of unwarranted suspicion, and a rejection of innovations and achievements by a significant portion of the population. It leaves our country open to the kind of inequality and perpetuation of violence that can be stoked by political figures during times of economic strife and geopolitical posturing.

Are we better than this? Yes, we are.

Is this part of our history that we have yet to thoroughly reckon with? Yes, it is.

That the seeds of Chinese Exclusion were sown during the time of Reconstruction, after the Civil War and the completion of the railroads, is telling. The hatred against Chinese raging out west coincided with the same time that the country was grappling with the aftermath of slavery and how to rebuild. But because so many of the same old Confederate politicians were reinstated, there was no possibility for real change—slavery became segregation, and politicians from across the country struck deals with each other quid pro quo to enact discriminatory exclusion laws.

If you were Chinese in America back then, you kept your paperwork close to you, and you tried not to cause waves.

Secrets were so commonplace within families that you learned not to ask too many questions.

Children had to learn to garner the strength to take a punch at school or in the playground, because that was better than getting Baba or Mama deported.

Being called *yellow* had different implications for Chinese people anyway—it was the color of royalty, like Huangdi, the Yellow Emperor.

But you could never be quite certain about your status, and when your loyalty would be questioned, and whether or not the political winds would shift and suddenly render you public enemy number one, as it did with Japanese Americans during World War II.

This is why for Asian Americans the constant questioning from *other* Americans trying to place our family origins, even if we wear the "right" clothing or speak with the "right" accent or graduate from the "right" schools—"Where are you from? No, where are you *really* from?"—is so unnerving, even threatening. It's an old, divisive sentiment questioning our right to be here, like anyone else, from the very soil upon which so many of us were born.

The idea of ourselves as *Asian Americans* would not come about until after 1965, amid the Civil Rights movement. Chinese American and Japanese American activists who had come together during marches and demonstrations to help African Americans suddenly reflected upon themselves and realized that despite the anger and distrust garnered during the Sino-Japanese war atrocities, especially among the older generations, there was a shared commonality of experience over how we were seen in the U.S. Not coincidentally, 1965 was also the year that the federal government introduced a new comprehensive Immigration Act, getting rid of the downright cruel 105-person quota for Chinese, and finally leveling the playing field.

I cannot help returning to all my original questions from childhood. Why was I the only Chinese American girl in my Queens neighborhood, when my family had been in the country since the days of the railroad? And why was it that on the rare occasion when I did encounter another Chinese American whose family had been around as long as we had in New York, I would discover that we were invariably related? The answers were right there in plain sight.

These were the effects of the Chinese Exclusion Act laws, and they were devastating. Between 1880 and 1920, there was a 25 percent drop in the Chinese American population—while the entire U.S. population more than doubled. From the Page Act and the paai wah expulsions onward, the steady decline in our numbers continued until the 1965 immigration reform. "They call it exclusion," wrote Chan Kiu Sing, a Methodist minister from Los Angeles, just after Chinese Exclusion was made permanent, "but it is not exclusion, it is extermination."

As one former resident of 37 Mott Street so succinctly put it, if the Chinese Exclusion Act had not been repealed, and "if John F. Kennedy hadn't opened up the Immigration Quota, most of us would be incestuously related." A contemporary of my father's, this retired chaplain met his wife through my aunt, and his own nephew married the daughter of his sister's best friend—*all 37 Mott Street families.*

I think about Grandpa Gene's response to my questions about what it was like spending three months in U.S. detention, during the last years of Chinese Exclusion.

"It wasn't bad," he had said.

Even back then, before I knew anything about this history, I didn't believe him.

It wasn't bad.

Perhaps he was thinking that at least he was alive, having escaped the atrocities of war.

Or perhaps you say that to your granddaughter, because you have to believe it yourself, in order to survive.

. . .

I never did get my dream relationship with my father.

One of the last times I saw Stanley, I tried to forgive him.

We were sitting in his office—the last one, on Lafayette Street.

It was like old times, me coming to his office, him sitting behind his desk like a fortress.

I had woken up that morning, our bedroom flooded with sunshine, convinced that I could do it.

"I've been wanting to say this for a long time," I said, sitting across from him. His office had not changed in the time that we had been apart, although the picture of his other granddaughter, in her Catholic school uniform, showed how much she'd grown. "I forgive you for what you did back then."

It was the accumulation of years of contemplation and intention. I was proud of myself for having even gotten to this point.

My father, sitting behind his desk, seemed visibly relieved.

"Thank you," he said, "but I don't think I did anything wrong."

It was like the needle suddenly flying off the record.

I imagine that when you give someone the gift of real forgiveness, you accept whatever response you receive.

That's when I knew I still had some work to do.

I stood up out of my chair.

"You know, it's very difficult to forgive someone who expresses absolutely *no remorse* for their actions," I said.

In that moment, as my father's face turned red, I knew that I would have to reckon with the fact that maybe I would never reach that point where I could truly forgive him.

Some months later, at home, I noticed something strange shimmering about my baby pictures.

I was flipping through Rose and Gene's old photo albums of my childhood, completely devoted to pictures of me as a baby from an old

Brownie camera that produced the kind of square photos so popular these days on social media. Maybe it was because I had been doing the research for so many years, and had seen photos of my father growing up at 37 Mott Street—mugging it up for the camera in overalls as a kindergartner, sporting his high school letterman's jacket on the roof, even his baby picture where he balls his fist near his face, looking at someone mischievously ("Chubby boy, why are you smiling?")—suddenly, I saw Stanley's face within my own staring out at me in every single one of my photos.

Photo #1: (Christmas) Nine-month-old Me, making a polystyrene mess with a plastic Santa on a sleigh ride, looking guiltily into the camera becomes . . . Baby Stanley with the *uh-oh* expression.

Photo #2: (Same Christmas) Baby Me smiling with a piece of twisted, golden challah bread in hand, turns into . . . Baby Stanley chomping down with his little teeth, a red holiday bow stuck to his fuzzy head, as if he were a present.

Stanley, 1931

Photo # 3: (Summer) One-and-a-half-year-old Me, walking across the grassy yard on shaky, chunky legs, is now . . . Little Stanley in pigtails and diapers, about to run out of the frame.

My father's face was there in every single photograph of my childhood, looking out at me through my own eyes.

"Get out of my baby pictures!" I screamed. "You were never there for me—and you don't deserve to be here now!"

When I showed my daughter the photos, she just looked at me.

"It's okay, Mom, you're made up of both of your parents," she said, with the matter-of-fact wisdom of an eight-year-old. "If your mother and father hadn't met, then you wouldn't have been born."

And then she added, "If you were not born, then I wouldn't be here."

She was right of course.

Not that long afterward, I purchased an antique Chinese puzzle ball made of sandalwood. It may not be as intricate or refined as ones fashioned in ivory for emperors—festooned with dragons and phoenixes, garden scenes, leaf motifs, and star latticework—but it still has the power to delight.

To hold a Chinese puzzle ball in your hand is to marvel at the artisanal craftsmanship, and wonder, How do they make these? How do they get these balls within each other? There are no slices through the layers, no gluing or fastening together of parts. They are sometimes called *Devil's workmanship balls* or *concentric balls* for the confounding ways in which they seem to mentally tease the viewer.

Puzzle balls are fashioned from a single piece of material—wood, stone, or bone—through which the maker fashions the layers by drilling a hole through each one and, using a series of small bent tools, carves layer upon smaller layer within, like tiny Russian nesting dolls.

It reminds me of what venerable Buddhist monk Thich Nhat Hanh once said about family members through the generations—they are the same, yet different.

So are individuals themselves, from birth to later maturity.

Ava, 1990s

Same, but different.

So many times I felt like the one standing outside looking in, trying to understand my family members' lives by peering into the darkest corners.

It was only as I drew closer to their stories, and was able to stitch them all together, that I began to understand that I was simultaneously the builder—fashioning the ball round and round in my hands with fiddly tools, rendering each layer the same, yet so very different from the previous one—all the generations of my family—as well as the puzzle ball itself, connected to all the various layers, including the very center ball, nestled within the darkest reaches, holding the very possibilities of another ball, a daughter, within.

. . .

THESE DAYS, CHINATOWN IS MINE.

It is Chinese New Year and Super Saturday—the day where every sizable kung fu school of note sends their lion dancers and students out into the streets to perform blessings for the New Year. I can hear the drumming from my open window, where in the courtyard below grows the tree of heaven, a hardy *Ailanthus* (made famous in *A Tree Grows in Brooklyn*), which folks out west say grows wherever Chinese resided, and which lives here right in our backyard.

I grab my jacket before dashing downstairs. *Chins always race downstairs,* a friend of the family once told me.

Once upon a time, my young grandfather Lung and his brothers did kung fu demonstrations on Mott Street for New Year as kids, while cheering spectators tossed them coins. Today, just like before, the head of the lion prances, back and forth, to the beat of drums and cymbals—sometimes it bows or prostrates three times in supplication, sometimes it climbs a chair to "eat" money, fruit, and lettuce. When the performers come out from under their head mask and tail curtain, switching partners, the most spirited players are often revealed to be teenage girls.

Chinese New Year is like a mini Mardi Gras, and outside at the newsstand on the corner of Mott and Mosco, where my family used to go sledding during snowstorms, DJ Yiu Yiu revs up the audience by spinning classic Mandarin and Cantonese vinyl from the 1940s and all the way up to the 2000s. A crowd has amassed—families, tourists, and old Chinatown hands—and everyone who isn't taking a video or snapping photos on their cell phone or gabbing to a neighbor is dancing to the music, a Mandarin version of Sheila E.'s "The Glamorous Life."

On the wall near the DJ booth is Chinatown's most recent mural—two women embracing, surrounded by gingerroot, jade, and flowers. Underneath an overlay of flying yellow cranes, the artists have stenciled in block lettering, "In the Future, Our Community Is Safe." In this time of scapegoating and violence against Asian women and elders, this mural is a precious wish for hope.

There are people here, especially old-timers, who knew my father and my family—some of whom have such bad memories of Stanley that they refuse to speak to me. Friends say that folks don't want to talk badly of the old man, but no matter.

There's a new generation in Chinatown, and now that Stanley has closed up shop, I'm finally free.

Once, I asked my grandfather Lung's youngest brother, Jocko, a nonagenarian born at Number 37 and living out in Pennsylvania, what he missed most about Mott Street.

"The community," he said, wistfully.

A visual artist I know waves to me from the crowd, before wrapping me in a hug. "Happy New Year! Where's your daughter?" she asks.

As I lean in to answer, someone pops a confetti blaster, and suddenly, with a bang, we are surrounded by multicolored paper descending through the air.

ONE FALL, A FEW MONTHS after my father retired, leaving Chinatown for good, I was lugging my neighbor's laundry up into the building while she was away. My neighbor lives in Yulan and Chin On's old apartment, and some Chinese New Years we have watched the parade from her fire escape, enjoying the panoramic view.

Oh, Great-Grandmother, I thought, as I entered the unit, tucking the laundry bag into a corner. *Give me a sign, something that I can recognize and understand.*

Outside, a car beeped its horn, loud and annoying. It was the kind of loud that would have New Yorkers of a certain era throwing their windows open and yelling, "Knock it off!"

I went to the window, where the view was spectacular.

Back then, Great-Grandmother Yulan could see both of our family stores, and both On Leong headquarters—the original on lower Mott, and the newer one right next door. All the important Chin places, plus her husband's favorite place to drink, the Port Arthur.

As I leaned against the sill, my eye meandered up Pell Street, past the Joe's Shanghai knockoff and all the hairdressing salons up the block. The American and Chinese flags over the Chin association building; the Hip Sing headquarters. A giant golden Pegasus, inexplicably hovering over the block, its wings outstretched and hooves aloft, crisscrossed by colorful hanging paper lanterns. The vertical hanging signage in English and Chinese neon made Chinatown look so much like Hong Kong. Even the lamppost shade was red and four-cornered, like a pagoda. I felt my great-grandmother's presence and her pleasure at my being here, and that's when I realized it:

If Yulan had been alive back then, she could have seen twenty-something me entering from the top of Pell Street that cold, wet February afternoon, preparing to meet my father at his office at the Mooney House for the very first time. She could have observed me pausing at the side door entrance, nervously looking up at that red brick building, hesitating before taking my hands out of my pockets and finally ringing the bell.

When the door opened, I stepped inside.

That day, I was so afraid of opening myself up and meeting my father—the man who had rejected us so many years before—and facing the potential of his rejection all over again.

I thought I was alone, doing this all by myself, but I wasn't.

Great-Grandmother Yulan was there, a ghostly presence, looking out and watching.

And perhaps, directly upstairs, Great-Grandmother Chun was there too, standing at the window of her sparkling apartment, smiling down in encouragement—and even my kid Grandma Rose, ducking under her mother's arm to get a better look.

And then, from across the hall, there's Grandmother Mak Lin throwing her window sash wide open.

Perhaps the jewelry store mother was there, and also, the wood-carver's wife, whose brother-in-law would marry a Doshim girl, my grandmother's younger sister.

I can see them all—the collective grandmothers and great-grandmothers, and aunties and wives, observing and witnessing from their apartments, the eyes and ears of the neighborhood.

Then, a short jump in time, like skipping stones across the lake of our lives, and there I am again, stepping out of the Mooney House, but now joined with my father on the street. I am trying to keep it all together—not lashing out in anger, not bursting into tears, because what is anger, but pain masquerading as bravado? The two of us walk toward Mott Street, me in the double-breasted peacoat I loved back then, and wore for several seasons until it fell apart, and in all black, and my father in his suit and long coat, lightly sidestepping puddles in those Italian leather shoes.

I can even see us crossing to the northern side of the block, near Mei Sum, the last coffee shop in the neighborhood remaining from my childhood—its Chinese signage reading right to left, a mirror image of its English one. Mei Sum has the best Cantonese-style jung, with succulent pork belly and a duck egg yolk in sticky rice all wrapped up in bamboo leaves.

We pause at the corner as my father indicates our building, and for the first time I regard it—*really* observe it—with soft, open eyes looking *up up up*, counting the green fire escapes to the fourth floor, trying to see *which apartment is ours—the one closest to the church, or the one to the right?* where the Adult Me—a mother, professor, writer—is standing alongside the ghosts of my grandmothers and great-grandmothers, looking on.

As the father and daughter round the corner, and continue their walk up the block, the mothers of Mott Street are watching.

They are watching, and they are pleased.

Acknowledgments

This book was created over the course of many years, building upon decades of research, including the tireless work of so many writers and academics before me to whom I am completely indebted. And because it takes a community, I must thank my readers who offered insight and guidance through so many points along the way, including Sarah Schulman, Jessica Hagedorn, Alice Elliott Dark, Sharon Gold, Martin Puchner, and Lydie Raschka.

There are writers whose brilliant work was like a sword that cuts through fire on days when I felt my own spirit flagging whom I'd like to thank, including Maxine Hong Kingston, Saidiya Hartman, Celeste Ng, Cathy Park Hong, Edmund De Waal, Lucy Sante, Margo Jefferson, Ta-Nehisi Coates, Hisham Matar, Julie Otsuka, Alexander Chee, Kimiko Hahn, Theresa Hak Kyung Cha, and Gloria Anzaldúa. Plus artists like Ruth Asawa and the collaboration of Charlie Chin, Joanne Nobuko Miyamoto, and Chris Iijima whose album *A Grain of Sand* was an anthem I played on repeat. To Iris Chang, who encouraged me, when this book was in its infancy, because "We need more Chinese American stories."

Three figures were instrumental in the creation of this book, including historian Scott Seligman, who first approached me about Dek Foon and helped me to understand his importance in the community during the second decade of Exclusion; Dorothy Rony Fujita, who patiently conducted my grandfather Lung Chin's oral history over the course of two years and documented his story for the Chinatown History Project; and Lung's friend Anne Dear Perryman, who kept the faith and his papers, and knew all along how important these stories were. A big round of thanks to you all.

Many thanks to my Chinatown family, especially Amy Chin and Peter Lau, who were key to my ability to conduct research in Toisan and in New York's Chinatown. To friends Linda Lew Woo, Helen Chin Eng, Dallas Chang, Gladys Yan, Alan Chin, Jan Lee, Mel and Richard Young, Deborah Lee, Danny Eng, and Mei Lum, Gary Lum and the entire WoW family; Thomas Sung, Vera Sung, and Jill Sung; Jane Chin, George Chew, Jan Lee, Geoff Lee, Vic Huey, Karen Zhou; the Think!Chinatown crew of Yin Kong, Kathy Wah Lee, Alice Liu, Rochelle Kwan, and photographers Ed Cheng and Cindy Trinh; the 21 Pell Street family, including Rob Gee, Pastor Bayer Lee, the late Mabel Lee, and her father, the Reverend Lee To; the American Legion family, including Tommy Ong, Gabe Mui, Honey Dupris, Karen Chan, Butchie Woo, and the late Peter Woo, who brought me into the fold.

So many colleagues helped with research, connections, and questions that guided the way. Thanks to Jeannie Pfaelzer, who allowed me to photocopy her entire catalog on the paai wah, Ted Gong and the 1882 Foundation, Charlotte Brooks, Carla Peterson, Ira Shor, Perla Guerrero, for discussions and a place to stay, and Krishnendu Ray, who opened access to a long-closed door. Special thanks also to Anne Mendelsohn, Peter Trachtenberg, and Kian Lam Kho for food and insights.

A big thank-you to the late Corky Lee, who not only documented us Asian American artists and activists, but brought us all together, and who worked tirelessly to introduce me to old Chinatown hands who knew my family. You are sorely missed.

Many institutions provided instrumental support during the research and writing stages. First and foremost, I want to thank the Dorothy and Lewis B. Cullman Center for Scholars and Writers at the New York Public Library, including Salvatore Scibona, Martha Hodes, Eyal Press, Hugh Eakin, Magda Teter, Nellie Hermann, Blake Gopnik, Barbara Weinstein, Sarah Bridger, Lynn

Melnick, Lauren Goldenberg, Paul Delaverac, among others. Thanks to Helen Bodian and Roger Alcaly, and Esther Allen for their support; and a special shout-out to librarians Rebecca Federman, Tal Nader, and Diane Dias De Fazio.

The Advanced Research Collaborative at the CUNY Graduate Center deserves thanks, as do my cohort of academic colleagues, including Linda Tropp, Robert Smith, Enrique Espada, Don Robatham, and Kay Powell. Thanks to the New York Foundation for the Arts for a nonfiction grant, the Fulbright Scholars Program, the Women Writing Women's Lives seminar, the Faculty Fellowship Publication Program at CUNY, the New York Institute for Humanities, and residencies that provided space for myself and my family like Marble House and Space at Ryder Farm; my cohort and their amazing children were so helpful, most notably, Hillary Frank and Sasha, and Djassi Johnson and Mirahl.

Special bow of gratitude goes out to the staff at the Chinatown History Project, now the Museum of Chinese in America, both past and present, including Jack Tchen, Charlie Lai, Beatrice Chen, Yue Ma, and Kevin Chu for all of your help and support in documenting the community.

Love and gratitude to my family, including my wonderful grandparents Rose Doshim and Gene Wong, my mother Laura Chin, and Kenith and Patricia Wong, and Wesley Wong. A special thank-you goes out to Ce Ce Chin, Bruce and Lucy Chin, Donald and Dori Chin for patiently answering so many questions, as well as Marcella Chin Dear, Anne Chan, Susan Chin, Penny Chin, Wendy Chin, Celeste Chin, Cheryl Chin, Loretta Wu, Lois Wu, Alison Ho, Tracy Lai, and Him Mark Lai. Stanley Chin and Lung Chin led me to this story in their own elliptical ways. A warm thank-you to Karen and Ruth Lisk, and the Lisk family. Many thanks to the late Philip Choy and Judy Yung for their work, and Judy's tour of Angel Island and the many conversations about our families; West Coast Chinese American friends who are champions of the Chinese railroad workers, some of whom are fellow descendants, including Sue Lee, Gordon Chang, Vic Lim, and Andrea Yee.

I want to thank friends who contributed hours of conversation and insight about this book, including Heidi Chua, Rick Sin, Maggie Ho, Matt Brim, Mara Faye Lethem, Dara Mayers, Monique Truong, Suki Kim, Maryann Feola, and Leslie Cribbs; and friends in the genealogy world, including Patrick Chew, Henry Thom, Tony King, Helen Chin, Lori Tan Chinn, Minerva Chin, and Ira Rezak for general guidance, interviews, and translation help these many years. Also, to the NY Chinatown Reunion and the tireless work of Richard Chu and the Dong Sisters for their help. Many thanks to my research assistants Sarah Huang, Shantal Rowe, and Obiageli Ukatu, who tirelessly unearthed articles and provided so much bibliographic help.

Gratitude to the community that is Sisters in Self-Defense, including my partner in crime artist Alison Kuo, photographer Tommy Kha, Dr. Emily Siy, Monica Liu, Sarinya Srisakul, Ping Choi, Lisa Quan, and all the sisters who have taught for and studied with us. The best thing about these sobering times was connecting with you all.

Every writer needs a coven of magical supporters, and much love to my own—Stacey D'Erasmo, Mary Bly, Alice Elliott Dark, Meg Tilly, Erica Ridley, and the amazing Sarah Gambito, whose Kundiman community supports so many Asian American writers. And to Tammy Delacort and her group, including Sherry Kempf, Rebekah West, Katy Perry, Kelly Huffman, Patty Wetterling, and others.

To my wonderful agent Frances Coady at Aragi, Inc. for her unfailing support and keen editorial eye as I traveled the world and back again for this book, and steadfast patience as I hammered out the chapters.

To the team at Penguin Press, especially my talented editor Virginia Smith Younce, who is endowed with her own innate powers of jujitsu—shaping this narrative and holding my hand when I was deeply entangled in the intricacies of all of its moving parts, and clearing the way for Mott Street to enter the world. Many thanks to Caroline Sydney for the clear-eyed edits and dedication to this book; to Juliana Kiyan, Megan Buiocchi, and Danielle Plafsky in publicity and marketing, who move with the power of ten thousand horses; to Lavina Lee and Sheila Moody in production editorial and copyediting; and the design team of Darren Haggar, Grace Han, and Meighan Cavanaugh for the powerful cover and interior design.

I could never have written this book without the love and support of Owen Brunette. Thank you for being steadfast during the seasons of lost passports, single-parenting, and the long birthing of books. I never met your father, but I feel like I know him through you. And darling Mei Mei, from the very beginning, you have expressed your creativity and own unique point of view—we continuously marvel at how effortlessly you light the way.

Bibliography

What you have in your hands is the culmination of several decades of research. As a child, I had an almost preternatural curiosity, interviewing family members, collecting stories, questioning the adults for nuggets of their experiences, and earning me the nickname *nosy*. While I kept a notebook from grade school onward, until I began the transcription process, many of these family stories were passed down orally, and some have only now entered the written record. Since the 1990s, I gathered whatever extant family documents remained, including books, letters, oral histories, photo albums, and handwritten documents. These, plus the oral stories, collected over the course of my entire life, provided the basis for this book.

CHAPTER ONE

There are many accounts of the building at 37 Mott Street both pre-and post the 1914 fire, including ones from family members like Rose Doshim Wong and Lung Chin. See also Bruce Hall's book *Tea That Burns.* Our earliest ancestor Yuan Son arrived to the U.S. in 1865, and like many railroad workers resided here under Lincoln's legacy.

Chinese Exclusion 1882, Forty-seventh Congress. Session I, Chap. 126, May 6, 1882.

Hall, Bruce Edward. *Tea That Burns: A Family Memoir of Chinatown.* New York: The Free Press, Simon & Schuster, 1998.

Lung "Pop" Chin oral history interviews, January 1988–February 1990. Interview conducted by Dorothy Rony Fujita, for the Museum of Chinese in America, New York.

Soennichsen, John. *The Chinese Exclusion Act of 1882.* Westport, CT: Greenwood, 2011.

Tchen, John Kuo Wei. *Chinese American: Exclusion/Inclusion*. New York: Scala Arts Publishers, 2014.

CHAPTER TWO

Although there was great acrimony between my families, they did keep tabs on one another. My grandmother read Lung Chin's obituary in *New York Newsday*, but in fact his obituary, which I later learned was written by his friend, the writer Anne Dear Perryman, appeared in several publications, including *The New York Times*. Luckily for me, I was able to contact Perryman in 2015, and not only had she been cowriting a book with Lung, but she had diligently kept his papers intended for a nonfiction book of his own. These included a stack of mostly undated notes he had penned willy-nilly across scratch pads and notebooks whose spines crumbled or tore apart in my hands; books on Chinese history, philosophy, and medicine; and some beautiful wood carvings. Although he never completed this story, his personal archive provided me with a solid scaffolding for many of the Chin family stories.

From 1988 to 1990, Lung gave his oral history to the Chinatown History Project (now MOCA), conducted by Dorothy Rony Fujita. When it was finally released to me in 2016, nearly twenty years after I first inquired about it, I listened to hours of interviews, and combed through its entirety. Part of it appears in the permanent collection of the museum as an installation piece in a room populated by Chin family store items. His oral history was another valuable source of information, and I am indebted to both Perryman and Fujita for their good work.

Chin, Ava, ed. "The Missing." In *Split: Stories from a Generation Raised on Divorce*. New York: McGraw-Hill, 2000.

Edward Mooney House, Landmarks Preservation Commission, August 23, 1966, Number 1, LP-0084.

"Lung Chin, 84, Is Dead," *New York Times*, March 29, 1990, B:10.

Lung Chin archives, in possession of the author.

Lung "Pop" Chin oral history interviews, January 1988–February 1990. Interview conducted by Dorothy Rony Fujita, for the Museum of Chinese in America, New York.

CHAPTER THREE

Currently, there are no known surviving first-person written accounts by a Chinese railroad worker on the transcontinental railroad documenting their experiences, although there were men who were literate. Violent periods on both sides of the Pacific, as well as neglect and a lack of appreciation of these records, have sadly led to their destruction. *The Diary of Dukesang Wong* is the closest that we have (Wong worked on the Canadian Pacific Railroad). The next best thing is the family stories. Most of what we know about my ancestor Yuan Son Wong (Wong Yuan Son) is based on oral stories my grandfather Gene Kai Fai Wong told my family. My search for Yuan Son's paper trail began in 1991, when, as an undergraduate, I traveled out to Salt Lake City, Utah, and visited the LDS Church's genealogy library to search for clues. I combed the census record for Chinese in Boise, Idaho, and found a reference to one Yuan Son as a gambler, which fit with one version of the story that he had opened a gambling parlor there. Other family members recalled hearing that Yuan Son had opened up a store. Through my research on gambling parlors of that era, I realized that his business was likely both—a store in the front and an adjacent gambling parlor in the back, with Yuan Son and his employees occupying the upstairs apartment.

Sometimes, my grandparents would say that Yuan Son had been "deported," but when I visited the Idaho Historical Society in Boise in 2018, and leafed through their jail ledgers, I could not find his name. Deportation is a legal term, including legal proceedings of which there would have been records, but there were none. Later, I would learn that this was not unusual—during the five years in which I canvassed the country searching for historical traces of family members, I could find no actual records of them in town or church archives. Whenever violence was enacted against them in America, many of the clerks, sheriffs, and judges responsible for bringing justice sided with the perpetrators; when instigators of violence were allowed to go free, most records on Chinese residents who were unlawfully pushed out, as Yuan Son was, were often buried or destroyed, especially after Chinese like the residents of Eureka, California, began suing towns for damage to their businesses and loss of property.

I visited Promontory Point, Utah, in 2006, 2018, and, most recently, in 2019, when I was invited to speak at the 150th anniversary of the completion of the Transcontinental Railroad; each time, I visited the areas where Yuan Son worked and camped out.

Note on Louis Beck's *New York's Chinatown*: While the profile on Dek Foon was enormously helpful, there are errors, including for place names. To determine Dek's date of arrival, I checked Beck's reporting against Dek and Chow's CEA files; given the dates, and the age of Dek's son, I believe in this case that the Exclusion documents are more accurate—placing Dek in California in March 1885.

Ambrose, Stephen E. *Nothing Like It in the World: The Men Who Built the Transcontinental Railroad 1863–1869*. New York: Simon & Schuster, 2000.

Beck, Louis J. *New York's Chinatown: An Historical Presentation of Its People and Places*. New York: Bohemia Publishing Company, 1898.

Chang, Gordon H. *Ghosts of Gold Mountain: The Epic Story of the Chinese Who Built the Transcontinental Railroad*. Boston: Houghton Mifflin Harcourt, 2019.

Chang, Gordon H., and Shelley Fisher Fishkin, eds. *The Chinese and the Iron Road: Building the Transcontinental Railroad*. Stanford, CA: Stanford University Press, 2019.

Chew, William F. *Nameless Builders of the Transcontinental Railroad*. Bloomington, IN: Trafford Publishing, 2004.

Hart, Arthur A. *Chinatown: Boise, Idaho, 1880–1970*. Boise, ID: Caxton Press, 2002.

Lee, Sue, and Connie Young Yu. *Voices from the Railroad: Stories by Descendants of Chinese Railroad Workers*. San Francisco: Chinese Historical Society of America, Autumn Press, 2019.

San Francisco Bulletin. 150th Anniversary Golden Spike 1869, Union Pacific site. www.up.com/goldenspike/sacramento-promontory.html.

Sun Ming Wong, CEA file, National Archives & Records Administration, Seattle, Washington.

"The Pacific Railroad from the End of the Track: The Great Ten-Mile Feat," *Daily Alta*, May 1, 1869.

Wong, Dukesang. *The Diary of Dukesang Wong: A Voice from Gold Mountain.* Edited by David McIlwraith. Translated by Wanda Joy Hoe. Vancouver: Canada: Talonbooks, 2020. This is the only known first-person account by a Chinese worker on the construction of the CPR.

Zwonitzer, Mark, and Michael Chin. "Transcontinental Railroad," *American Experience,* WGBH, Boston, 2003.

CHAPTER FOUR

Uncovering Louis Beck's profile of Uncle Dek helped launch my interest in Dek Foon. Much of what I know about his early years comes from a combination of conversations with Grandma Rose at her home in Flushing, and the written record. Beck, a journalist by trade, mainly obtained his information from local beat police officers, and I now know he got a few details wrong about Dek Foon, including where he lived before he started up his laundry business in Nevada City (Marysville, California, and not Millsville). The contemporary literature was extremely biased against Chinese, but Beck offered rare praise—calling Dek Foon "a self-made man" and "a Christian and one of the best known and highly respected men in Chinatown."

I read about the paai wah from the 1870s–1880s, including the coordinated attacks on Seattle's Chinese community from eyewitness accounts of the period, newspaper articles, and books like Beth Lew-Williams's *The Chinese Must Go!,* and Jean Pfaelzer's *Driven Out,* which details attacks on Chinese throughout the West. I had several conversations and email correspondence with Wingston Chan, a descendant of Chin Gee Hee. While there are varying accounts of Mrs. Chin Gee Hee's name, due to the fact that there were many wives (common for wealthy men of that period), the family confirmed that she was Lenoi Louie (Lui). Madame Louie's story was told by Chin Gee Hee to the Chinese consul, who relayed it to the secretary of state in 1888. Nothing survives from her point of view. When faced with the deafening silence in the record, I felt compelled to allow Lenoi Louie to permeate my consciousness, and write from her point of view.

I am particularly indebted to Wingston Chan, Lew-Williams for her scholarship, and to Pfaelzer, who allowed me to photocopy her entire archive on the paai wah, and to Cowboy Wally Hagaman in Nevada City for conversations. Also, to writer Scott Seligman for uncovering Dek Foon's CEA file in the New York NARA offices.

"Anti-Chinese Legislation in California." July 8, 1880 (unnamed publication). Bruce E. Hall Collection, Museum of Chinese in America, New York.

Beck, Louis J. *New York's Chinatown: An Historical Presentation of Its People and Places.* New York: Bohemia Publishing Company, 1898.

Bonner, Arthur. *Alas! What Brought Thee Hither? The Chinese in New York 1800–1950.* Teaneck, NJ: Associated University Presses, 1997.

Casey, Marion R. "37 Mott Street: The Nealis Family from Co. Sligo." Resurrecting the Ethnic Village, NYU. https://ethnic-village.org/the-nealis-family-from-co-sligo/#_edn4.

Chang Yen Hoon to Thomas Bayard, March 3, 1888, *Papers Relating to the Foreign Relations of the United States,* Part 1 (Washington, DC: Government Printing Office, 1889).

Chew, Lee, with Joseph Singleton. "The Biography of a Chinaman," *The Independent,* February 19, 1903.

"Chinamen Coming East." March 4, 1880 (unnamed publication). Bruce E. Hall Collection, Museum of Chinese in America, New York.

"Chinamen Driven Out," *Morning Mercury*, February 12, 1886.

"Chinese Haunts in New York." n.d. (unnamed publication). Bruce E. Hall Collection, Museum of Chinese in America, New York.

"Chinese in New York City, A Description." February 16, 1874 (unnamed publication). Bruce E. Hall Collection, Museum of Chinese in America, New York.

"Chinese Widowers." 1882 (unnamed publication). Bruce E. Hall Collection, Museum of Chinese America, New York.

Daniels, Roger. *Anti-Chinese Violence in North America*. New York: Arno Press, 1978.

Dek Foon, CEA file, 24/1102, New York, and 2500/5043, Boston, National Archives & Records Administration.

Hagaman, Wallace R., and Steve F. Cottrell. *The Chinese Must Go! The Anti-Chinese Boycott: Truckee, California: 1886*. Nevada City, CA: The Cowboy Press, 2004.

"Is It a Chinese Exodus? Rapid Growth of the Almond-Eyed Element in New York." 1879 (unnamed publication). Bruce E. Hall Collection, Museum of Chinese in America, New York.

"It Is Said the Chinese Population Is Increasing," *Daily Transcript*, December 23, 1885.

Kinnear, George. "Anti-Chinese Riots at Seattle, WN., February 8, 1886." *Seattle Post-Intelligencer*, reprinted in hardcover, February 1911.

Lee, Erika, and Judy Yung. *Angel Island: Immigrant Gateway to America*. New York: Oxford University Press, 2010.

Lew-Williams, Beth. *The Chinese Must Go: Violence, Exclusion, and the Making of the Alien in America*. 3rd ed. Cambridge, MA: Harvard University Press, 2018.

Lew-Williams, Beth. "The Remarkable Life of a Sometimes Railroad Worker: Chin Gee Hee, 1844–1929." In *The Chinese and the Iron Road: Building the Transcontinental Railroad*, edited by Gordon H. Chang and Shelley Fisher Fishkin, 329–345. Stanford, CA: Stanford University Press, 2019.

"More Chinese Driven Off," *Evening Herald*, March 1, 1886.

Nokes, R. Gregory. *Massacred for Gold: The Chinese in Hells Canyon*. 4th ed. Corvallis: Oregon State University Press, 2009.

Page Act, Forty-third Congress, Session II, Chap. 141, 1875.

Pfaelzer, Jean. *Driven Out: The Forgotten War Against Chinese Americans*. Berkeley: University of California Press, 2007.

Rev. Huie Kin. *Reminiscences*. Peiping, China: San Yu Press, 1932.

Salisbury, Harrison. *China: 100 Years of Revolution*. New York: Holt, Rinehart, & Winston, 1983.

Sun Ning difangzhi, 1893, official difangzhi records, sections from 1373–1570s, detailing pirate raids, insurgencies, famine, typhoons, and other natural disasters. Translated by Hilary Chan.

"The Chinese in New York." March 6, 1880 (unnamed publication). Bruce E. Hall Collection, Museum of Chinese in America, New York.

"The Chinese Quarter Expanding." 1880 (*New York Daily Tribune*). Bruce E. Hall Collection, Museum of Chinese in America, New York.

Van Norden, Warner M. *Who's Who of the Chinese in New York*. New York, 1918.

Wingston Chan interviews via phone (September 19, 2022, October 14, 2022, and

October 23, 2022), and email correspondence (September 7–13, 2021, and September 8, 2022, October 9, 2022, October 11, 2022, and October 24, 2022).

Yung, Judy. *Unbound Feet: A Social History of Chinese Women in San Francisco.* Berkeley: University of California Press, 1995.

CHAPTER FIVE

I first encountered Wong Chin Foo's writing via Philip Lopate's *Writing New York* anthology, and was surprised to learn that a nineteenth-century Chinese writer was writing for some of the best New York publications of the day. It was only later through the pivotal Chinese Exclusion/Inclusion exhibit at the New-York Historical Society in 2015 and correspondence with historian Scott Seligman, author of a biography of Wong Chin Foo, who showed me CERL letterhead listing Uncle Dek as a member of the League's board, that I began to get an inkling of the importance of this civic engagement.

"An Awkward Slip," *San Francisco Morning Call*, January 27, 1893.

"Chinamen Free Their Minds: Protest in Public Meeting Against the Registration Act." Bruce E. Hall Collection, Museum of Chinese in America, New York, 1892.

"Chinamen Protest Vigorously: A Mass Meeting at Cooper Union—Speaking Against the Geary Law." 1892 (unnamed publication). Bruce E. Hall Collection, Museum of Chinese in America, New York.

Chinese Equal Rights League. "Appeal of the Chinese Equal Rights League to the People of the United States for Equality of Manhood." New York, July 27, 1893.

"Denis Airs His Eloquence," *New York Times*, October 19, 1887.

Garrison, William Lloyd. "Speech of Wm. Lloyd Garrison at the Mass Meeting of the Chinese Equal Rights League." Tremont Temple, Boston, November 18, 1892.

Gold, Martin B. *Forbidden Citizens: Chinese Exclusion and the U.S. Congress: A Legislative History.* Alexandria, VA: TheCapitol.Net, 2012.

"Kearney Interrupted by Chinamen," *New York Tribune*, October 19, 1887.

Lopate, Phillip. *Writing New York: A Literary Anthology.* New York: Library of America, 1998.

"Money for Exclusion," *San Francisco Chronicle*, January 27, 1893.

New York City Census, 1895.

"Not Criminals: Chinese Demand Repeal of Geary Act," *Boston Daily Globe*, November 19, 1892.

Seligman, Scott. *The First Chinese America, The Remarkable Life of Wong Chin Foo.* Hong Kong: Hong Kong University Press, 2013.

Tchen, John Kuo Wei. *Chinese American: Exclusion/Inclusion.* New York: Scala Arts Publishers, 2014.

"The Chamber of Commerce Protests." 1892 (unnamed publication). Bruce E. Hall Collection, Museum of Chinese in America, New York.

"The Sentiment Expressed in the Methodist General Conference on the Subject of the Chinese Exclusion Act," *New York Times*, May 8, 1892.

"Wong Chin Foo and Denis: The Sand-lots Orator and the Mandarin Meet," *Chicago Daily Tribune*, October 23, 1887.

CHAPTER SIX

Stories of Chin On abound in the Chin family, but I read of his harrowing border crossing first from Lung's essay, which had been circulated at the 1985 family reunion picnic in Bradley Beach. His accounts place his father's crossing at Buffalo, but he later amended his account in an interview with Dorothy Rony, disclosing that Chin On actually took the route to Malone, New York—Lung chose Buffalo in his storytelling because by the time of my father's generation, no one knew the importance of Malone, and Buffalo was the largest nearby city.

Both Lung and his younger brother Calvin attest that their uncle Hing and father were elected president and secretary of On Leong, but none mention Tom Lee—not because Lee wasn't important, but because his heyday was in the era long before they were born, and Lee passed away when Lung and his younger brothers were children. By the time they were coming of age, their father and uncle were among the top daai lop jai bigshots in On Leong.

Bonner, Arthur. *Alas! What Brought Thee Hither? The Chinese in New York 1800–1950.* Teaneck, NJ: Associated University Presses, 1997.

Calvin Chin papers, written in California, n.p., undated.

Chin, Lung. "A Family Chronicle: The Chin Kai Mings: The First 700 Years." New York, 1985, n.p.

Culin, Stewart. *The Gambling Games of the Chinese in America, Fań T'án: The Game of Repeatedly Spreading Out, and Pák Kòp Piú or, The Game of White Pigeon Ticket.* Philadelphia: University of Pennsylvania Press, 1891.

Lung Chin archives, in possession of the author.

Lung Chin, *Chinatown, My Chinatown*, edited by Dorothy Rony Fujita, n.p.

Lung Chin oral history interviews (January 1988–February 1990), conducted by Dorothy Rony Fujita, Museum of Chinese in America.

Seligman, Scott D. *Tong Wars: The Untold Story of Vice, Money, and Murder in New York's Chinatown.* New York: Viking Press, 2016.

Van Norden, Warner M. *Who's Who of the Chinese in New York.* New York, 1918.

CHAPTER SEVEN

I am grateful that Lisk family descendants shared with me their perspectives on Dek and Elva, the dissolution of Elva and Doran's marriage, and Elva's being intersex. Information about Dek and Elva's marriage and later years was also provided by Doshim family members and Dek Foon's descendants in Hong Kong.

Bonner, Arthur. *Alas! What Brought Thee Hither? The Chinese in New York 1800–1950.* Teaneck, NJ: Associated University Presses, 1997.

Civil War record on Benjamin Lisk, U.S. Returns from Military Posts, 1806–1916.

Dek Foon, CEA file, 24/1102, New York, and 2500/5043, Boston, National Archives & Records Administration.

Faber, Anna Shifrin. "A Vessel for Discrimination," *Georgetown Law Journal* 108 (2018):

1363. https://www.law.georgetown.edu/georgetown-law-journal/wp-content/uploads/sites/26/2020/05/Faber_A-Vessel-for-Discrimination-The-Public-Charge-Standard-of-Inadmissibility-and-Deportation.pdf.

Gold, Martin B. *Forbidden Citizens: Chinese Exclusion and the U.S. Congress: A Legislative History*. Alexandria, VA: TheCapitol.Net, 2012.

"Ju Sing Weds," *Brooklyn Daily Eagle*, July 30, 1887.

Karen Lisk interview, in person, July 8, 2018; correspondence June 26, 2018, and July 30, 2018.

Kevles, Daniel. *In the Name of Eugenics*. New York: Knopf, 1985.

Marriage certificate, Elva Lisk and William Doran, May 26, 1895, State of New York.

New York State Census, 1875.

U.S. Federal Census, 1880.

CHAPTER EIGHT

Several parts of this chapter about the Kishinev fundraisers are based on English-language and Yiddish newspaper articles that reported on the fundraisers in 1903 and 1905 (see next page). Scott Seligman's contemporary articles were also very helpful.

I had always imagined or hoped that Chin On and Hing were at the Port Arthur peace dinner, but because he was in San Francisco during the April 1906 earthquake, it's unlikely he was there; plus, even if he was in New York, according to the press reports, all the bigwigs sat it out—even Tom Lee.

I was ruminating about Chin On's near-death escape, and reading about other firsthand accounts of the earthquake, when I saw images of the City Hall in ruins. I had long known that the destruction of the Hall of Records was a significant event in the history of Chinese immigration, but it was only when I saw the buildings and recognized them as the same ones before which Denis Kearny argued so vehemently against Chinese immigration that I began to understand the full significance, and ironies, surrounding this particular site.

"A Chinese Dinner," *The Deaf-Mutes' Journal*, November 27, 1902.

"Aid for Kishineff Victims," *New York Times*, May 13, 1903.

"American Bounty for Kishineff Sufferers," *New York Times*, May 15, 1903.

Bonner, Arthur. *Alas! What Brought Thee Hither? The Chinese in New York 1800–1950*. Teaneck, NJ: Associated University Presses, 1997.

"Chinamen Get Gold Medals," *The Sun*, November 21, 1903.

"Chinese Help for Jews," *New York Times*, May 12, 1903.

"Chinese Help the Tsar's Martyrs," *The Forward*, May 7, 1903. Translated by Ira Rezak.

"Chinese Play for Jews," *New York Daily Tribune*, May 12, 1902.

Chin On, CEA file, 12486/9-3, National Archives & Records Administration, San Bruno.

"Dinner Begins with Dessert," *New York Tribune*, November 19, 1902.

Genthe, Arnold. "Earthquake and Fire." In *As I Remember*. New York: Reynal & Hitchcock, 1936. https://sfmuseum.org/1906.2/genthe.html.

"Gold Medals Given to Chinese by Jews," *Washington Times*, November 21, 1903.

"Hail Foster, J., Peacemaker," *New York Sun*, March 29, 1906.

"Hip Sings Sign Treaty: On Leong's Turn Next—Then Peace Is Expected to Dwell in Chinatown," *New York Times*, February 7, 1906.

Jack Chin letter to descendants, July 24, 1989, n.p.

"Judges Guests at a Chinese Banquet." *New York Times,* February 18, 1903.

"King David in Chinese Garb." *The Sun*, December 4, 1905.

Lung Chin oral history interviews (January 1988–February 1990), conducted by Dorothy Rony Fujita, Museum of Chinese in America.

Lym, Glenn. "Scapegoat: The 1871–1906 San Francisco City Hall." Here6, Lymarch, You-tube.

"More Details of the Kishineff Atrocities," *New York Times*, May 15, 1903.

"Most Exclusive Club in New York's Chinatown," *New York Times*, January 1, 1905.

"On Leong Tongs and Sing Tongs Will Be Good: Rival Feuds of New York's Wicked Chinatown Sign Agreement to Quit Carrying Revolvers," *Buffalo Courier-Express*, February 3, 1906.

Schwartzenberg, Susan. "Going Public: The San Francisco Civic Center." In *Reclaiming San Francisco: History, Politics, Culture*. San Francisco: City Lights, 1998.

Seligman, Scott D. "The Night New York's Chinese Went Out for Jews," *The Forward*, January 26, 2011.

Seligman, Scott D. *Tong Wars: The Untold Story of Vice, Money, and Murder in New York's Chinatown*. New York: Viking, 2016.

"The Benefit in the Chinese Theater," *The Forward*, May 12, 1903.

"The Chinese Benefit," *Jewish World*, May 12, 1903.

"The Oriental Club Dines," *New York Times*, March 1, 1904.

"The Tongs to Give Up Gambling and Shooting," *New York Times*, February 3, 1906.

"To Aid Kishineff Sufferers: Jews Arranging Benefits for Russian Co-Religionists—Sympathy Shown by Chinese Colony," *New York Times*, May 8, 1903.

"Tong's Dinner Peaceful; On Leongs Stayed Away: Not One Member of the Hostile Faction Appeared," *New York Times*, February 12, 1906.

"Tongs Hold Peace Confab," *The Sun*, January 31, 1906.

"Tonight the Benefit from the Chinese," *The Forward*, May 11, 1903.

Wu Doshim's Northfield Mount Hermon school records under "Ing Shim," 1901–1902.

Zipperstein, Steven. *Pogrom: Kishinev and the Tilt of History*. New York: W. W. Norton, 2018.

CHAPTER NINE

In 2017, my family and I moved to China so that I could research the book as a Fulbright Scholar, and it was there that I took several trips to Hong Kong. Much of the medical history of early colonial Hong Kong, the plague, and the missionary hospitals was based on books like Frank Ching's *One Hundred and Thirty Years of Medicine in Hong Kong* and Arthur Starling's *Plague, SARS, and the Story of Medicine in Hong Kong*. A special note of thanks to Elizabeth Zinn from Hong Kong University and her colleagues who helped me confirm that Great-Grandmother Chun had been trained at Nethersole Hospital.

Much of the section dealing with Doshim's immigration woes is based on his Chinese Exclusion act file, which was one of the hardest to locate. Most files are located in the city where the person primarily resided, but in Great-Grandfather Doshim's case, it was at his

1909 port of entry, Seattle, where his biggest case file was located—within a shadow database that the Seattle NARA offices was no longer using. I want to thank the volunteers at NARA for their tireless work to grant me access, especially Lily Eng.

Benedict, Carol. "Bubonic Plague in 19th-Century China," *Modern China* 14 (April 1988): 107–155.

Ching, Frank. *130 Years of Medicine in Hong Kong.* Singapore: Springer, 2018.

George, Janet. "The Lady Doctor's 'Warm Welcome': Dr. Alice Sibree and the Early Years of Hong Kong's Maternity Service 1903–1909," *Journal of the Hong Kong Branch of the Royal Asiatic Society* 33 (1993): 81–109. http://www.jstor.org/stable/23890094.

"If You're Chinese, It's 4604," *New York Sun*, February 13, 1907.

Pryor, E. G. "The Great Plague of Hong Kong," *Journal of the Hong Kong Branch of the Royal Asiatic Society* 15 (1975): 61–70. http://www.jstor.org/stable/23881624.

Salisbury, Harrison. *China: 100 Years of Revolution.* New York: Holt, Rinehart, & Winston, 1983.

Starling, Arthur E. *Plague, SARS, and the Story of Medicine in Hong Kong.* Hong Kong: Hong Kong University Press, 2006.

Wu Doshim CEA file, NARA RG 85, Box: RS059, Case No. RS2314, National Archives & Records Administration, Seattle, Washington.

CHAPTER TEN

Chun and Doshim's courtship, immigration saga, and eventual life in Brooklyn with Dek and Elva—even the short scene at the store that refused to serve Chun—were based on oral stories told to me by Grandma Rose. As a resident of Hong Kong and a "subject of the crown," it was easier for her mother to gain entry into Canada than directly into the U.S. itself.

To better understand the Elsie Sigel murder and the manhunt for Leon Ling, I pored over Bonner's *Alas!*, newspaper articles, and Mary Ting Yi Lui's book *The Chinatown Trunk Mystery.* I traced Doshim's journey via his CEA file, where he led authorities off the family's trail by traveling to Seattle solo; I held my breath when officials asked why my great-grandfather was there, when they expected him to go through Malone, New York, where his file had been sent.

For the numerous historic ways of undercover entry into the country, see the articles cited.

Bigelow, Poultney. "The Chinaman at Our Gates: A Personal Inspection of the Port of Entry on the Canadian Frontier," *Collier's Weekly*, September 12, 1903.

Bonner, Arthur. *Alas! What Brought Thee Hither? The Chinese in New York 1800–1950.* Teaneck, NJ: Associated University Presses, 1997.

"Chinamen Shipped in Hay," *Daily People*, November 3, 1900.

"Chinese Came Through in Coffins," *New York Herald*, April 25, 1895.

"Chinese Enter; Bribery Found, Secret Service Officers Tell of Regular Traffic Over Mexican Border," *Chicago Daily Tribune*, August 25, 1901.

"Chinese Importations: Two Violators of the Exclusion Act Caught at Buffalo." 1890 (unnamed publication). Bruce E. Hall Collection, Museum of Chinese in America, New York.

"Chinese Subjects of Queen Victoria." Bruce E. Hall Collection, Museum of Chinese in America, New York, n.d.

Lui, Mary Ting Yi. *The Chinatown Trunk Mystery: Murder, Miscegenation, and Other Dangerous Encounters in Turn-of-the-Century New York City.* 2nd ed. Princeton, NJ: Princeton University Press, 2005.

Ng Wu Chow, CEA file, 24/1034, National Archives & Records Administration, New York.

"Smuggling Chinamen in Sleepers." June 16, 1891 (unnamed publication). Bruce E. Hall Collection, Museum of Chinese in America, New York.

"Smuggling Chinamen: Profitable Business," *New York Tribune*, November 29, 1901.

"Smuggling Chinese Across the Border," *New York Herald*, September 11, 1891.

"Smuggling in Chinese: Bribed Witnesses and False Fathers Are Utilized," *Washington Post*, February 10, 1901.

"Smuggling of Chinamen: Suspected of Coming Over the Canadian Border in Disguise—One Dressed as a Woman." 1897 (unnamed publication). Bruce E. Hall Collection, Museum of Chinese in America, New York.

"The Invading Chinamen," *New York Tribune*, June 17, 1898.

"The Smuggler Chinee Is Peculiar," *Washington Post*, May 21, 1911.

"To Stop Chinese Influx: Detention Stations to Be Opened on the Canadian Border—One at Malone, N.Y.," *New York Times*, April 30, 1903.

"Uncle Sam's Soldiers as Chinese Smugglers," *New York Herald*, December 28, 1891.

"Ways of the Wily Celestial," *Washington Post*, August 29, 1909.

Wu Doshim CEA file, NARA RG 85, Box: RS059, Case No. RS2314, National Archives & Records Administration, Seattle, Washington.

CHAPTER ELEVEN

In spring of 2017, I took three trips to Toisan and visited our ancestral villages. Most of the family stories here are based on Lung Chin's papers and oral history, and Jack Chin's written narrative. In addition, a great-aunt gave me a copy of the Chin genealogy *jiapu*, from which I gleaned the biographical details about our most-revered male ancestors.

These stories, including those about Kai Ming, were a source of wonder and pride for young Grandfather Lung as he yearned to understand himself within the context of his father and family. Of all of the families whose genealogies I collected, only the Kai Ming Chin genealogy provided a mini narrative of our "great men" through the entirety of the Ming dynasty. They were proud of this lineage for various reasons—the Ming period was revered by Han Chinese as the last dynasty of Chinese rulers (squeezed between Yuan Mongol and Manchurian emperors); and because the first Ming emperor elevated military families like ours to the nobility, rather like samurai in feudal Japan.

Chin family genealogy zupu, Kai Ming Chins, Toisan, China. Translated by Alex Li.

Chin On, CEA file, 12486/9-3, National Archives & Records Administration, San Bruno.

Glick, Carl. *Shake Hands with the Dragon.* New York: Whittlesey House, McGraw-Hill Book Company, 1941.

Jack Chin, CEA file, 12486/8-6, National Archives & Records Administration, San Bruno.

Jack Chin letter to descendants, July 24, 1989, n.p.

Keay, John. *China: A History.* New York: Basic Books, 2011.

Lee, Yulan (Lee Shee), CEA file, 12486/8-4, National Archives & Records Administration, San Bruno.

Lung Chin archives, in possession of the author.

Lung Chin, CEA file, 12486/8-5, National Archives & Records Administration, San Bruno.

Lung "Pop" Chin, Chin On ID papers, from Museum of Chinese in America.

Lung "Pop" Chin oral history interviews, January 1988–February 1990. Interview conducted by Dorothy Rony Fujita, for the Museum of Chinese in America, New York.

CHAPTER TWELVE

The long journey from Toisan to Hong Kong and across the ocean to the West Coast of America to Angel Island is recounted in Lung Chin's accounts from his papers and oral history with Dorothy Rony Fujita, and Jack Chin's document addressed to the family. Even though the brothers traveled together, they remembered different parts of their experiences. In the summer of 2015, we camped out as a family on Angel Island, and expert Judy Yung was kind enough to give us a private tour of the facilities. For testimonies and the poetry of Angel Island, I consulted the work of Him Mark Lai, Judy Yung, and Erika Lee; I based the medical examination on accounts in Lee and Yung's *Angel Island.* Many thanks to Cousin Wendy Chin, who interviewed Lung as part of a school project and learned about the youngest Chin daughter who had been left behind.

Billings, W. C. "The Medical Application of the Immigration Law." In *Eugenics in Race and State.* Baltimore: Williams and Wilkins, 1923.

Chin family genealogy zupu, Kai Ming Chins, Toisan, China. Translated by Alex Li.

Chin On, CEA file, 12486/9-3, National Archives & Records Administration, San Bruno.

Jack Chin letter to descendants, July 24, 1989, n.p.

Lai, Mark Him, Genny Lim, and Judy Yung. *Island: Poetry and History of Chinese Immigrants on Angel Island 1910–1940.* Seattle: University of Washington Press, 2014.

Lee, Erika, and Judy Yung. *Angel Island: Immigrant Gateway to America.* New York: Oxford University Press, 2010.

Lee, Yulan (Lee Shee), CEA file, 12486/8-4, National Archives & Records Administration, San Bruno.

Lung Chin archives, in possession of the author.

Lung "Pop" Chin oral history interviews, January 1988–February 1990. Interview conducted by Dorothy Rony Fujita, for the Museum of Chinese in America, New York.

CHAPTER THIRTEEN

As mentioned in the first chapter, the importance and history of Sun Lau has been written about in Bruce Hall's *Tea That Burns,* as well as supported by family and former residents alike. While I've had to imagine opening day, the importance of the church for Chun and Elva cannot be overstated, nor can the tensions over Chun as a Hakka in a building full of Toisanese families. Then, as now, there are different levels of "Chinese"-ness—who is accepted and who is not—and this section, based on conversations with my grandmother who raised me, reveals that.

Chin On's womanizing, terrifying violence, and abusive nature toward his wife and children were based on Lung Chin's papers, and conversations and interviews with various family members, including Jocko Chin, my father, Stanley Chin, and others. The stories about the friendship between the Doshim and Chin children were from Jack Chin, and supported by family photographs. The story of Normon's death on Mott Street was based on family stories and his death record.

Batlan, Felice. "She Was Surprised and Furious: Expatriation, Suffrage, Immigration, and the Fragility of Women's Citizenship, 1907–1940," *Stanford Journal of Civil Rights and Civil Liberties* 15 (2020): 315.

Boissoneault, Lorraine. "Literacy Test and Asian Exclusion Were the Hallmarks of the 1917 Immigration Act," *Smithsonian Magazine*, February 6, 2017.

Bredbenner, Candice Lewis. *A Nationality of Her Own: Women, Marriage, and the Law of Citizenship.* Berkeley: University of California Press, 1998. http://ark.cdlib.org/ark: /13030/ft0g500376/.

Chin On, CEA file, 12486/9-3, National Archives & Records Administration, San Bruno.

"Expatriation Act of 1907." See Chapter 2534, Section 3, "That any American woman who marries a foreigner shall take the nationality of her husband . . ." https://immigration history.org/item/an-act-in-reference-to-the-expatriation-of-citizens-and-their-pro tection-abroad/.

Hall, Bruce Edward. *Tea That Burns: A Family Memoir of Chinatown.* New York: The Free Press, Simon & Schuster, 1998.

Hover, Ernest J. "Citizenship of Women in the United States," *American Journal of International Law* 26 (October 1932): 700–719.

"Immigration Act of 1917 (Barred Zone Act)." Immigration History. https://immigration history.org/item/1917-barred-zone-act/.

Jack Chin, interviews, Bradley Beach, Summer 2000.

Jocko Chin, interviews, King of Prussia, Pennsylvania, January 2015.

Lung Chin archives, in possession of the author.

Normon Doshim death certificate, 1915, New York City Municipal Archives.

U.S. Federal Census, 1920.

Wu Doshim, CEA file, NARA RG 85, Box: RS059, Case No: RS2314, National Archives & Records Administration, Seattle, Washington.

Wu Doshim, U.S. World War I draft registration card, dated September 12, 1918, from New York, NY Roll 1765675, Draft Board 094.

CHAPTER FOURTEEN

While researching Chun's midwifery training, I remembered Grandmother Rose's stories about how her mother helped keep the family and their immediate neighbors safe. Grandma was a toddler during the 1918 flu outbreak, but the stories filtered down to her and then eventually to me. My writing the second half of the book in large part during the COVID-19 pandemic led me to consider this time period perhaps more carefully, and viscerally, than I would have before. Chins being targeted was reported in Bonner's *Alas!*, and the need for the family to flee is addressed in Lung's papers. The personal accounts of the raids on Chinatown are based on Doshim family stories, and the following newspaper articles.

"450 Chinese Seized; Tong Peace Signed," *New York Times*, September 15, 1925.

"600 Chinese Are Seized to End Tong War," *Brooklyn Daily Eagle*, September 15, 1925.

Aimone, Francesco. "The 1918 Influenza Epidemic in New York City." NIH: National Library of Medicine, *Public Health Reports* 125 (Suppl. 3; 2010): 71–79.

Bonner, Arthur. *Alas! What Brought Thee Hither? The Chinese in New York 1800–1950.* Teaneck, NJ: Associated University Presses, 1997.

Chin, Calvin. "Chin Kai-Mings in America." San Francisco. Undated, n.p.

"Chinatown's Mayor Dead: Tom Lee Was a Factional Leader in the Old Tong Feuds," *New York Times*, January 11, 1918.

Jack Chin letter to descendants, July 24, 1989, n.p.

Lung Chin archives, in possession of the author.

Lung Chin oral history interviews (January 1988–February 1990), conducted by Dorothy Rony Fujita, Museum of Chinese in America.

"New York Tong Violence," *Guanghai Journal,* 1927. Translated by Hilary Chan.

"Rival Tong Chiefs Agree on a Truce," *New York Times*, August 29, 1925.

"Tong Heads Warned Agree to Stop War: Hip Sing and On Leong Leaders Art Threatened with Deportation," *New York Times*, November 20, 1924.

Wilson, Michael. "What New York Looked Like During the 1918 Flu Pandemic," *New York Times*, April 2, 2020.

CHAPTER FIFTEEN

Yuan Son's life, in both the U.S. and Toisan, is based on Gene Wong's stories, told over the course of my childhood, and supplemented by my own travels to the Sierra Nevada in 2016 and his village in Toisan in the spring of 2017. There, I interviewed residents and extended family members, and collected the Wong genealogy zupu, detailing the family lineage. I also consulted Gene Wong's (Sun Ming Wong) CEA file in Seattle. Information about Chinese opera in Chinatown was based on interviews with Rose Wong and Helen Chin Eng. Dek and Elva's life in Hong Kong was based on trips to Maryland and Hong Kong in 2019 where I tracked down and interviewed Dek's grandsons and extended family members. For an understanding of colonial life in this period, I read John M. Carroll's *A Concise History of Hong Kong.*

Carroll, John M. *A Concise History of Hong Kong.* Lanham, MD: Rowman & Littlefield, 2007.

Dek Foon, CEA file, 24/1102, New York, and 2500/5043, Boston, National Archives & Records Administration.

Elva Foon, CEA file, 2500/5044, National Archives & Records Administration, Boston.

Gene Wong, a.k.a. Sun Ming Wong, CEA file, 7030/11729, National Archives & Records Administration, Seattle, Washington.

Gooley, Lawrence. "B. A. Rolfe: A Pioneer in Radio," *Adirondack Almanack*, December 12, 2014.

Helen Chin Eng interviews, March 13, 2016, July 24, 2016, September 25, 2016.

Jack Chin letter, July 24, 1989, n.p.

Lee, Erika, and Judy Yung. *Angel Island: Immigrant Gateway to America.* New York: Oxford University Press, 2010.

Lung Chin oral history interviews (January 1988–February 1990), conducted by Dorothy Rony Fujita, Museum of Chinese in America.

Ng Woon Tong and Jo Kammer, Dek Foon's descendants, interviews February 15, 2019, in person and via phone, and May 25–30, 2019, in person, Hong Kong.

Wong family genealogy zupu. Translated by Hilary Chan.

CHAPTER SIXTEEN

Depictions of Mak Lin and Lung Chin's arrival to Mott Street, Chin On's financial ruin, and Yulan's heroic tenacity are based largely on Lung Chin's remembrances from his oral history and essays, and interviews with family members. The conflict over Rose's enrollment in college is based on family lore. Information on Dek Foon's deteriorating heart condition comes from family stories and his death certificate. For Japanese atrocities in China during World War II, see Iris Chang's *The Rape of Nanking*. In 2016, I traveled to Seattle's NARA to read Gene's and Doshim's files, and to visit the former Immigration Station where Gene had been held. I also recorded an interview with him in November 1996 to document this experience.

Yulan's passing is rendered as remembered by family members. Gene and Rose's early courtship was described by Rose Doshim Wong and Kenith Wong, their eldest son. Gene's address book in New York had only a few addresses in it, including the restaurant where Uncle George worked and the Church of All Nations where Gene took classes and where they were married.

Chang, Iris. *The Rape of Nanking: The Forgotten Holocaust of World War II*. New York: Basic Books, 1997.

Chin family films, c. 1920s–1940s, shared by Donald Chin.

Chin, Lung. "A Family Chronicle: The Chin Kai Mings: The First 700 Years," New York, 1985, n.p.

Dek Foon, obituary, *Boston Globe*, April 3, 1938.

Donald Chin interview, in person, May 2015, Monterey, CA.

Elfman, Lois. "Mabel Ping-Hua Lee 1916: A Pioneer of the Suffrage Movement," *Barnard Magazine*, Fall 2020.

Gene Wong, a.k.a. Sun Ming Wong, CEA file, 7030/11729, National Archives & Records Administration, Seattle, Washington.

Gene Wong interview, in person, November 1997.

Gene Wong papers, in possession of the author.

Ging Hawk Club scrapbook, compiled by Lillian Dong Louie, 2004.096.001, "The Gift of the Gods" program pamphlet, 3.001.4, Museum of Chinese in America.

Glick, Carl. *Shake Hands with the Dragon*. New York: Whittlesey House, McGraw-Hill Book Company, 1941.

Gold, Martin B. *Forbidden Citizens: Chinese Exclusion and the U.S. Congress: A Legislative History*. Alexandria, VA: TheCapitol.Net, 2012.

Grunfeld, Katharina Kroo. "Hunter College" entry, The Shalvi/Hyman Encyclopedia of Jewish Women, Jewish Women's Archive.

Handbook for Overseas Chinese in the United States, 1946 (1988.19.120), Idaho Historical Society.

Karen Lisk email correspondence, April 10, 2022.

Lung Chin, *Chinatown, My Chinatown*, edited by Dorothy Rony Fujita, n.p.

Lung Chin oral history interviews (January 1988–February 1990), conducted by Dorothy Rony Fujita, Museum of Chinese in America.

Recipe for Western Cooking, 1914 (1988.19.121), Idaho Historical Society.

Ringle, Ken. "The Forgotten Holocaust," *Washington Post*, December 11, 1997.

Stanley Chin interviews, in person, January 6, 2015, December 21, 2015, December 30, 2015, September 2016, October 19, 2016, January 11, 2017, October 21, 2018.

U.S. Federal Census, 1940.

Wong family genealogy zupu. Translated by Hilary Chan.

Wu Doshim, U.S. World War II draft registration card, registered April 27, 1942. National Archives, St. Louis, Missouri.

Yang, Jia Lynn. "Overlooked No More: Mabel Ping-Hua Lee, Suffragist with a Distinction," *New York Times*, September 19, 2020.

CHAPTER SEVENTEEN

Most of this final chapter was based on personal experience, including my trip to Promontory Summit, Utah, in 2019 to celebrate the 150th anniversary of the completion of the transcontinental railroad, and to honor Yuan Son and the other railroad workers. Information on Elva's latter years was provided by family members and her death certificate; I consulted texts written by authors like Herculine Barbin and Hida Viloria to better understand my aunt's perspective and the challenges for intersex people today. Many thanks to former and current Mott Street residents, especially Lung Chin, Jack Chin, and James Moy, whose spirits still resound along the block.

Chin, Jean Lau, and Daniel Lee. *Who Are the Cantonese Chinese? New York City Chinatown During the 1940s–1960s*. Charleston, SC: CreateSpace Independent Publishing, 2014.

Coolidge, Mary Roberts. *Chinese Immigration: 1860–1945*. New York: Henry Holt and Co., 1909.

Department of State letter to Sun Ming Wong, August 23, 1996. In possession of the author.

Elva Foon, death certificate no. 17329, 1945, Department of Health, Vital Records, City of New York.

Foucault, Michel. Translated with an introduction by Richard McDougall. *Herculine Barbin: Being the Recently Discovered Memoirs of a Nineteenth-century French Hermaphrodite*. New York: Vintage Books, 2010.

Franklin Delano Roosevelt's "Statement on Signing the Bill to Repeal the Chinese Exclusion Laws," December 17, 1943. The American Presidency Project, University of California, Santa Barbara.

Gold, Martin B. *Forbidden Citizens: Chinese Exclusion and the U.S. Congress: A Legislative History*. Alexandria, VA: TheCapitol.Net, 2012.

James Moy interviews via phone, March 27, 2018, and January 9, 2019.

Jocko Chin interview, in person, King of Prussia, Pennsylvania, January 2015.

"Kiu Sing Chan Residence." Significance statement, 2014. Historic Places L.A., L.A. Historic Resources Inventory. SurveyLA: Boyle Heights Historic Resources Survey.

Viloria, Hida. *Born Both: An Intersex Life*. New York: Hachette, 2017.

Index

Note: Italicized page numbers indicate material in photographs or illustrations.